K

CHURCH AND SOCIETY IN SPANISH AMERICA

D1737825

Cedla
Centrum voor Studie en Documentatie van Latijns Amerika,
Centro de Estudios y Documentación Latinoamericanos,
Centro de Estudos e Documentação Latino-Americanos,
Centre for Latin American Research and Documentation

The Centre for Latin American Research and Documentation (Cedla) conducts and coor-
dinates social science research on Latin America, publishes and distributes the results of
such research, and assembles and makes accessible documentary and scholarly materials
for the study of the region. The Center also offers an academic teaching programme on
the societies and cultures of Latin America.

Keizersgracht 395-397 ek Amsterdam; The Netherlands
Fax: +31 20 625 5127; E-mail: cedlapublications@cedla.uva.nl

CHURCH AND SOCIETY IN SPANISH AMERICA

A.C. Van Oss

ⓐ

Aksant
2003

Reprints from the following publications have been used with permission:

'Mendicant expansion in New Spain and the extent of the colony (sixteenth century)'
    Boletín de Estudios Latinoamericanos y del Caribe, Vol. 21 (December 1976) pp. 32-66.
'Comparing colonial bishoprics in Spanish South America', *Boletín de Estudios
    Latinoamerica-nos y del Caribe*, Vol. 24 (June 1978), pp. 27-66.
'Architectural activity, demography and economic diversification: regional economies of
    colo-nial Mexico', *Jahrbuch für Geschichte von Staat, Wirtschaft und Gesellschaft
    Lateinameri-kas*, Vol. 16 (1979), pp. 97-145.

This publication was made possible by a grant from the Unger van Brero Foundation. The
mission of this foundation is to advance the study of social-economic history by providing
scholarships for fieldwork and bestowing grants to publications. It was founded in accor-
dance with the testament of Mrs Elsa Angeniza Wilhemina van Brero in 1967.

CEDLA LATIN AMERICA STUDIES NO. 90

ISBN 90 5260 053 8

Cover design: Jos Hendrix, Groningen
Typesetting: Hanneke Kossen
Printed and published in the Netherlands

Aksant Academic Publishers, www.aksant.nl

Acknowledgements

Adriaan van Oss died in May 1984. He was a promising, young historian who left nineteen publications, including an important monograph on the ecclesiastical history of Central America: *Catholic Colonialism. A Parish History Guatemala, 1524-1821*, published in 1986 by the Cambridge University Press. The monograph is still recognized as a major work, even though it has been out of print for several years. Now, eighteen years later, some of his more timeless articles have been reprinted in this volume; or appear now for the first time in English. As there seems to be a renewed interest in the colonial Church because of its institutional and economic importance, CEDLA feels that interested scholars will welcome this new material.

Although he was deeply engrossed in the theme of Catholic Colonialism, Van Oss's interests included other completely different topics. At his death, he had left a collection of 21 manuscripts, in various stages of completion. These were written in three languages: English, Spanish and Dutch. Van Oss was a polyglot, and in his private life as well he made notes and remarks in each of these languages. In a concept paper for one of his last articles he sometimes changed in the middle of a sentence from English into Spanish, and vice versa. English was, however, his mother tongue.

The corpus of Van Oss is characterized by a unique historical method. He combined the history of the Church and the arts, especially architecture, with economic and social history in an amazing, nearly quantitative manner. In one article, for example, through an extensive series of maps and tables, the geographic extension and withdrawal of the mendicant clergy is traced. This made him conclude that conflicts between the regular orders and the secular clergy at the end of the century stemmed from a declining Amerindian population rather than a loss of missionary fervor, as the early Franciscans at the time had believed. The article on architectural activity, demography and economic diversification in colonial Mexico was composed from the top of a stepladder that was placed in the center of his room at CEDLA. On the floor were a series of graphs and tables, and sitting at the top of the stairs Van Oss recognized a series of regional economies of colonial Mexico, that were later drawn as maps. The method was also used for what he called a 'primitive geography' of sixteenth-century Venezuela, and for the comparison of the various characteristics of the bishoprics in Spanish South America.

In another article, Van Oss concluded that it was time to reject the mercantilist views of colonial Central America that had emphasized long-distance trade and imperial connections. He suggested instead a model of local self-sufficiency, unified by Church and by various forms of cultural adaptation. He investigated the distribution of settlements in the region, its self-sufficiency as a colony, its seaports, and the population in the interior. This article shows that the Spanish urban culture that was transplanted to the region flourished, even when it did not continue to have intensive economic ties with the metropolis. In fact, urban history was an interest Van Oss developed alongside his 'primitive' historical geography and parish history. In two of his articles, the unique grid of the colonial cities was mirrored to stratification models and ethnic composition. Moreover, Van Oss believed firmly that the fact the colonizers established their cities in the highlands, suitable for agriculture and domestic trade, rather than settling on the Atlantic coast, proved that Latin America was not the commercial exporting colony as believed by most economic historians in the 1970s.

In short, Van Oss's intriguing semi-quantitative methodology, combined with close reading of difficult sources (see his elaboration of Vasquez's Chronicle in this volume), makes his work an example for historical research. The method is curiously pre-computer, pre-digital, and thus easily replicable for other young historians, provided they take the time to collect data, serialize them into graphs and tables and criticize the results with close reading of qualitative sources. The last chapter on the Church in Hidalgo during the turbulent Cristero Revolt in Mexico shows that the method may also serve more recent sources. But more important than the method, the conclusions of the articles themselves in this volume are still of great historical importance, and no doubt will serve the historian of the Church as well as economic history of the colonial era. Van Oss's work supports the recent tendency to look at the domestic interior of Latin America, to judge the colony from the inside, as it were. In his view, Catholic Colonialism and the 'typical' Spanish town made up the face of Latin America's colonial heritage.

This collection of essays has been funded by a grant from the Unger van Brero Foundation, for which we are extremely grateful. The original texts were retyped and scanned by many different people during the time it has taken to put the manuscript into digital form. Proof-reading was done by Beatrice Simon. Editing and final corrections were made by Suzanne Verkoren and Kathleen Willingham. Great care has been taken to reproduce the many illustrations that A.C. Van Oss originally made for this book. A small number of these could not be reproduced here because of limits in the production process, but this has not, we believe, detracted from the intellectual legacy of A.C. Van Oss.

CEDLA Editorial Board

TABLE OF CONTENTS

The life and work of Adriaan C. Van Oss*

Adriaan van Oss used to give me copies of quotations from books and articles that had struck him as especially meaningful. His favorite author, J.L. Borges, was a real gold mine of such citations. Years ago he gave me a copy of the following passage:

'Un hombre se propone la tarea de dibujar el mundo. A lo largo de los años puebla un espacio con imágenes de provincias, de reinos, de montañas, de bahías, de naves, de islas, de peces, de habitaciones, de instrumentos, de astros, de caballos y de personas. Poco antes de morir, descubre que ese paciente laberinto de líneas traza la imagen de su cara.

(Borges, Buenos Aires, 31 de Octubre de 1960)'

In the margin Adriaan had written: 'Faire de l'histoire'. In this conception historical writing is considered as the creation of a dream world, in which, ultimately, the author pictures himself. Let me hasten to explain that Adriaan did not adhere to this pessimistic view of the work of the historian. However, we may well ask to what extent the historical writings of Adriaan van Oss do reflect his own personality.

There were two sides to his nature: on the one, hand, the adventurous young man who liked to roam about in the Spanish-speaking world; and on the other hand, the patient, hard working student in a quiet corner of a record-office or library. His special taste for adventure came from his seafaring family: his grandfather, his uncle and, in his youth, his father too, were officers on a Dutch steamship line sailing to Latin America. Thus in a way there were traditional connections with that part of the world. After long periods of hard work Adriaan had to break out of the uneventful reading-room to discover and see new things, especially to get new visual impressions.

His health was precarious: he had suffered since childhood from severe asthma, and this probably explains the other side of his personality. In his youth he was already an avid reader. Like many other historians, he belonged to the group of children who devour books at an early age. In spite of his asthma he was a good sportsman, and in college won many championships in swimming, thanks to his will power and perseverance.

In his work he was efficient and systematic, and everything was well-organized, perhaps due to his American upbringing. From his mother he had received the gift of being a good teacher; he knew perfectly how to stimulate his students. His personality, of course, was most clearly expressed in his choice of subjects for historical research. First however, we must turn our attention to the course of his life and career.

He was born in Troy, N.Y. on November 23, 1947. At that time his father still had Dutch citizenship. His mother was American, but descended from a very old Dutch family that had emigrated to the New Netherlands in the colonial period. He spent his youth in Royal Oak, near Detroit, and in upstate New York with his grandparents on his mother's side. He was awarded his bachelor's degree in political science at Amherst College in 1969. His parents wanted him to become a lawyer, but he decided to follow a different course. During the early seventies young people wandered all over the world, and so did he. Like many other young people, he made a trip through Mexico, Guatemala and Honduras, all the way to Bogotá. There he stayed for nearly one year, meanwhile visiting Ecuador and Peru.

At the end of 1970 he left Bogotá for Amsterdam with two Dutch students, for it was a magnet for young people of many nationalities. He worked at various jobs, and at the same time studied Spanish grammar and Spanish and Latin American literature. This rather irregular life ended at the beginning of 1972, when he gained employment at the *Centro de Estudios y Documentación Latinoamericanos*, CEDLA, in Amsterdam. He became editorial secretary of the *Boletín de Estudios Latino-americanos y del Caribe*, the bi-annual journal published by CEDLA. He also edited two issues of a directory of *Latinoamericanistas en Europa*, in 1973 and in 1976.

His job was an administrative one, but with his inborn intelligence he soon changed it into a position of a more scientific nature. He was greatly interested not only in Spanish and Latin American literature, but also in the history of art, especially the architecture of churches and monasteries, and in history of religion and popular belief. Little by little he became a historian, and began to publish articles and reviews of books in the *Boletín*. It was interesting to observe his gradual development from an adventurous young man to a very diligent scholar who brought many new ideas and methods to his chosen field of study.

His love for traveling and wandering remained, but his trips were now limited to the holidays. Travel began to serve scientific purposes, related to special projects. In this way he traveled in Mexico, collecting data for his *Inventory of 861 Monuments of Mexican Colonial Architecture*. He took pictures of the churches, monasteries, etc. and made notes on every characteristic detail. On the roof of the convent in Ixmiquilpan he met Inés Maldonado, an archaeologist and art historian from Rosario, Argentina; she later became his wife.

In the Netherlands his American Bachelor's degree was an impediment to promotion to a higher scientific position. The board of the CEDLA Institute made it possible for him to attend graduate school for eighteen months in the Department of History of the University of Texas at Austin. There he attended the workshops of well-known scholars including Stanley Ross, Richard Graham and Thomas Reese.

In 1980 he became a candidate for Ph.D. He had scarcely returned to the Netherlands when he learned he had been granted two fellowships to work on his doctoral dissertation: the Fulbright-Hays doctoral dissertation research fellowship, plus a fellowship from the Social Science Research Council and the American Council of Learned Societies. At the same time he was appointed lecturer (*Wetenschappelijk medewerker*) in the Department of History of the University of Leiden, with a special assignment in Latin American History. Despite some difficulties, it was possible to postpone the Leiden appointment for two years.

As the subject for his dissertation van Oss had chosen the history of the Church in the rural parishes of Guatemala during the colonial period. He collected the data in the archives in Guatemala City and with his wife visited most of the parishes in the country. At the same time they made a wonderful collection of pictures and slides of the exterior and interior of the churches. After a year of intensive work he returned to Austin to complete the dissertation, entitled: *Catholic Colonialism: a Parish History of Guatemala, 1524-1821* At the end of 1982 he received his Ph.D. and in May, 1983 was granted the Outstanding Dissertation Award of the University of Texas. This was the first time a historical dissertation had ever received this honor. Further, during his stay in Guatemala, van Oss had been elected a corresponding member of the *Academia de Geografía e Historia de Guatemala*.

In September 1982 he had assumed his position at the University of Leiden. His courses in Latin American history were a great success, attended by many students. His seminars were inspiring and stimulating. It is clear that Adriaan van Oss would have become one of the leading figures in this field in the Latin American Department.

In 1984 he was involved as secretary in organizing the first conference of Spanish and Dutch historians in Leiden. On May 2, during this conference came his sudden death, probably caused by asthma. The distress was great and general. A multitude of family, friends and students attended his funeral in Oegstgeest, a town near Leiden. A good man, a bright young scholar – irreplaceable – had gone; it was a grievous loss for his wife, his parents, his friends and his students, but also for the historical sciences, especially those of Latin America.

At the age of 36 he was carried off, in the prime of his scientific life. Much work was left in press or in manuscript. When we sum up his works, we find that his principal subjects were the Church, ecclesiastical institutions, the clergy, religious life, architecture and architectural activity, printed books and pamphlets, the cities, demography, and economic activities. The focus of his work is mostly on Spanish America in general, and Central America, Mexico and Guatemala in particular.

His preference was for the colonial period, when the Church still dominated human life. He did not feel at home in the more modern centuries after Independence, although he did write about that period. Shortly before his death he had finished a long survey of the history of Latin America in the nineteenth century. Other topics concerned eastern Texas in the 1830s, Minas Gerais (1889-1937), the Church in Hidalgo in the 1920s and modern Argentine street names. The last two in particular are a demonstration of his inventiveness and his refreshing, untraditional way of research. In writing about the building and repair of churches in Hidalgo during the vigorous anti-religious campaign of the central government in Mexico, he showed the wide gap between legal and political theory and the practices of daily life. He did so using an unexpected source: a list of monuments. In another paper, street names were used as a source of the history of the Argentine mentality, an expression of patriotism.

Adriaan van Oss had many new, illuminating ideas, and he applied new methods to research in Latin American history. In his first article, *The Mendicant Expansion in New Spain and the Extent of the colony,* he related the conversion activity of the friars to population density. The monks went first to the regions with the greatest concentrations of population. Van Oss distinguished between a first period, of extension to the edge of the population concentrations, followed by a second period of intensification, filling the gaps between the center and the frontiers. He also demonstrated that the then existing network of roads was an important factor in the process of conversion.

In a study of architectural monuments in Peru, he made graphs of building activity over three centuries (1534-1834). These graphs are very important, as they reflect not only demographic changes, but also fluctuations in business cycles. This idea was elaborated in his work on Mexico. He made an inventory of 861 colonial monuments, and then related building activity to demography and economic activities. On a smaller scale he used building activity in studies of Acámbaro, Hidalgo and Venezuela.

Increases and decreases in building activity gave an overall impression of the economic situation. In colonial Latin America, food prices were of only local or limited regional significance, often diverging greatly over even short distances, due to high transport costs. The prices of plantation products, on the other hand, were dependent on European markets. For these reasons prices can be used only in a limited sense to determine the economic situation. Van Oss discovered that building activity could also be used for this purpose. I think this is very important, but there is more. The three factors, population concentration, economic activities and building activity, can also be used in research on centers and peripheries. High economic or building activity generally goes together with population concentration. Later research showed that this rule does not hold universally, but is only in force when there is a market economy.

In his study of South American bishoprics, van Oss related the careers of the bishops to episcopal revenues. On this basis, he could reconstruct the paths of promotion of the colonial bishops. The economic situation of the bishoprics was also reflected in the construction and magnitude of the episcopal cathedrals.

There are some overlapping articles on the colonial cities. He was interested in the origin and the spread of the chessboard city plans, and found that in these gridiron plans other patterns of rhomboid or diamond-like form are hidden. Within the city plans, centers, middle zones and peripheries can be distinguished. In Tunja (Colombia) in 1623 there were three zones: The residential quarters of the *encomenderos,* the *vecinos* and the Indians. The *encomenderos* resided in the center of the town, near the *plaza* with the official buildings and the principal churches; *vecinos* sometimes lived a little farther from the *plaza*; and the Indians had their houses in the outskirts of the town. Even in modern Sucre (Bolivia) the pattern of distribution is the same, and within Argentine cities, groups of street names and hotels again indicate three distinct zones.

The Central American colonies were autarkic. Export of products was of little importance. The colonies were not typically colonial in the sense that they were exploited for the profit of the motherland. There were no large military occupational forces either. How was it possible that Spain could govern these large and distant regions over such a long period? Adriaan van Oss attributed this to the role of the clergy. In his dissertation he explained the great significance of the clergy, especially the friars, in the rural districts. They not only met their religious obligations, but also performed many cultural, social and administrative tasks. In his view Spanish domination in America was more the result of a spiritual crusade than of a military conquest.

At the local level the clergy executed many tasks that were done by civil servants in other governments. Even their incomes surpassed those of the government officials. Although the crown had decreed that the Christian faith should be presented in its purest form, uncontaminated by worldly interests, a whole system of various contributions sprang up with the first conversions. Viewed in the most prosaic terms, parochial incomes made the Church the greatest business of the colonial period.

The regular clergy could control the rural population through their knowledge of the Indian languages. The secular clergy, on the contrary, attempted to hispanize the population according to the wishes of the central government in Spain. During the eighteenth century almost all regular parishes were secularized. This brought to an end the ecclesiastical state within a state: a republic of priests and Indians.

The subject that interested Adriaan van Oss most in colonial history was the Church, or more precisely, the monasteries, the friars and the Indians. Perhaps he saw it as a Utopia, which could not be realized because of the hostility of the outer world and the frailty of the human spirit. He was pained by the great gap between Christian ideals and the practices of ordinary daily life.

In his work he emphasized the importance of continuity in the historical process. Each generation stands on the shoulders of its predecessors. According to his view, historical development is slow and gradual, leaving little room for revolution. Perhaps this strong feeling for continuity also explains his interest in the history of architecture. In this field 'revolutions' are rare, and gradual development is the norm.

Most notable in his work is the diversity of subjects. He tried to combine the cultural, social and economic aspects of life in Latin America in one holistic view. It was a long cherished ideal of his to write, together with me, a handbook of Latin American history in which he would cover the fields of religion, culture and the arts, and I would deal with the economic and social aspects. The title of the first volume was to be *Culture and Society in Colonial Latin America*. It was our intention that this should be a holistic history of Latin America. Much of Adriaan van Oss's work can be considered spadework in anticipation of this book – a dream that did not come true. The loss is irrevocable, and to many of us it still remains incomprehensible.

B.H. Slicher van Bath

Note

*   A similar version of this biography was published in the *Jahrbuch für Geschichte von Staat, Wirtschaft und Gesellschaft Lateinamerikas*, 22 (1985).

A FAR KINGDOM: CENTRAL AMERICAN AUTARKY AT THE END OF THE EIGHTEENTH CENTURY

Two types of colonialism

'Is it mainly greed that drives men to build empires?' Martin Wolfe, in his introduction to a collection of essays on *The Economic Causes of Imperialism*, answers this question in the affirmative: 'somehow man's implacable search for gain is at the bottom of it. Indeed, this one reason the odor of imperialism is so rank.'[1] Under the influence of mercantile theories of empire, many of us have joined Wolfe in attaching an exploitative, parasitic meaning to the terms empire and colony absent in their original acceptations. In its classical sense, the word colony has to do with the cultivation of the land, and therefore the settling of new areas. Colonization meant the transplantation of peoples and cultures without specifying the economic bases of the new communities thus formed.

The Greeks and Romans colonized the Mediterranean, implanting their institutions and languages. At the same time, however, their imperial economies were primitive systems in which the greatest part of the population engaged in subsistence agriculture, and barely maintained commercial ties with the imperial metropolis. Land transport was especially costly and inefficient, and only luxury goods and government supplies could generally be traded over long distances. No effective system of banking and credit ever evolved, and even the money economy was only weakly implanted in most colonial areas.[2]

Plato, in the *Laws*, describes an ideal colony on the island of Crete as being as nearly as possible self-sufficient, geographically isolated and located at a distance from the coast. He goes so far as to maintain that trade is actually inimical to good colonialism. When the Athenian learns that Clinias has been entrusted with the planning of a new Magnesian colony on Crete, the first question he asks is whether it is to be 'an inland State, or situated on the sea-coast'. According to Plato, the ideal colony must be situated in the mountains, and as nearly as possible self-sufficient,

> For the sea is, in very truth, a right briny and bitter neighbor ... for by filling the markets of the city with foreign merchandise and retail trading, and breeding in men' souls knavish and tricky ways, it renders the city faithless and loveless, not to itself only, but to the rest of the world as well.[3]

It is only the more recent sense of 'colony' that stresses, in contradiction of Plato, the economic conception of a strategic outpost used by the imperial power for the commercial exploitation of the hinterland. In this view, the colonial settlement is first and foremost an extractive funnel, a transfer station between the underdeveloped periphery and the overseas metropolis.

Both types of colonialism took place in North and South America, reflecting themselves in different kinds of settlements. The extractive type prevailed along the Atlantic coasts, around the bays of Chesapeake and Todos os Santos. Rio de Janeiro, described at the beginning of the nineteenth century as 'the principal emporium of Brazil'[4] and the populous cities of the British colonies in North America all owed their preeminence to their strategic positions as ports.

But in other parts of the New World the second type of colonialism prevailed, developing in relative isolation from the mother country. Whether by geographical accident or cultural design, this type dominated much of Spanish America. This paper takes the case of Central America to argue that most Spanish settlements in the New World were colonial in the classical meaning of the word without necessarily fitting the extractive model.[5] Spanish culture was transplanted and thrived even in the absence of continued extensive economic contact with Spain. Colonial Central America presents us with the paradox of a narrow strip of land caught between two seas, populated and governed by Europeans, which just as Plato's Magnesia turned its back to the coast, and therefore to intensive commercial ties with the metropolis.

Distribution of settlements

This inward orientation can already be appreciated in the distribution of settlements as they acquired form during the colonial period. Of the 764 cities, towns, and villages (*ciudades, villas,* and *pueblos*) registered by the Guatemalan geographer Domingo Juarros towards 1800, I have been able to locate and map 614.[6] If the Captaincy General of Guatemala had been a trade-oriented colony, then its cities would have been strategically situated with respect to the Atlantic coast. The contrary is the case. The great majority of the settlements were closer to the Pacific than to the Atlantic. Even more significantly, only a tiny number of settlements, and no city or town of consequence, were located on either coast.

Most settlements nestled in the cool highlands, and the principal towns, including the capital city, tended to straddle the continental divide, especially where it passed through the Guatemalan provinces of Sacatepéquez, Chimaltenango, Soloá, and Totonicapán. In these provinces almost one-quarter of all settlements mentioned by Juarros huddled together on less than one-twentieth of Central America's land area.

The colonial settlements did not favor the warm and humid coastal plains, as in a plantation economy for export. In this respect a 1579 map showing towns and roads in the Pacific coastal province of Suchitepéquez may be considered representative.[7] The towns, each symbolized by a tiny checker-board recalling the famous grid pattern of streets typical of Spanish urbanism in America, can be seen clustered among the mountains at the top of the map. The sea is indicated by scrollwork at the bottom. Only one road descends to the coast, where no settlement is to be found, and the captions make clear that to the colonial Guatemalan mind, the coastal lowlands were not in the first instance considered useful for plantations in tropical export products, but as grazing land for cattle and horses.

Demographically oriented inwards upon itself, Central America was ill-disposed for external trade. The contrast with truly maritime-oriented regions could hardly be more striking: in Catalonia, Valencia, Guipúzcoa, Vizcaya, or Asturias, to name a few Spanish examples, the pattern was exactly the opposite. There the towns clustered around natural harbors and in the river valleys which connected them with the sea; the mountains were the backland. In the Americas we find some examples of this kind of coastal orientation as well. Two splendid ones are the bays of Chesapeake (Virginia) and Todos os Santos (Bahia). In both, the towns and villages hugged the shorelines, only abandoning them where navigable rivers or streams wound their way further inland.[8] But Central America shared nothing in common with this type of distribution. Its nature was more hermetic. In this respect it had more in common with the Andean highlands of South America than with Brazil or the North American colonies. Of great importance must have been the original distribution of the Indian population at the time of the Conquest. In Central America and the Andes this was a far greater factor than in Brazil or North America, where Indian populations had always been sparse.

And in contrast to the mining regions of Latin America, such as the Bolivian *altiplano*, Minas Gerais in Brazil, or Mexico's arid north, it was not gold and silver that lured the colonists of Central America to the highlands. Aside from Tegucigalpa's short-lived and poverty-stricken silver industry, precious metals never achieved more than incidental status in the colonial economy.[9]

Pedro de Alvarado, the first European to explore these lands was sorry not to find the cities of gold of legend, but was pleased to find another kind of wealth. He wrote to Hernán Cortés of Guatemala's 'much corn land' and many people: 'believe it Your Grace, that this land is more populated and has more people than all the lands, that Your Grace has governed up to now'.[10] Indeed, the 'corn land' of the highlands provided the economic base for Spanish colonization.

A self-sufficient colony

Colonial Central America has been described as a 'classic case' of a dependent, monocultural economy. Its history has been written in terms of the export cycles of two cash crops: first cacao and later indigo.[11] A sixteenth-century 'cacao boom' had spent itself by the late 1570s, and affected the coastal lowlands, which as we have seen were sparsely settled. Towards 1800, indigo held the position of honor. In the peak year of 1797, some 1,344,000 pounds of the dyestuff left Central American ports, providing a small group of Guatemalan merchants with the means to dress themselves in silk, brocade and beaver hats.[12]

Because the Creole elite depended on the export of indigo for its foreign exchange, it has been assumed that indigo was also the axis about which the economy in general turned. For that reason, the history of indigo production in the Captaincy General of Guatemala has been more carefully studied than almost anywhere else, while by contrast, the workings of the internal economy remain largely a mystery. Historians have treated this side of economic life as hardly more than a nebulous backdrop to the more dramatic export trade.[13]

Central American geographers of the period, however, saw the matter in a completely different light. While they were by no means ignorant of the lucre to be derived from external commerce, they gave it a minor place in their accounts. For Domingo Juarros and Pedro de Cortés y Larraz – who left the most detailed geographical descriptions we have from the end of the eighteenth century – the indigo trade was simply one more facet of economic life in general.[14] Even at the peak of the indigo trade, Central America's ties to the outside world were weak, and such ties as there were only affected limited areas in any significant way. Far from being completely dependent upon the vicissitudes of the external market, Central America was a largely self-sufficient agrarian society, thrown back on its own resources, isolated from the rest of the world.

Juarros, writing about 1800, paints a surprisingly varied picture of an essentially closed economy, mentioning more than a hundred different products or economic activities a total of 238 times, spread over sixteen provinces.[15] The vast majority of his references are to domestic agrarian production and local trade, not to the outside world. Indigo is only mentioned for three provinces (San Salvador, Sonsonate and Nicaragua), shipbuilding and drydocks for one (Realejo), smuggling for two (Honduras and Nicaragua), and there is only one reference to licit maritime trade (Sonsonate). Moreover Sonsonate's trade was not with Spain, but with Central America's southern neighbor, Peru. Only about three percent of Juarros's references to economic activities have to do with indigo or external trade. In fact, Juarros devotes more words to wild game and hunting than to the entire subject of indigo.

Three decades earlier, Pedro de Cortés y Larraz, archbishop of Guatemala, recorded the results of his visit to the 123 parishes of his see between 1768 and 1770.

Among other aspects of Guatemalan material and spiritual life, Cortés y Larraz also compiled data on the most important economic activities of each parish. His description of the archdiocese lists only fifty products as opposed to Juarros's hundred-plus; the archbishop was, of course, mainly interested in agricultural production, since this formed the base upon which his tithe income depended. While the geographical area he described is limited to eleven of the sixteen Central American provinces, it includes both the demographic heartland and the major indigo producing regions, and thus provides access to a cross-section of the economy at that time (Table 1).

Table 1   *Economic activities per parish, according to Cortés y Larraz, 1768-1770*

Activities mentioned	Parishes for which mentioned	
	Number	*Percent*
Maize	117	20.8
Cattle (*ganado, ganado mayor*)	73	13.0
Beans (*frijoles*)	69	12.3
Sugar	46	8.2
Local and regional trade in foodstuffs and crafts	29	5.2
Indigo	28	5.0
Wheat	27	4.8
Cacao	21	3.7
Fruit	20	3.6
Vegetables	15	2.7
Cotton	15	2.7
Salt	12	2.1
Fish	11	2.0
Sheep	9	1.6
Chili (*chile*)	9	1.6
Traffic in firewood	7	1.2
Woven mats (*petates*)	7	1.2
Small livestock (*ganado menor*)	5	0.9
Cords, nets, rope	4	0.7
Cotton textiles	2	0.4
Garbanzos	2	0.4
Bananas	2	0.4
Chian	2	0.4
Reed	2	0.4
Sisal	2	0.4

Table 1   *Continued*

Activities mentioned	Parishes for which mentioned	
	Number	Percent
Others (mentioned for one parish each): local Trade in snow; local trade in flowers; rice; cattle fair; straw hats; palm-leaf hats; reed hats; iron mills; tobacco; *annatto*; stone-cutters; carpenters; forges; pepper; furniture (wooden); pottery; pigs; wool; woolen textiles; honey; chickens; peas (*chicharos*), health spa; horses; trade with Peru	24	4.1
All activities mentioned	536	99.8

Source   Cortés y Larraz, *Descripción geográfico-moral de la diócesis de Goathemala.*

Of all the references made by Cortés y Larraz to economic activities, 83 percent have to do with agriculture for direct consumption, and local and regional commerce. Indigo accounts for another five percent. The final twelve percent have to do with the cultivation of several cash crops, which according to market conditions might either have been consumed within Central America or exported. Such products were sugar, cacao, pepper, *annatto* and tobacco. Pepper, *annatto*, and tobacco need not concern us greatly; Cortés y Larraz only mentions them for one parish each. Sugar and cacao, on the other hand, were being produced in 46 and 21 parishes respectively.

About these two crops it is impossible to be certain, but indications are that they were not exported in significant quantities around 1800. The decline of cacao as an important export product in the face of competition from Venezuela and Guayaquil, about which Juarros complains at one point, has been documented in detail by Mac-Leod, and sugar had never really been a Central American export product. The main sugar markets had always been the Central America cities themselves.[16] We know from a Nicaraguan document of 1800 that while a substantial portion of Nicaragua's sugar and cacao production was being sold to other provinces, none of it was being exported outside of Central America.[17] It therefore seems safe to add sugar and cacao to the list of agricultural products for internal consumption.

Around 1770, indigo was being cultivated in fewer than one-fourth of the Guatemalan parishes. In no parish was indigo a monoculture in the strict sense; in almost all of them it was simply one of a series of agricultural products. Only in the parish of San Miguel (in eastern El Salvador) does Cortés y Larraz single it out as the most important crop:

> The soil of this parish is very fertile for everything, but although maize, cattle, and vegetables are grown here, the principal crop is indigo, which is harvested in much abundance and is the chief object of everyone's labour on the haciendas.[18]

Although indigo could theoretically be grown at a variety of altitudes and in almost any type of soil,[19] in practice its cultivation was limited to the coastal lowlands of the Pacific, where the warm climate especially suited it. Although Cortés y Larraz nowhere makes special mention of the marketing of the indigo harvest, Floyd tells us that it was funneled from the plantations through the hands of Guatemalan merchants to ports on the Atlantic coast for shipment to Europe.[20]

On the subject of trade with Europe, Cortés y Larraz is as silent as Juarros. Nowhere does the archbishop mention it. The only reference to maritime trade at all concerns the Peruvian trade. Ships navigating the pacific coast between Peru and Acapulco sometimes stopped at Acajutla, in the parish of Sonsonate. Nevertheless, the visible effects of the Peruvian trade on Sonsonate's economy were negligible:

> ... The soil [of Sonsonate] is suitable for everything, and several rivers pass through it, but little is grown, and there are more forests than cultivated grounds; because of this the people are poor and there is much nudity, even though they could be very rich, on the one hand because of the fertility of the soil, and on the other because it is where the ships that come from the other America disembark ...[21]

Indeed, if it were correct to speak of Central America around 1800 as a monoculturally dependent economy, then the monoculture upon which it depended would have to be maize, not indigo. Maize was grown in every single parish of the archdiocese of Guatemala, and this single crop alone accounts for one-fifth of all the economic references made by Cortés y Larraz. If we add to maize all the other references to foodstuffs for direct local consumption (beans, cattle, wheat, fruit, vegetables, salt, fish, sheep, chili, small livestock, garbanzos, bananas, *chian*, rice, pigs, honey, chickens, and peas), it becomes apparent that the local subsistence sector was the keystone of Guatemala's colonial economy, accounting for two-thirds of all Cortés y Larraz's references to economic activities.

In the densely populated areas, agriculture and husbandry for direct consumption were supplemented by a lively network of regional trade relations. Magnets for this kind of commerce were the large markets in the cities of Guatemala and San Salvador, and the town of Quezaltenango.[22]

Guatemala was the nerve center of the most intensive market activity. Foodstuffs arrived at the daily market from all the nearby towns, and from several more distant ones. The trade radius for the market in foodstuffs stretched more than fifty kilometers in some directions. Maize, fruit, and wheat were brought from Hermita, Comalapa, and Patzicia, and fish from the towns and villages on the shores of the lakes of Atitlán and Amatitlán. The capital was not only dependent upon the rural towns for its feeding, but also for energy. One of the branches of trade most often mentioned by Cortés y Larraz was the supply of firewood for the hearths, kitchens, kilns, and bakeries of the city. At least seven rural towns supplied this wood commercially.[23]

Almolonga was so specialized in catering to the needs of the Guatemalan capital that it seems to have neglected its own agriculture, the only crop of importance being maize. But Almolongan men made regular trips down the mountains to the Pacific coast, returning with fish and lowland fruits for resale in the capital. The women of the town, in the meanwhile, occupied themselves in the manufacture of tortillas, which they carried to the market twice daily, along with Almolongan woven mats.[24] Such local and regional trade had to struggle with an extremely primitive system of overland communications.

As everywhere, crafts and industries were especially concentrated in the larger towns and cities. The capital was renowned not only for its wide variety of textiles, including the finest sorts as well as the ordinary cotton fabrics 'worn by all the poor people of the realm', but also for its tobacco factory, its porcelain ('some of it so fine that it resembles that made in Germany'), and its artisans, in particular musicians, silversmiths, and sculptors.

Some towns gained renown for certain specialized branches of production: San Sebastián del Tejar was known for its tiles, used in the construction of houses, and Panajachel supplied the necessary ropes and nets for the fishing villages on the shores of Lake Atitlán. Furniture produced in Cobán, the capital of Verapaz, found its way to distant markets, as did the cotton and woolen textiles manufactured in San Pedro Soloma, to the north of Huehuetenango. Cotton from Cahabón, the most remote village of Verapaz, was transported to Cobán, whence it was distributed among the towns and villages of the 'entire province'. Santa María, on the outskirts of Guatemala, specialized in finer wares, flowers and ice gathered from nearby volcanic slopes.[25]

In some towns, the presence of a pilgrimage church or a thermal bath gave rise to a kind of early tourist industry, often catering especially to inhabitants of the capital city. The most famous pilgrimage in the archdiocese of Guatemala directed itself to the 'Black Christ' of Esquipulas, mentioned by both Cortés y Larraz and Juarros. Twice a year, on the 15th of January and during Holy Week, great numbers of pilgrims descended upon the church and accompanying fair. According to Cortés y Larraz, their number could rise to 20,000; according to Juarros, 85,000 visitors were not unusual.[26]

The most popular bathing resorts, favored by city-dwellers, were San Juan Amatitlán, whose waters were a specific for a number of different ailments, and Concepción Escuintla, where Archbishop Cortés y Larraz was shocked to find men and women bathing together: 'an unhappy health, that which must be sought at the expense of honesty and salvation'.[27]

Thus in both of the geographical descriptions studied here, the references to the internal economy far outweigh those to external commerce. The modern emphasis on the indigo trade as the centerpiece of the late-eighteenth-century economy of Central America seems incompatible with the relatively minor place accorded it by Juarros and Cortés y Larraz.

The peripheral character of indigo and maritime trade can be illustrated by comparing the presence or absence of indigo plantations and ports with the approximate population densities of Central America's twenty-nine *partidos* around 1800 (Table 2).

Table 2 *Population densities 1800, by* partidos *and incidence of indigo and ports*

Partido	Population density (persons/km²)	Indigo	Port
Sacatepéquez	30.20	-	-
Totonicapán	29.53	-	-
Chimaltenango	19.01	-	-
San Salvador	17.50	X	-
Atitlán	11.45	-	-
San Vicente	8.92	X	-
Realejo, Subtiava	8.69	-	Realejo
Sonsonate	7.61	X	Acajutla
Sololá	6.56	-	-
Santa Ana	6.44	X	-
Quezaltanango	5.65	-	-
San Miguel	4.74	X	-
Guazacapán	4.71	-	-
Chiquimula	4.50	-	-
Verapaz	3.89	-	-
León	3.73	X	Río San Juan
Acasaguastlán	3.49	-	Golfo Dulce
Huehuetenango	3.47	-	-
Suchitepéquez	3.34	-	-
Tegucigalpa	1.58	-	-
Escuintla	1.56	-	-
Matagalpa	1.47	-	-
Cuidad Real, Tuxtla, Soconusco	1.35	X	San Fernando
Comayagua	1.00	X	Omoa, Trujillo
Nicoya	0.77	-	-
Costa Rica	0.74	-	-
Total	2.79		

Sources On population and population density, Van Oss, 'The population of Central America towards 1800', unpublished essay (Table 3); on ports active about 1800, *Gazeta de Guatemala*, 1800-1802; on indigo, Juarros, *Compendio de la historia de ciudad de Guatemala*; Zavala, 'Descripción por menor de la provincia de Nicaragua'; 'Noticia de las provincias y partidos que tiene el reyno de Guatemala, con sus respectivas producciones', Serrano y Sanz, ed., *Colección de libros y documentos*, pp. 319-320; Guitiérrez y Ulloa, *Estado general de provincia de San Salvador.*

There is a negative correlation between population density on the one hand, and indigo production and the incidence of ports on the other. The indigo regions were
less densely inhabited than the areas where indigo was not produced, *partidos* with
ports were even less densely populated, and *partidos* with both indigo plantations
and a port were the least populous of all:

    Population density in *partidos* with
 - neither ports nor indigo: 3.80   persons per km²   (16 *partidos*)
 - indigo: 2.41   ”   ” ”   (10 *partidos*)
 - ports: 1.94   ”   ” ”   (9 *partidos*)
 - both indigo and ports: 1.77   ”   ” ”   (6 *partidos*)

Until now, we have not discussed the actual value of the indigo trade. But a simple
calculation shows that while income from the exports of Central American indigo at
its peak was certainly sufficient to allow a small group of Guatemalan merchants to
live on a high foot, its contribution to the whole economy could never have loomed
very large.

    In order to calculate the value, we must first know the quantities. Smith has pro-
vided them in the form of a table showing the registered exports of indigo from Central American ports during each year of the late eighteenth century.[28] They are represented in Table 3 in simplified form: yearly averages by five-year periods.

Table 3   *Registered exports of Central American Indigo 1772-1882 by five-year periods*

Period	Average annual indigo export (in pounds)
1772-1776	561,000
1777-1781	834,800
1782	n.a.
1783-1787	832,400
1788-1792	1,112,200
1793-1797	1,037,400
1798-1802	913,800

Source   Smith, 'Indigo Production and Trade in Colonial Guatemala', p. 197.

Registered indigo exportation reached its peak during the decades of the 1790s.
Smith's figures are based on records of the Sales Tax Administration, and thus do
not take contraband into account. Floyd believes that contraband may have
accounted for an additional 100,000 pounds a year.[29] At its peak then, indigo was
exported at a rate of 1,000,000 to 1,200,000 pounds per year. If we assume, along
with Floyd, that a negligible proportion of the indigo was consumed within the confines of the isthmus itself, then the export figure represents the total production
figure.[30]

What was this worth? The question is made more complicated by the fact that three different grades were sold: *flor, sobresaliente,* and *corte,* in descending order of value. Between 1790 and 1800, the officially set price of one pound of flor varied between 12.5 and 16 reales, that of *sobresaliente* between 9.5 and 13, and that of *corte* between 7 and 10.5 (1 peso = 8 reales).[31] Of all the indigo classified by the Indigo Growers' Association in 1791 and 1794, 85 and 94 percent respectively was of the *corte* grade.[32] The Intendant of the province of San Salvador, Antonio Gutiérrez y Ulloa, asserted that the most commonly sold grade was *corte,* and the normal price for indigo was 11 reales (1.375 pesos) per pound.[33] At 11 reales per pound, the gross value of Central American indigo exports during the peak period of exportation would have been in the neighborhood of 1,650,000 pesos. Related to the population of Central America at the time, the per capita value would have been about 1.79 pesos.

What was this worth in real terms? Price data for Central America during the period is scarce, even for the cash crop indigo, as we have seen. Nevertheless, scattered prices for maize allow us to translate the price of a pound indigo into an amount of maize of equivalent value. According to reports in the *Gazeta de Guatemala* in 1802 and 1803, maize prices ranged between a low of 2.5 and a high of 5.25 pesos per *fanega* in different places and dates.[34] At this rate, the per capita indigo export of Central America at its peak would have had a gross value of between .34 and .71 *fanega,* or about one bushel of maize a year.

Overland communications

In an export-oriented economy, the points where all roads meet are the entrepôts. The dock or railhead is like a spider in its web. Starting there the various strands diverge, and are most dispersed in the production regions. Where they converge again, there is the port. Central America did not fit this model. A map of overland routes and navigable waterways described in several colonial sources (Figure 1) testifies to this failure.[35] Instead of providing the main points of articulation, the ports were the outer fringes of a network which radiated from the demographic centers of the interior.

Nor were the roads themselves in condition to bear much traffic. They had to be negotiated on foot or muleback; the geographical descriptions make no mention of wheeled transport along them. Indeed, what were called roads (*caminos*) were sometimes hard to distinguish from the surrounding landscape. Of 143 different trajectories described by Cortés y Larraz, more than half (73) included 'violent' climbs or descents (*cuestas violentas, barrancas, precipicios, derrumbaderos,* etc.). Sixty-five involved crossing one or more rivers without the aid of a bridge, usually by wading, but once on a chair borne by four Indians immersed up to their chests in the water, and twice in a kind of sack (*surrón*) shot from one side to the other along a suspended cord. At some crossings canoes were available. On 39 of the routes, loose rock or landslides formed hazards, and 17 were marshy (*ciénagas, barreales, atascaderos*). Heavy brush and woods were obstacles on 21 of the routes.[36]

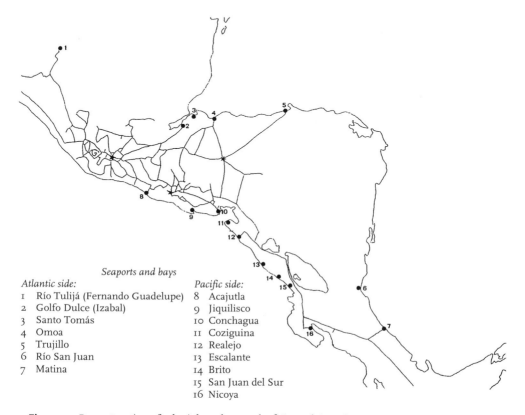

Seaports and bays

Atlantic side:
1 Río Tulijá (Fernando Guadelupe)
2 Golfo Dulce (Izabal)
3 Santo Tomás
4 Omoa
5 Trujillo
6 Río San Juan
7 Matina

Pacific side:
8 Acajutla
9 Jiquilisco
10 Conchagua
11 Coziguina
12 Realejo
13 Escalante
14 Brito
15 San Juan del Sur
16 Nicoya

Figure 1   *Reconstruction of colonial road network of Central America*
          * 'Capitals': Antigua, San Salvador, Comayagua.

In his account, Cortés y Larraz complained of having unnecessarily scaled and descended a mountain between Zacualpa and Joyabaj because his guides lost the road.[37] Similarly, the road between Amatitlán and Sinacantán was difficult to follow: 'often the road cannot be recognized'.[38] At least eight stretches of road were qualified as 'labyrinths of mountains'.[39] Between San Juan Ixcoi and Soloma the road was 'so sad that it seems that the sadness becomes palpable... All around is a confusion of mountains, causing horror at the thought that it must be penetrated'.[40] Between Tacuilula and Guanagazapa the road was covered by a kind of vine, which caught the feet of the mule, while the rider had to protect his face from the overhanging brush.[41]

It is easy to guess the effect of these obstacles to trade. The highland population centers had to live on their own resources. Even in 1850, Central American roads were unimproved tracks unsuited to wheeled traffic. In that year the otherwise optimistic Englishman John Baily soberly concluded that the difficulty of overland transportation formed an insurmountable barrier to commercial penetration of the Guatemalan highlands. He calculated that a mule train leaving Guatemala City for the Atlantic coast took three to five weeks to reach the nearest roadstead at Lake Izabal, and that the cost of the mule train alone was up to four times the sea freight charge from Izabal to Europe.[42]

Seaports

In light of colonial Central America's inward orientation and its primitive road network, we need not be surprised at the absence of booming port cities of the type familiar from the history of Europe's mercantile expansion. This type of city can hardly be said to have existed in Central America. On the Atlantic coast east of Trujillo towards 1800, no port was even inhabited, although some had been founded with high expectations during the early colonial years. Such were San Gil de la Buena Vista, which had its beginnings as early as 1523, or Triunfo de la Cruz, which failed in spite of its name and good natural harbor, capable of handling the largest boats. They, along with a port such as Cartago, further to the east, had succumbed to the disadvantage of being separated from the population centers by long, hot lowlands. At Matina (Costa Rica), a small fort had been constructed around 1743 to protect the port, whence ships once embarked for Portobelo and Cartagena. But by 1800 it had been judged more prudent to abandon it.[43]

To the west of Trujillo there were Omoa and the Golfo Dulce (Lake Izabal). Omoa was a good and protected bay, capable of holding twenty or twenty-five ships at a time. Indeed, it was fortified during the second half of the eighteenth century. Nevertheless, a plan dated 1768 offers poignant testimony to the isolation of an important Central American port: it shows a fort with a path leading out, identified as the road to San Pedro Sula; but the path curves under the shadow of the walls and heads directly to the sand beach, thereby avoiding the vast shaded area surrounding the fort on all other sides, identified as 'swampy, impenetrable woods'.[44] A little stone fort was also constructed at the mouth of Lake Izabal, but aside from that there seems to have been no permenent settlement. Heat, humidity, and disease made human occupation of the Atlantic coast difficult. At Omoa the only permanent population was 'a village of negroes, who are the only ones who can suffer the climate'.[45]

Trujillo itself was the only port on the Atlantic side which ever had true urban pretensions. Founded in 1524, and the original site of the Honduran episcopate, by the early seventeenth century it came to boast a hospital and a fort with seventeen pieces of artillery. Nevertheless, the crenellated city wall, bustling harbor life, and ecclesia magna portrayed in John Ogilby's atlas (London, 1671) were pure fantasy.[46]

The city had in fact been destroyed by Dutch pirates in 1643, and remained deserted until 1789. More accurate than Ogilby's drawing was a 1770 Spanish map showing the 'ruins of Trujillo'. Towards 1800 it was still a town in its very beginnings, with eighty or a hundred Spaniards and three hundred negroes.[47]

On the Pacific side, most of the ports were located in the provinces to the southeast, away from the densely populated provinces of what is now the Republic of Guatemala. The province of Escuintla, directly south of the city of Guatemala, did have a bay, which some referred to as 'Puerto de Guatemala'. But others objected that it in no way deserved the name, as it offered no protection to any ship that might harbor there. Ajacutla, the port of Sonsonate, was an open bay as well, but nevertheless served as a stopping point for ships navigating between Peru and Acapulco. Realejo, further down the coast was Nicaragua's principal port, and according to Juarros, the best in the realm. It was adequate for even the largest ships, offered total security against storms, and counted 'a thousand' embarkations, in addition to dry-docks and other facilities for ship-repair.

For every port actually used, there were several which were rarely, if ever, visited by larger vessels. Such were Juquilisco and Conchagua, Coziguina, San Juan del Sur, Brito, Escalante and Nicoya.[48] In some cases the natural situation of these ports was excellent; the reason they were not frequented was that little trade could be had there.

Acajutla, the most important Pacific port, remained rustic in spite of the Peruvian trade. The facilities consisted of two unguarded shacks which served as warehouses. Cortés y Larraz, who visited it about 1770, reported having seen a frigate from Peru while he was there. Despite its small draft, it was anchored at a distance from the coast, apparently for fear of running aground in the surf. Even at a distance, however, it was a great attraction for the local children, who offended the stern bishop's sense of propriety by splashing in the waves all day, 'entirely naked, idle, and lacking breeding and shame'. It was explained to Cortés that there was no way to keep the children out of the water as long as a ship was to be seen. 'And how long do they usually stay?' asked Cortés. 'And they told me six months, eight, or even more'.[49]

For the active ports there are no statistical series on the volume of trade. Nevertheless, there are indications. Floyd was able to document a total of 24 ships docking at Omoa and Santo Tomás (Golfo Dulce) during the four years from 1789 to spring 1793; or about six ships a year at the two ports. Since ships doing one of these two ports would often do the other as well, the number actually arriving from outside the realm would be even lower.[50]

Another impression of the volume of maritime trade can be had from the regular reports of ships' arrivals, departures, and sometimes cargoes, published in the *Gazeta de Guatemala*. I have consulted 36 issues of a total of 135 numbers actually published between 14 April 1800 and 25 October 1802.[51] These issues contain reports on the arrival of 28 ships and 4 departures over a 30-month period. If the issues consulted are representative, the total number of ships to visit the Central American ports would have been on the order of 105 during the whole period, or 42 per year. The two leading Atlantic ports were Trujillo (9 arrivals, 2 departures) and Omoa (5 arrivals, 1 departure), followed by San Fernando Guadalupe (río Tulijá, Ciudad Real; 3 arrivals), the Golfo Dulce (1 arrival, 1 departure), and the río San Juan (1 arrival). On the Pacific side, Acajutla (Sonsonate) was the most frequently visited port (5 arrivals), followed by Realejo (4 arrivals), whose 'thousand' embarkations apparently were often idle.

No Central American port seems to have received more than one ship a month on the average, an impression confirmed by a contemporary calculation of the amount of all the imports and exports moving through Trujillo in 1800. According to this source, ten ships arrived during the year in question, and thirteen departed.[52] (The difference between the numbers of arrivals and departures need not be cause for concern; there were often long layovers).

It requires a great stretch of the imagination to consider such colonial ports as agressive commercial outposts of the World Economy. Instead, they might be more realistically seen as a neglected and slightly pathetic mercantile appendage to the dominant highland provinces.

Inland towns

In contrast to the huts and shacks of the coast, true towns and cities developed inland, independent of external commercial relations. How large were they? Although fragmentary, Juarros is again the best source, providing the total populations of some 49 inland settlements late in the colonial period. Some were impressively large. The colonial capital, with about 25,000 inhabitants, was approximately the same size as the city of New York at the same time, and Quezaltenango, San Salvador, and Cobán – with 11,000 to 12,000 inhabitants each – were comparable in population to such North American colonial cities as Charleston and Newport.[53] And behind such large urban centers, we find a whole array of smaller, but for the time certainly respectable towns, most often in the neighborhood of 3,000 to 5,000 inhabitants, as can be seen in Table 4.

According to the data provided by Juarros, Central America towards 1800 was urbanized to a considerable degree. Of its one millions inhabitants some 7 percent lived in cities of 10,000 inhabitants or more, and a least 20 percent lived in agglomerations of 4,000 or more.[54]

The very existence of even small towns testifies to an intensive colonial presence. Although during the Classic period, the lowland Maya may possibly have produced true urban population centers, there is general agreement that in the highlands, open and undefended settlements of any consequence were largely abandoned during the

Early Postclassic 'time of troubles' in favor of defensive hilltop sites incapable of housing significant permanent populations. On the eve of the Spanish Conquest, the indigenous population lived scattered in single dwellings or tiny hamlets.[55]

Table 4 *Distribution of inland settlements by size, according to Juarros*

Population	Number of settlements
10,000 and more	5
7,000-9,999	7
4,000-6,999	15
1,000-3,999	18
fewer than 1,000	4
Total	49

Only occasionally were colonial towns founded on previously settled sites. They were new creations, founded in some cases to house Spanish colonists or mixed-bloods (*mestizos, mulatos, pardos, ladinos*), but in others the population was predominantly Indian. Indian towns were the result of Catholic missionary zeal, founded by Franciscan, Dominican, Mercedarian, or secular *doctrineros* for the purpose of spreading the faith and implanting, as they said, Christian polity among the natives. In spite of Spanish protective legislation encouraged by the missionaries, and aimed at isolating Indian communities from the disturbing influence of non-Indian colonists, nevertheless, the early distinction between towns for Indians (*pueblos de indiso, reducciones*) and for non-Indians (*pueblos de españoles, villas de ladinos*) soon broke down. Not only did Spaniards and ladinos infiltrate the Indians zones, but the new non-Indians towns and cities rapidly acquired indigenous population of their own. The process of racial mixture took place on a massive scale, not only in the cities, but also in the rural areas. The purely Spanish segment of the urban population formed a small minority. By the late eighteenth century most towns were neither 'Spanish' nor 'Indian', but racially mixed.[56] The statistics in Table 5 have been collected from Juarros to give on impression of the late colonial ethnic composition of those towns for which such information is available.

    In spite of inferior numbers, Spanish cultural influence penetrated the farthest corners of the colony. The Church was the primary instrument of cultural dominion, a kind of Trojan horse of Hispanism, which once admitted to the new territories forever left its stamp, introducing not only Christian doctrine, but an array of other cultural baggage as well. A perfect example is the modest Dominican reduction of Coapa (Chiapas), founded towards 1528 and destroyed by pestilence in 1680. Recent excavations have uncovered a regular grid pattern of streets 6 meters wide dividing blocks 66 meters on a side, according to the Spanish colonial style. At the center was a *plaza mayor* and, of course, the Dominican convent and church. Christianity eliminated most of the items associated with pre-Columbian religion, the only ceremonial holdover being a spike-ornamented and lime-painted incense burner. Aside from the incense burner, only domestic pottery in the indigenous style persisted, but this was also in the process of being replaced by glazed pottery in the Spanish tradition. Even the most humble house excavated had examples of this new colonial type.[57]

Table 5 *Inland towns for which Juarros gives racial competition*

Town	Spanish [a]	Mixed [b]	Indian	Total
San Salvador	614	10,860	585	12,059
Quezaltenango	464	5,536	5,000	11,000
Granada	863	5,675	1,695	8,233
Cartago	632	7,705	-	8,337
San José	1,976	6,350	-	8,326
León	1,061	6,366	144	7,571
Santa Cruz Chiquimulilla	-	1,108	6,144	7,252
San Miguel Totonicapán	-	454	6,395	6,849
Villa Vieja	1,848	4,807	-	6,655
San Miguel	239	5,300	-	5,539
San Juan Sacatepéquez	75	336	5,000	5,411
Zacatecolula	209	3,087	1,592	4,888
San Vicente	218	3,869	-	4,087
Aguachapa	164	1,383	2,500	4,047
Villa Hermosa	610	3,280	-	3,890
Sonsonate	441	2,795	185	3,421
Chiquimula de la Sierra	296	589	2,000	2,885
San Antonio Retalhuleu	32	826	1,761	2,619
Guazacapan	18	346	1,720	2,084
Nueva Segovia	151	453	-	604

[a] Españoles europeos y criollos
[b] Mestizos, mulatos, pardos, ladinos.
Source Juarros, *Compendio de la historia de la ciudad de Guatemala.*

The physiognomy of the new towns reveals more about the nature of colonial society. In contrast to the military-defensive aspect not only of the pre-Columbian hilltop sites, but also typical of Spanish urbanism in the Peninsula itself, Central America's colonial towns were open to the surrounding landscape and favored level valley sites. No inland town or city of the colonial period was ever fortified against attack, the only permanent works of military architecture being the modest fortifications on the Atlantic coast. With the exception of the fifteen years of civil war which followed the

Conquest, rebellions were very rare. In this respect, Spanish colonization introduced an era of peace in Central America unknown there during the period preceding the Conquest, but also unknown in Europe of the same period. In contrast to Europe's mercantile colonies, which were always vulnerable to shifts in the European balance of maritime power, highland Guatemala was relatively untouched by such fluctuations, and was never military threatened.

As is well known, the regular, open-grid street pattern prevailed in Spanish America, a standard program almost universally observed. In Central America the grid pattern was also applied. The major cities all follow it, but what is perhaps surprising is the degree to which even small towns and villages conformed to the model. Today the pattern still survives as in the colonial period, although smaller communities usually only have a few central streets laid out gridwise; the system breaks down on the peripheries. Of course there are exceptions, such as the large town of Santiago Atitlán, which perhaps due to its accidented location on the lakeshore, has a more haphazard street arrangement.[58] The idea, nevertheless, was there: a 1585 plan of this Indian village shows it stiffly laid out in eight blocks about a central *plaza mayor*. The most prominent building is the Franciscan convent, *el monasterio*.[59]

This aspect of the plan, at least, is completely accurate; Santiago Atitlán even today is dominated by the same whitewashed church on the uphill side of the plaza. In fact the center of every town, large or small, was its plaza and its church. Just as the opening Title of Spain's *Laws of the Indies* reads 'On the Holy Catholic Faith', so every colonial town was spatially arranged around and about its church, the plaza itself serving as a capacious church yard. This single image is perhaps the most remarkable constant feature of the Spanish colonial city, not only in Central America, but in all the New World dominions.

If the church was at the center of even the smallest and most remote villages of the colony, the profusion of churches in the colonial capital was truly remarkable. Of 44 public buildings known to have existed in 1773, the year that Antigua Guatemala was devastated by earthquake, no fewer than 41 were ecclesiastical structures, and of these no fewer than 17 were permanent monastic communities (Table 6).[60]

And any one of several ecclesiastical buildings surpassed the most impressive work of civil architecture in size and grandeur. The plot of land occupied by the convent of San Francisco, for example, was roughly twice the size of that allotted to the building housing the colonial administration and the mint.[60]

The primacy of the religious community in colonial life can also be illustrated by means of another simple statistic. Of some 2,700 printed works known to have been printed in Guatemala during the colonial period, almost 80 percent were either ecclesiastical or devotional works, or theses defended at the theologically-oriented University of San Carlos, as opposed to only about 13 percent civil or military decrees.[62]

This need not surprise us once we take into account the huge monastic community. It is not as yet possible to estimate, even roughly, the total number of persons living behind cloistered walls in Antigua, but we do know, for example, that in 1690, the Franciscan convent housed as many as 100 friars, and that the nuns' convent of La Concepción not only provided refuge for 255 nuns and novices, but also for 700 servants.[63] Today, even with most of the colonial religious constructions lying in ruins, no visitor to Antigua can escape the sensation of walking through a monastery writ large.

Table 6 *Public structures in Antiqua, Guatamala, 1773*

Type, name	Number
Churches and convents for men: San Agustín, Belén, San Francisco, La Merced, Compañía de Jesús, La Recolección de Cristo, Santo Domingo	8
Churches and convents for women: Santa Catalina, Beaterio de Belén, Santa Teresa, El Carmen, La Concepción, Santa Clara, Capuchinas, Santa Rosa de Lima, Beaterio del Rosario	9
Church and hospital: San Pedro	1
Churches (including cathedral): Cathedral, Los Remedios, San Cristóbal el Bajo, San Sebastián, El Calvario, La Candelaria, Santa Cruz, San José el Viejo, Santa Ana, Santa Isabel, de la Virgen, San Lázaro, Santa Cruz del Milagro, Santa Lucía	14
Chapels and hermitages: Espíritu Santo, Nuestra Señora de los Dolores del Cerro, Santísima Trinidad, Benditas Animas, de los Pasos, Cruz de Piedra	6
Other ecclesiastical: University of San Carlos, Diocesan Seminary, Archepiscopal Palace	3
Non-ecclesiastical: Palace of the Captains General (seat of the colonial Administration), City Council (Cabildo), Customs house and tax office	3

Source   Markman, 1966 (see note 60).

Conclusion

Central American culture during the colonial period had nothing to do with the stereotype of the colonial settlement as 'a port and a fort'. Geographically it avoided the sea routes in favor of isolated highland valleys. Fully in keeping with the autarkic ideal of classical antiquity, it inclined towards self-sufficiency instead of commercial ties with the outside world.[64] Racial and cultural mixture was the rule in a colony based on permanent settlement, and not the lure of mercantile speculation. The unifying cultural bond was the Catholic Church, especially the monastic orders. In contrast to trade-oriented coastal factories, Central American towns had no need of fortifications, a fact which surprised the seventeenth-century English traveler Tomas Gage, who thought that everything worth anything could be robbed. Having heard of the fame of the Guatemalan capital, he expected 'strong walls, towers, forts or bulwarks to keep out an aspiring or attempting enemy', but instead found himself entering the city 'without entering through walls, or gates, or passing over any bridge, or finding any watch or guard to examine who I was'.[65] The European image of the colony should take account not only of the grim and somewhat guilty view proposed by theories of colonial exploitation, but also of the telling surprise of a Thomas Gage, who discovered that not all the riches of the Indies were capable of being loaded into a caravel.

Notes to Chapter 1

1   Martin Wolfe, ed., *The Economic Causes of Imperialism* (New York: Wiley 1972), p. 1.

2   Richard Duncan-Jones, *The Economy of the Roman Empire: Quantitative Studies* (Cambridge: The University press 1974).

3   Plato, *Laws*, transl. H.G. Bury, 2 vols. (London: Heineman 1926), Book 4, p. 257.

4   John Mawe, *viagens ao interior do Brasil principalmente aos distritos do ouro e dos diamantes*, trad. S. Benevides Viana (Rio de Janeiro: Zelio Valver, 1944), pp. 105-112.

5   From the first moment of the Spanish Conquest two distinct motives vied for primacy in the minds of the conquistadors: on the one hand the desire to extract (*rescatar*) treasure from the Indians with as little extraneous involvement as possible; and on the other, the instinct to settle permanently (*poblar*), physically incorporating the New World within the Crown of Castile. In their extreme forms, the two attitudes were incompatible. Hermán Cortés, First letter to Charles, V, 10 July 1519, *Cartas y documentos*, ed. Mario Hernández Sánchez Barba (México: Porrúa, 1963), pp. 3-32; Bérnal Díaz del Castillo, *Historia verdadera de la conquista de la Nueva España*, ed. Joaquín Ramírez Cabañas, 2 vols. (México: Porrúa 1968), Chapters 19 and 42.

6   A.C. van Oss, 'The population of Central America towards 1800' unpublished essay (Figure 1).

7   Juan de Estrada, Mapa de la costa de Zapotitlán y Suchitepéquez, 1579, Manuscript Collection, Nettie Lee Benson Library, University of Texas at Austin, JXI-XX-9. Published in A.C. van Oss, *Catholic Colonialism: a Parish History of Guatemala*, 1524-1821, Ph.D Dissertation The University of Texas at Austin, (Ann Arbor, University Microfilms International, 1982), p. 70, Fig. 6.

8   Joan Blaeu, *Blaeus grooten atlas oft wereltbeschrijving in welcke 't aerdrijk, de zee en hemel, wort vertoont en beschreven*, VIII (Amsterdam: Johan Blaeu 1665), unpaginated; Dauril Alden, 'The Population of Brazil in the Late Eighteenth Century: A Preliminary Study', *Hispanic American Historical Review*, (*HAHR*), 43, no. 2 (1963), map on p. 189; Lewis Cecil Gray, *History of Agriculture in southern United States to 1860* (Washington: Carnegie Institution, 1933), 1, p. 14. In North Carolina, the term 'back country' was used to designate 'the regions *back* of the coastal settlements – that is, the interior ... the area west of the fall line', Charles Christopher Crittenden, *The Commerce of North Carolina 1763-1789* (New Haven: Yale University Press, 1936), p. 85.

9 Murdo J. MacLeod, *Spanish Central America: A Socioeconomic History, 1520-1720* (Berkeley: University of California press, 1973), pp. 253-263.

10 Pedro de Alvarado, *An Account of the Conquest of Guatemala in 1524*, transl. and ed. S.J. Mackie, with a facsimile of the original text in Spanish (New York: The Cortés Society, 1924), p. 65.

11 MacLeod, *Spanish Central America*, p. 385; Manuel Rubio, 'El añil o xiquilite', *Anales de la Sociedad de Geografía e Historia de Guatemala*, 26 no. 3-4 (1952) 313-349; Robert S. Smith, 'Indigo Production and Trade in Colonial Guatemala' *HAHR*, 39, no. 2 (1959) 181-211; Troy S. Floyd, 'The Guatemalan Merchants, the Government, and the *Provincianos*, 1750-1800' *HAHR*, 41 no. 1 (1961), 90-110; Elisa Luque Alcaide, *La Sociedad Económica de Amigos del País de Guatemala* (Sevilla: Escuela de Estudios Hispano-Americanos, 1962), pp. 28-32.

12 Smith, 'Indigo Production and Trade', p. 197; Floyd, 'The Guatemalan Merchants', p. 91.

13 Dauril Alden, 'the Growth and Decline of Indigo Production in Colonial Brazil: A Study in Comparative Economic History', *The Journal of Economic History*, 25, no. 1 (1965), 40n. Francisco de Solano gives a poetic assessment of indigo's role in Central America's economy: 'producto vertebral sobre el que gira la fama, el prestigio, la riqueza y la economía de Guatemala... La expresión más brillante del comercio de toda la Capitanía de Guatemala y ... el sostén de la economía colonial de la región, ...' 'La economía agraria de Guatemala, 1768-1772', *Revista de Indias*, no. 123 (1971), pp. 308-309.

14 Pedro Cortés y Larraz, *Descripción geográfico-moral de la diócesis de Goathemala*, ed. Adrián Recinos, 2 vols. (Guatemala: Sociedad de Geografía e Historia de Guatemala 1958); Domingo Juaros, *Compendio de la historia de la ciudad de Guatemala*, 3rd ed., ed. Victor Miguel Díaz, 2 vols. (Guatemala: Tipografía Nacional, 1937).

15 'Descripción geográfica del Reyno de Guatemala adornada con algunos rasgos de historia natural y política de los lugares de dicho Reyno', in Juarros, *Compendio*, 1, 10-94.

16 Juarros, *Compendio*, 1, 19; MacLeod, *Spanish Central America*, 235-252, 291, 302-303.

17 Juan de Zavala, 'Descripción por menor de la provincia de Nicaragua', *Colección de libros y documentos referentes a la historia de América*, ed. Manuel Serrano y Sanz, Tomo VII (Madrid: Victoriano Suárez, 1908), p. 325.

18 Cortés y Larraz, *Descripción geográfico-moral*, 1, p. 159.

19 MacLeod, *Spanish Central America*, pp. 180-181.

20 Floyd, 'The Guatemalan Merchants', pp. 90-91.

21 Cortés y Larraz, *Descripción geográfico-moral*, 1, p. 77.

22 One of the most enthusiastic passages in Juarros' *Compendio* is dedicated to the marketplace of Quezaltenango: 'Es sin duda el pueblo mas famoso, rico y comerciante de todo el Reino, y que hace conocidas ventajas á muchas de sus Villas, y Ciudades... Hai en Quezaltenango obradores de todos oficios, 30 fabricas de pañetes finos de diversos colores, estameñas, salyales y cordellates, en que trabajan 190 oficiales: y muchos telares de ropa de algodón... Su plaza es la mas bien proveida, y de mayor comercio despues de la de Guatemala: se regula su venta anual en 1800 *fanega*s de

trigo: 14000 pesos de cacao, 50 mil de panelas: 12 mil de azucar: 30 mil de texidos de lana: 5 mil de telas de algodón; y a proporción los viveres'. Vol. I, pp. 49-50.

23 Cortés y Larraz, *Descripción geográfico-moral*, I, pp. 27, 29, 30, 35, 38, 40, 48, 192; II, pp. 79, 86, 93, 162, 172, 179, 183, 209, 281.

24 Ibid., I, p. 38.

25 Ibid., I, pp. 35-38; II, pp. 12-13, 22, 123-124, 168.

26 Ibid., I, p. 265; Juarros *Compendio*, I, p. 32.

27 Cortés y Larraz, *Descripción geográfico-moral*, II, pp. 241-242; Juarros, *Compendio*, I, pp. 21, 57.

28 Smith, 'Indigo Production and Trade', p. 197.

29 Floyd, 'The Guatemalan Merchants', 91n.

30 Ibid., 101: 'Indigo was an export commodity destined almost entirely for Cádiz ...'

31 Smith, 'Indigo Production and Trade', 201-202.

32 Ibid., 185.

33 Antonio Gutiérrez y Ulloa, *Estado general de la provincia de San Salvador, Reyno de Guatemala* (año de 1807), 2nd ed. (San Salvador: Ministerio de Educación, 1962), p. 139.

34 *Gazeta de Guatemala*, 12 July 1802, folio 174: 3 pesos per *fanega* in Sololá, 20-24 reales per *fanega* in Salamá; 25 October 1802, folio 274: 20 reales per *fanega* in Cojutepeque; same issue, folio 275: 3 pesos per *fanega* in Metapán; 6 June 1803, folio 243: 3 reales per *almud* in San Salvador and Santa Ana, 2 reales per *almud* in Metapán, 2.5 reales per *almud* in Olocuilta and Zacatecolula, 3.5 reales per *almud* in Cojutepeque. Conversion factors: eight reales to the peso and twelve *almudes* in a *fanega*. One *fanega* is 2.58 bushels. Manuel Carrera Stampa, 'The Evolution of Weights and Measures in New Spain', *HAHR*, 29, no. I (1949) pp. 15-16.

35 Juan de Pineda, 'Descripción de la provincia de Guatemala. Año 1594' Serrano y Sanz, ed., *Colección de libros y documentos*, pp. 415-471; Antonio Vázquez de Espinosa, *Compendio y descripción de la Indias Occidentales*, ed. Charles Upson Clark (Washington: Smithsonian Institute, 1948) parr. 569-757; Cortés y Larraz, *Descripción geográfico-moral*; Gutiérrez y Ulloa, *Estado general*; Luis Diez Navarro, 'Informe sobre la Provincia de Costa Rica presentado por el Ingeniero don Tomás de Rivera y Santa Cruz. Año de 1744', *Revista de los Archivos Nacionales*, 3 (San José, 1938), pp. 579-600; Juan de Estada, Mapa de la costa de Zapotitlán y Suchitepéquez, 1579, MS. JGI.xx, Nettie Lee Benson Library, University of Texas at Austin.

36 Cortés y Larraz, *Descripción geográfico-moral*, I and II.

37 Ibid., II, p. 68.

38 Ibid., II, p. 215.

39 Ibid., I, pp. 57, 247, 261-262; II, pp. 5-6, 98-99, III, 121-122, 128.

40 Ibid., II, pp. 121-122.

41 Ibid., II, p. 235.

42 John Baily, *Central America: Describing Each of the States of Guatemala, Honduras, Salvador, Nicaragua, and Costa Rica: their Natural Features, Products, Population, and Remarkable Capacity for Colonization* (London: Trelawney Saunders 1850), pp. 19-28.

43 Juarros *Compendio*, I, pp. 33, 35, 42, 46.

44 Ibid., 1, pp. 31, 33, 36-37; plan of Omoa in 1768 reproduced along with others in appendices to José Antonio Calderón Quijano, 'El fuerte de San Fernando de Omoa: Su historia e importancia que tuvo en la defensa del Golfo de Honduras', *Revista de Indias*, 3 no. 9 (1942) pp. 515-548 and *Revista de Indias*, 4 no. 11 (1943) pp. 127-163.

45 Juarros, *Compendio*, 1, pp. 36-37.

46 John Ogilby, *América: Being the Latest, and Most Accurate Description of the New World* (London, 1671). The drawing in reprinted in Adriaan C. van Oss, 'El régimen autosuficiente de España en Centro América', *Mesoamérica*, 3 (1982) 80, Figure 2.

47 Juarros, *Compendio*, 1, pp. 34-35; España, Servicios Geográficos y Militar del Ejército, Estado Mayor Central, *Cartografía de Ultramar*, Carpeta 111, Láminas (Madrid: Imprenta del Servicio Geográfico del Ejército, 1955), Num. 123.

48 Juarros, *Compendio*, 1, 27, 39, 43-44.

49 Cortés y Larraz, Descripción geográfico-moral, 1, p. 77.

50 Floyd, 'The Guatemalan Merchants', 98n.

51 Conserved in the Library of the University of Texas at Austin. Of the 135 issues actually published between 14 April 1800 and 25 October 1802 (numbers 152 through 286), 36 are available at the repository. The issues consulted are those of 14 and 21 April and 12 May, 1800; 19 January, 16 and 23 March, 31 August, 17, 21, 24, and 28 September; 1, 5, 8, 12, 15, 19, 22, 26, and 29 October, 1801; 22 February, 8 March, 5 and 26 April, 3, 17, 24, and 31 May, 14 and 21 June, 5 and 12 July, 9 August, 2 and 25 October, 1802; also the supplement to no. 286, not dated but must be from November 1802.

52 *Gazeta de Guatemala*, 17 September 1801, folio 562.

53 Juarros, *Compendio*, 1, pp. 10-74; Carl Bridenbaugh, *Cities in Revolt: urban Life in America, 1743-1776* (New York: Knopf, 1955), p. 216.

54 Population of 49 towns from Juarros, *Compendio*, 1.

55 Marshall Joseph Becker, 'Priest, Peasants, and Ceremonial Centers: The Intellectual History of a Model', *Maya Archaeology and Ethnohistory*, ed. Norman Hammond and Gordon R. Willey (Austin: University of Texas Press, 1979), pp. 3-20; Gordon R. Willey, Gordon F. Ekholm and René F. Millon, 'The Patterns of Farming Life and Civilization', *Handbook of Middle America Indians*, ed. Robert Wauchope, Vol. 1 (Austin: University of Texas Press, 1964), p. 463; Stephan F. de Borhegyi, 'Settlement Patterns of the Guatemalan Highlands', Handbook of Middle American Indians, ed. Wauchope, Vol. 2 part 1 (Austin, 1965), pp. 70, 73.

56 Magnus Mörner, 'La política de segregación y el mestizaje en la Audiencia de Guatemala', *Revista de Indias*, 24, no. 95/96 (1964), pp. 137-151; Sidney D. Markman, 'Pueblos de Españoles and Pueblos de Indios in Colonial Central America', *Verhandlungen des XXXVIII Internationalen Amerikanistenkongresses*, Band IV (München: Kommissionsverlag Klaus Renner, 1972), pp. 189-199; Jorge Luján Muñoz, 'Indios, ladinos y aculturación en San Miguel Petapa (Guatemala) en el siglo XVIII', *Estudios sobre política indigenísta española en América*, Vol. 1 (Valladolid: Seminario de Historia de América, Universidad de Valladolid, 1975), pp. 331-346; Jorge Luján Muñoz, 'Fundación de villas de ladinos en Guatemala en el último tercio del siglo XVIII', *Revista de Indias*, 36, no. 145/146 (1976) pp. 55-81; Jorge Luján Muñoz, 'Reducción y funda-

ción de Salcajá y San Carlos Sijá (Guatemala en 1776)', Separata de *Anales de la Socie-dad de Geografía e Historia de Guatemala*, 49 (1976).

57   Thomas A. Lee, Jr., 'Coapa, Chiapas: A Sixteenth-Century Coxoh Maya Village on the Camino Real', *Maya Archaeology and Ethnohistory*, ed. Hammond and Willey, pp. 208-222.

58   William T. Sanders, 'Settlement Patterns', *Handbook of Middle American Indians*, ed. Wauchope, vol 6 (Austin, 1967), p. 80.

59   Mapa a colore del lago de Atitlán 1585, Manuscript Collection, Nettie Lee Benson Library, University of Texas at Austin, JGI-XX, fol. 306.

60   Sidney D. Markman, *Colonial Architecture of Antigua Guatemala* (Philadelphia: American Philosophical Society, 1966), pp. 93-211.

61   J. Joaquín Pardo, Pedro Zamora Castellanos y Luis Luján Muñoz, *Guía de Antigua Guatemala*, 3a ed. (Guatemala: Pineda Ibarra, 1969), plano 11.

62   A.C. van Oss, 'Printed culture in Central America, 1660-1821', in this volume.

63   Nómina y lista y relación jurada del número de religiosos, que tiene esta provincia del Santísimo Nombre de Jesús de Guatemala, con distinción de parcialidades calidad de los sujetos, y otras noticias, concernientes, el perfecto conocimiento, que se pretende, hecha este año de 1690. Manuscript Collection, Nettie Lee Benson Library, University of Texas at Austin, G19 gol. 83; Markman, *Colonial Architecture*, p. 166.

64   Aristotle, *Politics*, transl. H.Rackham (London: William Heinemann 1932; repr. 1967), Book VII, Chapters 4 and 5.

65   Thomas Gage, *Travels in the New World*, ed. J.E.S. Thompson (Norman: University of Oklahoma Press, 1958), p. 176.

2

Vázquez's chronicle as a source for the history of religion and architecture in colonial Guatemala

Prime sources for the history of colonial religion and architecture are the hundreds of religious chronicles and geographical descriptions written by Spanish and Creole churchmen of the period. The value of such sources in general is well known and need not be justified further here. For Guatemala the fundamental works of this type include the description written by Remesal, Fuentes y Guzmán, Ximénez, García de la Concepción, Cortés y Larraz, and Juarros.[1] To the same series belongs the *Crónica de la Provincia del Santísimo Nombre de Jesús de Guatemala* written by the Franciscan friar Francisco Vázquez towards 1700 and published in two volumes by the Franciscan printing shop in Guatemala in 1714 and 1716.[2] The purpose of this paper is to briefly explore some of the possibilities and peculiarities of Vázquez's account of the Franciscan Order in Guatemala from its beginnings in 1524 through the date of publication.

The author

Francisco de Asís Vázquez de Herrera was an *hijo de provincia,* born in the city of (Antigua) Guatemala in 1647 and accepted into its Franciscan convent at the age of fifteen or sixteen. Ordained as a priest in 1669, he executed a variety of offices during his ecclesiastical career before being officially appointed Chronicler of the Province (of the Holy Name of Jesus of Guatemala) in 1683. As early as 1681 he had already begun compiling his work; Vázquez wrote not only from personal experience, but also had access to the archives of his Order. Most of the writing seems to have been done during the 1690s, but corrections were made up until the very time of printing, and even afterwards: the manuscript version contains additions, often in handwriting different from that of Vázquez, referring to developments which took place as late as 1720. Vázquez himself seems to have died in 1714, although the exact date of his death is not known.[3]

Literary aspects and organization

With its 305 chapters sprawling over more than 1,600 folio pages in the original edition, the *Crónica* is the most long-winded single work published in Guatemala during the colonial period. Its purpose is frankly apologetic and didactic. In part it is a Franciscan riposte to the Dominican history of Guatemala written by Remesal a hundred years earlier. Without once mentioning Remesal by name, Vázquez is early referring to his Dominican rival when he deplores 'la ponzoña que derramaron algunos malsines' and 'libros ... forjados de noticias y relaciones apasionadas de hombres sediciosos'.[4] Vázquez, in singing the glories of his own Order in Guatemala, is not above pulling the rug out from under the foremost historian of the rival Dominicans.

The Franciscan ideal of simplicity finds little echo in Vázquez's prose style, which favors long and confusing sentences and paragraphs, overdrawn comparisons and metaphors, and flights of pedantic oratory punctuated by lengthy quotes in Latin of murky significance. The narrative is liberally sprinkled with attempted Gongorisms ('Ladrillo fué misterioso de este espiritual seráfico edificio'), and the 292-word sentence with which Vázquez chooses to open his work prefigures a style of writing in which clarity of meaning is sacrificed at the altar of literary 'elegance'. Part of the problem is the prolixity common to writers of the period, but even among chroniclers Vázquez is heavy reading, witness the acid commentary of the editor of the *Gaceta de Guatemala* in 1797; 'Al padre Vázquez, fuera de no tener ninguna de las bellas prendas de Remesal y de Fuentes, le fue dado un estilo tan duro, tan cansado, tan insoportable, que a quien lea dos hojas de su libro sin vomitar, bien pueden dársele eméticos a pasto'.[5]

Vázquez has divided his Chronicle into five books, which ostensibly correspond to the Pentateuch. His history of the Franciscan enterprise in Guatemala is one of Christian beginnings and preparations for redemption. Sporadically, but with great fervor, Vázquez urges his readers to consider the early Franciscans as barefoot soldiers of God, spreading the law of salvation among the idolatrous Indians, hitherto in the devil's bondage. Old-Testament imagery permeates the *Crónica*; there are relatively few allusions to the New Testament or to the lives of the Saints. The Franciscan fathers in Guatemala, as portrayed by Vázquez, bear less resemblance to the gentle man of Assisi than to the Patriarchs of Israel whom Vázquez evokes literally at every turn: Gideon, Joshua, Melchisedek, Jonah, Caleb, Elijah, Abraham, Noah, Moses, Isaac, Jacob, Ezekiel, Elisha, Phinehas, Levi, Mattithiah, Job, Tobiah.

This symbolic program is not systematically carried out, but laid on as ornament. The five-book division is arbitrary and incidental to the content. A practical guide to the actual organisation of the work is as follows:

Book 1   Development and organisation of the Franciscan Province of Guatemala from the arrival of the first missionaries in 1524 until its erection as an autonomous province in 1565.

Book II   Development and organisation of the Franciscan Province from
               1565 through 1600.
Books III and IV Biographical sketches of a great number of Guatemalan Francis-
               cans, 1524 through the late seventeenth century.
Book V   Subdivided into three treatises. Treatise I deals with Franciscan
               missionary efforts in the frontier regions of Honduras and Nica-
               ragua; Treatise II with the organization and development of the
               Franciscan Province 1600-1716: and Treatise III with the foun-
               dation of the Tercera Orden de Penitencia in Guatemala.

Books III and IV are the most laden with trivia and also in some respects represent a
literary low point, although some biographical details are so incredible as to provide a
measure of unintended comic relief. Books I and II, and V are rich in useful historical
information, which when pieced together give us a coherent picture of many aspects
of Franciscan activity in colonial Central America.

The social, economic, and ecological setting

Late eighteenth-century ecclesiastical accounts, such as those by Cortés y Larraz and
Juarros (see note 1), show a lively interest in the ethnic, demographic, economic, and
ecological characteristics of the Guatemalan land and people. This was, after all, the
setting in which the Church had to deploy itself, and the limitations imposed by the
natural environment were of vital concern. The attitude of Vázquez is more heroic in
this respect; he is biblically vague about the natural obstacles to missionary work,
stressing Franciscan stoicism and virtue in the face of adversity without really telling
much about the nature of that adversity.

The *Crónica* is almost devoid of population data, although missionary work is
always extremely sensitive to population distribution and fluctuations. Indeed, we do
hear of the occasional failure of a *doctrina* through local population decline, or of the
rapid growth of another, but Vázquez hardly ever deals in numbers, however approximate. One of the few exceptions is that he mentions a figure of 1,000 Indians for
the village of Santiago Atitlán about 1680, but in the absence of comparative data either for different villages at about the same time, or for the same village at different
times, little can be done with such an estimate.[6] There are scattered indications of
epidemics, especially if they affected the capital or nearby Almolonga.[7] A bizarre disease affected the Indians of the Pacific coastal region, leaving large numbers of blind
in the adjoining Franciscan *doctrinas* of Suchitepéquez, Patulul, and Ziquinalá.[8]

Information on agriculture and economy is similarly scarce, and limits itself to
scattered details. For example, Vázquez mentions the extremely rapid multiplication
of cattle during the early years of the colony, and the fertility of the soil of the valley

of Guatemala, responsible for yield ratios of 100:1, according to the *Crónica*.[9] On transportation and distribution of products, on markets, there is not a word. Almost the only reference to transportation possibilities is a description of the (very bad) road between Sololá and Panajachel.[10]

As an ethnographer Vázquez is, if possible, worse. Far from sharing the curiosity, if not admiration, any missionary must have for the people he attempts to proselytize, Vázquez rarely goes further than repeatedly expressing contempt for native laziness, concupiscence, and treachery. Once converted to Christianity – this is roughly Vázquez's attitude – Indians remain weak and sorry creatures, always in danger of relapse to earlier pagan ways and never to be completely trusted. In their pagan state Indians are 'bloodthirsty wolves' in constant communication with the devil. Vázquez takes sharp issue with the Dominican writers Las Casas and Remesal, who attribute a benign character to the Indians, and blamed Spanish colonists for impeding the work of evangelization:

> Y se concluye que el embarazo a la predicación y fundación de conventos, no le pusieron los conquistadores, sino que lo causaron los indios, *por no salir de sus enormes torpezas, crueldades, brujerías, latrocinios, prestigios, idolatría supersticiones, homicidios y vicios, con que el demonio, con quien conversaban y comunicaban, se hacía servir y reverenciar ...*[11]

If Vázquez's insight into native society thus does not go beyond a superficial moral judgment, his view of Spanish society, as reflected in the pages of the *Crónica* is hardly more profound. Spaniards and Creoles are with few exceptions portrayed as pious, generous, hard-working individuals, practically interchangeable. About the workings of the society, or life in the city of Guatemala, Vázquez is elliptical or silent. Spanish colonials are dealt with exclusively in function of their relations with the Franciscan Order. Society consists of two groups: on the one hand a large group of friends and benefactors, and on the other a small group of 'sowers of dissention' and troublemakers. Only in a few particularly egregious instances does Vázquez dirty his hands with the latter group.

Religious life

It is of course in the area of describing ecclesiastical, and above all Franciscan, theory and practice that Vázquez makes his most important contribution. Here he is truly an invaluable source, although his undeniable prejudices and unabashed glorification of his own Order make him anything but an impartial witness. In all matters involving the least degree of personal interpretation he should be used with extreme caution. My impression is that he is a man perfectly capable of lying in order to promote the good cause.

A systematic study of the *Crónica* would, in my opinion, provide a fine point of departure for a number of specific topics, although the already mentioned limitations of the work make it necessary to supplement Vázquez's word with evidence from other sources. In the area of missionary methods we might mention the effect of personal conduct upon effective proselytization; the obstacle posed by ignorance of native languages, and Franciscan attempts to overcome this barrier; the (lack of) effectiveness of the Spanish policy of *reducciones* among the Indians; and the extirpation of idolatry. Part of Vázquez's bitterness towards the Indian population might be explained by the fact that at the time he wrote, more than 150 years after the first missionary activities in Guatemala, Christianity still had only a tentative foothold in many parts of Central America. The relativity of Christianity's success in Central America is symbolically illustrated by the fact that Vázquez chose to model his chronicle on the first five books of the Old Testament. In placing the burden for this shortcoming on the Indians' shoulders, Vázquez avoids responsibility for his Order, but part of the explanation must be sought in the missionary process itself.

Vázquez's observations on established parish life are also a vein which might profitably be mined. The introduction, frequency and manner of administering the sacraments of Baptism, Communion, Marriage and Extreme Unction are all questions discussed at least in passing by Vázquez. At Almolonga, burials took place inside the church, and not in the churchyard.[12] Even in the smallest towns, processions were often associated with the liturgy.[13] In a large town, such as San Salvador, processions could be very elaborate, with arches decorated with flowers and musical accompaniment. In San Salvador the feast of the Holy Sacrament lasted eight days.[14] Such festivities were organized and paid for by the confraternities which sprang up in every town and village. Membership in the confraternities was open to Indians, and to women as well as men. In one case at least, even children were encouraged to join.[15] Some Indians complained about the expense involved in joining a confraternity, but expenses were usually modest. The Confraternity of San Nicolás Tolentino in Santiago Cotzumaluapan paid eight reales for one Mass every month, and three pesos for the titular feast each year.[16] In no case, according to Vázquez, did any village confraternity spend more than 20 pesos per year.[17] Confraternities often sprang into being spontaneously around a given image; such was the Confraternity of the Santa Cabeza, for example, in the city of Guatemala. Here the image in question consisted of the remnants of Crucifixion destroyed by pirates in Trujillo in 1643.[18]

Although Guatemala's Franciscans were highly active in the spiritual care of 'the world', the heart of any monastic order is its conventual life. Life in the convent is thus also a subject which receives detailed treatment, if not critical scrutiny, in the pages of the *Crónica*. Vázquez reproduces, for example, the original statutes and constitutions of the Province of Guatemala adopted in 1567, as well as the rules for novices of 1582.[19] It is difficult to form an opinion on the degree of observance of the rules. On the one hand, Vázquez claims that observance even went beyond the mini-

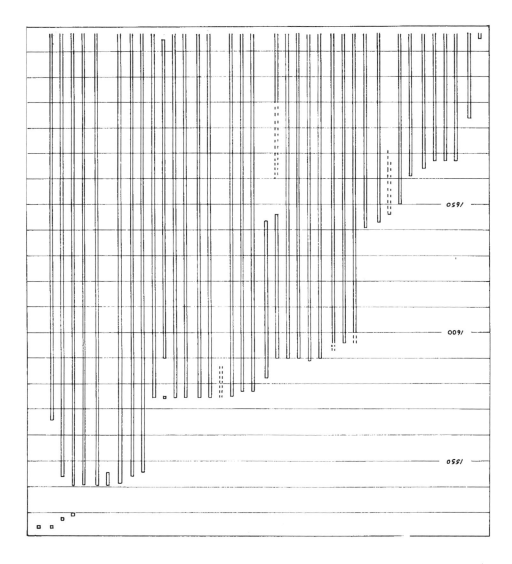

Figure 1   *Franciscan establishments in existence 1524-1716, according to Vázquez*

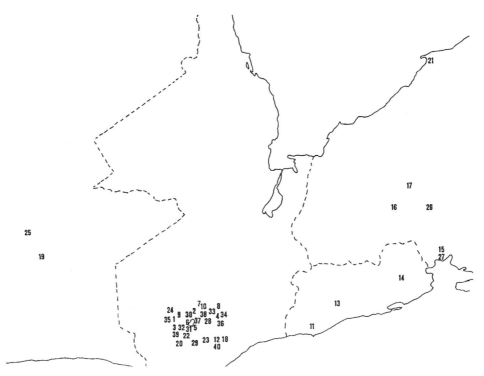

Figure 2 *Map of Franciscan establishments, Province of Guatemala, 1524-1716, according to Vázquez (for numbers, see Figure 1)*

mum guidelines provided by the statutes (his lives of the Franciscan religious are an interminable series of fasts, nightly disciplines, hairshirts, and even auto-crucifixions); on the other hand he does not omit to mention that the rebuilding program carried out in the Guatemalan convent between 1684 and 1689 included cells for demented friars and for punishment of 'such that deserve it'.[20]

Works of conventual hygiene and cleanliness receive great attention; such works were performed by the friars themselves, almost uninterruptedly it would seem.[21] And among the more humble monastic offices, that of porter receives special attention; the lives of two porters are described in some detail.[22]

In the pre-university period of Guatemalan history, the training of religious had to take place in the convents themselves. The first chair of Latin in Guatemala City's Franciscan convent was instituted in 1548.[23] In 1573/75 attempts were being made to elevate the program of studies to *colegio* level, and Fray Juan Casero was the first Franciscan in Guatemala to read Latin and Theology on a regular basis.[24] By 1583 Guatemala was no longer completely dependent on 'imported' religious from Spain or Mexico, since priests could be trained and ordained in the Guatemala province.[25]

As one of the 'mendicant' orders, the Franciscans were at least in theory completely dependent for their material sustenance on what they could 'beg' from the laity. In part, donations took the form of altar fees, which had fixed values. Royal largesse was also a source of income. A Royal Cédula of 1533, for example, ordered that one-fourth of the tribute payments collected in Guatemala be applied to the expenses of building churches. A 1575 Cédula decreed that Franciscan *doctri-neros* receive a yearly stipend of 50,000 maravedís from the royal treasury, the same amount paid to secular *doctrineros*. Since such payments were subtracted from tributes collected in Guatemala, some *encomenderos* resisted these provisions.[26] The King also might make special, once-only donations, such as the 3,000 pesos he gave for the reconstruction of the convent in Almolonga towards 1582, or the donation to every newly founded Franciscan convent after 1575 of one silver chalice, enough wine to celebrate Mass the first year, and oil for the lamp of the Holy Sacrament.[27] Municipal governments might also make certain facilities available; in Guatemala the *Ayuntamiento* granted a water allotment to the Franciscan convent in 1544, and increased the allotment in 1573.[28] Personal donations came in all sizes. The President of the Guatemalan *Audiencia* personally donated all the meat consumed by Guatemala's Franciscan community beginning in 1573.[29] Large donors were given special seating privileges in the church, and sometime burial privileges. In recognition of their large donations to the Guatemalan convent, the Medrano, Solórzano, and Alvárez de la Vega families were given special burial vaults in the sumptuous Loreto chapel lateral to the church.[30] Modest gifts were common, as in Tegucigalpa, where Diego Juárez and Diego Hernández each promised a bell, and Luis de Achiaga, Carlos Ferrufiño, and Alonso Rodríguez Bravo gave a hundred *tostones* each.[31]

Historical geography of the Franciscan Order

Between 1524 and 1716 the Guatemalan Franciscan Order expanded from their original temporary chapel in Salcajá to a system of 34 convents with a total religious population of more than 200 friars. Vázquez narrative allows us to chart this development.

Figure 1 shows the chronology of the Franciscan establishments, as reconstructed from Vázquez.[32] Except in the cases of the first four ephemeral missions of the 1520s, the establishments are permanent convents, with at least two resident friars and a vote in the meetings of the Provincial Chapter. The chronology of foundation of new convents shows that Franciscan expansion in Guatemala proceeded gradually, and lacked the explosive character observed for the mendicant orders in New Spain during the same period.[33] Until about 1600, the limiting factor was the number of available Franciscans. During the sixteenth century the Guatemalan province was entirely dependent upon recruitment abroad, mostly in Spain. And in this recruitment it had to compete with more populous and less isolated New Spain to the north. Guatemala did not fare especially well in this competition. In 1559, for instance, there were already some 380 Franciscans in New Spain, compared with only about 29 in Guatemala.[34] Regularly throughout the sixteenth century, Guatemala's Franciscans complained about the lack of religious personnel at their disposal, and repeatedly requested reinforcements.[35]

The permanent Franciscan presence in Guatemala dates from 1540 or 1541; the earlier attempts at religious colonization during the 1520s had been frustrated by the continuation of Indian uprisings from 1526 through the 1530s. It was during the period 1540-1600 that the greatest number of convents were founded. New foundations took place in waves or phases. There were three such waves during the sixteenth century, each associated with the arrival of a new shipload (*barcada*) of Franciscan friars in Guatemala. Thus the wave of foundations which took place between 1540 and 1545 was made possible by Franciscan missions of 5 and 28 religious in 1540 and about 1543, respectively; the wave of the mid-1570s followed a shipment of 40 friars in 1571; and the wave of the 1590s was associated with the arrival of 23 or 26 religious in 1593.[36] Until 1600, the number of convents founded was a pure function of the arrival of new recruits to the Franciscan province. The locations chosen by the Franciscans for their establishments (Figure 2), while including far-flung outposts as remote from Guatemala as Chiapas and eastern Honduras, were heavily concentrated in the central Guatemalan highlands. This Franciscan heartland had been staked out during the first wave of expansion in 1540-1545. The second wave of expansion, 1566-1582, was responsible for the creation of the most remote outposts, and testifies to an early expansionist optimism on the part of the Franciscans. With the exception of Ciudad Real in Chiapas, the Franciscan outposts were a disappointment; especially those in eastern El Salvador and Honduras ran into difficulties almost at once.[37] Disillusionment with the outlying areas reflects itself in the third wave of expansion, 1589-1600; by the 1590s Guatemalan Franciscans had decided to consolidate their possessions in the heartland instead of pursuing the optimistic imperialism rehearsed in the second wave. By 1600 the maximum limits of territorial expansion had been reached for all practical purposes.

Sixteenth-century expansion gave way to a period of consolidation which lasted through the entire seventeenth century. After 1600, emphasis shifted from opening up new territories to building on, and improving, existing possessions. This can be seen first of all in the relationship between the number of convents, which ceases to grow after 1600, and the total religious population, which continues to rise. Until the 1590s, each new shipment of friars was followed by a wave of new foundations. But the arrival of 20 new religious in 1608, and 30 in 1610 did not lead to the establishment of new convents; they went to augment the size of already existing ones.[38] The population of the main convent in the city of Guatemala tripled in size between the late sixteenth and early eighteenth centuries. Such new foundations as there were arose out of the interstices between the convents of the central Guatemalan highlands. By 1716 Vázquez was able to boast of a tightly knit ring of Franciscan houses:

> Todos los referidos pueblos y Guardianías están en tal disposición situados, que saliendo de Guatemala por Itzapa, se va haciendo un cordón y dando vuelta por la costa, hasta llegar a Guatemala encadenándose unos pueblos con otros ... sin que haya despoblado en todo el ámbito dicho.[39]

The shift from early expansionism to subsequent consolidation was accompanied by a shift in Franciscan mentality. The shift can be traced in the imagery employed in the Franciscan biographical sketches of Vázquez. Whereas the founding fathers are described as militant knights of Christ, adventuring into the wilderness in search of souls, the fate of the later Franciscans was to stay put and to build. Here is a short sampler of images, one group occurring all earlier than page 140 of book III, the second group taken from the pages thereafter:

> *The founding fathers*: dichoso soldado de Cristo; capitán valiente de la milicia seráfica; caza de almas por los montes; sagrados paladines del Evangelio; cazador de almas; soldados de Cristo; valeroso soldado de Cristo; valerosísimo soldado de Cristo.[40]

> *The builders:* ladrillo misterioso de este espiritual seráfico edificio; cimientos del edificio de las virtudes; levantar el edificio de la vida evangélica; como diestro arquitecto levantó el edificio de la perfección.[41]

By the end of the sixteenth century some of the evangelical fervor had gone out of the Franciscan enterprise in Guatemala. A period of stabilization set in, and with it, Franciscans began to devote more energy to the improvement and care of their conventual architecture.

Vázquez on church architecture

Vázquez documents building campaigns and describes the architecture in greater or lesser degree on many Franciscan edifices up to the time he wrote, as well as providing incidental data on many other colonial buildings both secular and ecclesiastic. On secular and religious, but non Franciscan, architecture, Vázquez should be considered a supplementary source, to be consulted with other chroniclers of the period. On the Franciscan buildings he is sufficiently thorough as to deserve consideration on his own. The *Crónica* by itself provides a fairly detailed portrait of Franciscan architectural production through the early eighteenth century.

Since outside the main convent of Guatemala City, the normal monastic community consisted of just two friars,[42] and even by 1690 the largest community outside the capital only housed five,[43] Franciscan simplicity in architecture was more than just an ideal, it was a rigorously self-enforcing rule of life. During the early period no Guatemala convent outside the capital could have even aspired to violate the letter of the Ordinances drawn up for the American provinces by the General of the Franciscan Order in Rome in 1541, which stipulated that no convent should contain more than six cells in each dormitory, that the conventual buildings should be 'very poor'. Cells could not be larger than eight feet (*pies*) wide by nine long, and cloister walks could not be wider than seven feet.[44] These rules, which have a certain academic ring in the setting of sixteenth-century Guatemala, were echoed by the Provincial Chapter of Guatemala in the original constitution (1567) with the further elaboration that:

> ... en ningún tiempo se permita el que se hagan de bóveda nuestras iglesias, salvo sobre el Altar Mayor, según lo que dispuso y permitió S. Buenaventura, cuyas constituciones damos aquí por expresadas. Y asimismo, que los edificios de nuestros conventos sean humildes y pobres, y las celdas de los frailes, chozas y tabernáculos de peregrinos y advenedizos, que no tienen casa propia, pues caminan al cielo. Y así, demás del tamaño y pequeñez que está mandado se hagan, no tengan otro adorno que una cruz de palo, que les sirve para dormir, y ningún fraile por sí, ni por otro, dé calor para que se contravenga a la pobreza de los edificios.[45]

The first 'convents' founded during the 1540s were adobe or wattle hermitages, without divisions or ornament. The house at Almolonga, which served as the first Franciscan headquarters in 1540 and 1541,

> apenas tenía un lienzo de horcones y bajareque, cubierto de paja, sin divisiones, ni forma de vivienda, como cosa que se había hecho para un mero hospicio de los religiosos ... era una porciúncula, en lo pequeño y pobre.[46]

The first structure in Guatemala City was an adobe church, with a dormitory for the two resident friars made of wattle, church and dormitory with thatched roofs, and the churchyard walled in by a hedge of nettles.[47]

This type of construction was common to the poorer convents even at the time Vázquez wrote. They were fire traps. The church at Samayac burned down in 1617 'de un fulminante rayo que la hizo cenizas'.[48] Fire also destroyed the thatched convent and church in Patulul in 1636; it was rebuilt immediately, presumably in the same style.[49] When the church and convent at San Bartolomé Suchitepéquez were destroyed by lightning in 1645, the village was too poor to reconstruct them, and the resident friar moved to nearby Santo Tomás. The little convent and church he managed to build there were struck down by lightning in 1681.[50] Similarly, the fire that destroyed the church and convent at Santiago Cotzumaluapa in 1715 occasioned a move to the adjoining village of Santa Lucía. In 1716 a church was being built next to the thatch-roofed convent.[51] If a storm failed to direct lightning to one of these humble structures, heavy rainfall might be sufficient to bring the roof down, as it did in the case of San Vicente's parish church in 1663.[52]

It was not until the final quarter of the sixteenth century that a number of the better-to-do convents were reformed and given more permanent buildings. The building campaigns which began after 1575 correspond to the onset of what we have called the phase of consolidation or stabilization of the Franciscan province of Guatemala. During the late 1570s and early 1580s the convents and churches of Comalapa, San Miguel Totonicapán, Quezaltenango, Sololá, Tecpán Guatemala, and Santiago Atitlán were all refurbished. These were all towns in the Franciscan heartland of central Guatemala; the buildings they received were a great improvement on the old structures, and lasted until Vázquez's time:

> Estas eran de calicanto y aquellas de lodo y carrizos tendidos; las nuevas de maderas y clavadas, y las antiguas de palos toscos y débiles atados con bejucos; las nuevas de teja, las antiguas de paja ...[53]

The Franciscan convent at Almolonga was also reconstructed around 1580; part of the cost of construction was paid by a special royal grant of 3,000 pesos.[54]

Outside the central Guatemalan highland region new construction also took place. In Ciudad Real, private donations made it possible to construct a 'very good and spacious' convent between 1577 and 1583. It was said to be large enough to house up to twenty friars, even though usually there were only four.[55] In 1578 two friars also set up housekeeping in Huitiupan 'los cuales edificaron su monasterio con portería, campanilla y refectorio'.[56] In Sonsonate, the founders of the Franciscan convent blithely ignored the prohibition against vaulted Franciscan churches. With the support of a large donation they undertook 'una obra muy suntuosa de arquería y bóveda, que se acabó, porque la bienhechora murió dentro de pocos años, y heredaron los albaceas ...'.[57] Other works were underway in San Salvador in 1580 and in Comayagua in 1694.[58]

If thunderstorms were the terror of the adobe and thatchwork churches, earthquakes were deadly for the more substantially built ones. According to Vázquez, the more substantially built a convent was, the more it had to fear from earthquakes. And earthquakes were so frequent in Guatemala that it is a marvel that Central Americans continued to build at all. Vázquez is extremely good at his accounts of earthquakes; the worst ones, according to him, occurred in 1565, 1575-77, 1585-86, 1651, 1663, 1676, and 1689. Between 1575 and 1590 there were so many earthquakes, Vázquez says, that 'en más de sesenta años, siguientes al de 1590, no osaban edificar templos, ni casas de suntuosidad, porque cuanto más recias las fábricas, tanto menos seguridad tenían, y en los edificios más fuertes era mayor el estrago'.[59]

Whether or not fear of earthquakes was the reason, there does seem to have been a period of decreased architectural activity following the campaigns of the final quarter of the sixteenth century. There were exceptions, however, as at Comayagua, where the 1620s and 1630s were exactly the period of greatest activity. The Cuardian, Diego del Saz,

> trabajó mucho en hacer la iglesia y convento de Comayagua, yendo él mismo con los cortadores de la madera a los montes a traerla, y cargando la piedra para la fábrica sobre sus mismos hombros ... Hízose ... el año de 1630 el noviciado, mucha parte de la portería, y la sala *De profundis,* y otras muchas obras, unas que se acabaron en ese tiempo, y otras que se principiaron.[60]

The convent in Guatemala City

The primacy of the main convent at (Antigua) Guatemala was such that at any given moment it was likely to have as many as twenty times the number of friars in residence than the second-largest convent in the province. Its architectural program reflected this primacy; by the time Vázquez wrote it was far and away the most elaborate Franciscan structure in Central America. Just as the conventual population of the main convent rose gradually, from two at the time of its foundation to around hundred at the beginning of the eighteenth century, so the complex of buildings which housed the community only took shape gradually. Vázquez is a good source of data for the architectural history of the convent.

The first building, which has been mentioned above, arose in a hurry. It could not have been begun before late 1541, and it was already in place by June, 1542. There was a small church and some kind of living arrangement; both buildings were of adobe and thatch. Guatemala's Franciscan community did not stay long in this provisional convent. Either in 1543 or 1544 they moved to a new site, some 200 meters to the north. After moving, the Franciscans continued to administer the original church as the Capilla de la Veracruz for Indians of the barrio de San Francisco. This chapel survived in deteriorated condition until the mid-seventeenth century, when it was torn down to make way for the church of San Felipe Neri (the Escuela de Cristo).[61]

At the new site, which remains the site of the church of San Francisco today, work was begun immediately on a more permanent building. The whole community lent a hand: 'Acudían a la obra del convento e iglesia los vecinos y conquistadores con mucho amor y voluntad'. Construction was still underway in 1548, but work must have been completed by 1552, because in that year a chapel was given in use to the Confraternity of the Veracruz, and the same Confraternity was allowed to use the chapter room for its meetings.[62]

Vázquez describes the structure as it must have looked upon completion:

> Cada lienzo del claustro no pasaba de doce varas, y en esta distancia había doce celdas en los tres lienzos, sacristía y refectorio, y alguna otra oficina del convento. Cada celda era de nueve pies de largo y ocho de ancho, al tenor y

letra de la constitución; que más parecía estufa para tomar sudores, o empare-
damiento en castigo de culpas, que vivienda de hombres. Las paredes princi-
pales eran de adobe, los tabiques y divisiones de bajareque ... de carrizos ten-
didos, atados con bejucos en horcones de palo, entrepuesto lodo. Cada celda
tenía una tronera o fenestra de una cuarta de ancho y alto, para la luz necesa-
ria para leer en algún libro; y en tal altura, que estaba más de dos varas del
suelo para quitar toda ocasión del más leve divertimiento ... Las puertecitas de
las celdas eran tan bajas, que el más pequeño del cuerpo, había menester in-
clinarse para entrar por ellas. Puertas y ventanas en muchos años no las hubo
de madera, sino fué en la iglesia y sacristía; en las celdas servían de puertas
unas esteras (que llaman acá petates) pendientes de dos estacas por lo alto.
Cosa encalada no la hubo, sino fué la iglesia y sacristía. El dormitorio tenía
vara y medio de ancho. La iglesia fué necesario hacer mayor de lo que quisie-
ran aquellos seguidores de la santa pobreza; y así tuvo treinta varas de largo y
ocho de ancho, por la continuada frecuencia de los fieles ...[63]

This second church and convent lasted for a quarter of a century essentially untouched, even though the earthquake of 1565 caused such damage that the church
had to be shorn up for more than ten years to prevent its thatched roof from caving
in, 'por estar sus débiles maderos vencidos, la paja podrida'.[64]

Finally the old church was torn down and rebuilt during the period 1578-1581,
the same period that several other central Guatemalan convents were undergoing
reforms. Just as in the 1540s, the entire city turned out to help:

Asistía, pues, personalmente el señor Presidente, sirviendo a veces de peón, y
a su ejemplo muchos caballeros y gente devota. Los religiosos, así sacerdotes
como de noviciado, cargaban mezcla, piedra y ladrillo.

The new church was thus far more solidly built than the older one, with walls of
stone and brick masonry. The nave of the new church was roofed in wood, but the
capilla mayor was given an amateuristically designed masonry vault, 'tan baja,
cuanto a todos se venía a los ojos'. A large lateral chapel was apparently also constructed to Saint Anne at the same time; it still existed in Vázquez's day, and was
known as the 'capilla de Indios'.[65]

If any work was done during the late sixteenth century to repair the conventual
living quarters, Vázquez does not mention it. Upon termination of the church in
1581 or 1582, no important construction was carried out until about 1600, when the
rich Loreto chapel was built. The exact dates of construction are not known for the
Loreto chapel, but it was certainly begun after 1594 and finished by 1605. The Loreto
chapel was housed in the south tower of the main façade of the church, which was
thus also presumably built at the same time. Decoration of the façade was also in
progress, since immediately prior to the building of the Loreto chapel, the space

which it was to occupy was being used to store stone efigies which were later to be placed in niches in the façade.[66] All signs thus point to a general reconstruction and enlargement of the west end of the church towards 1600.

The Loreto chapel, which no longer exists, lives on in Vázquez detailed description:

> Su forma es cuadrada y de cuadratura perfecta, tiene de ancho veinte y dos palmos y otros tantos de largo, la puerta principal mira al norte, y sale a nuestra iglesia junto a la puerta principal de ella, en la pared frontera meridional está el hermoso retablo. En el lado hacia el poniente tiene una hermosa, clara y bien dispuesta ventana guarnecida de dos rejas de fierro, la una que sirve de preservar la vidriera de que consta todo lo claro, alambrada con todo primor y la otra más interna en que se entretejen los vidrios. Demás de estas dos rejas férreas que están embebidas en la pared sale otra reja de fierro volada a modo de balcón que hermosea la ventana y hace sobresalir toda la obra. Entra el sol a besar las aras en el verano equinoccio.
>
> En la pared hacia el oriente solamente tiene una puertecilla, bastante para salir el sacerdote a decir misa, porque a aquella parte tiene su sacristía. Todo el pavimento y paredes está vestido de unos vivos vistosos azulejos que se trajeron para una obra tan insigne de la Nueva España. ... Las paredes son fuertes, anchas y muy pulidas, y tan recias, que sobre la capilla está otra mansión que la suele habitar el religioso que cuida del reloj y despertar a maitines; y por último una espaciosa torre que fué de las campanas, y por haberse hecho años después otra igual, a la otra parte de la portada, sirve de reloj que está superior a la capilla. La cumbre o cielo de la capilla es de media bóveda con muy aseados y bien dispuestos lazos, perfiles, listas y molduras, que parece una media esfera, donde el oro como ascuas, lo colorido de hermosas pinturas de muy delicado pincel, todo el óleo, hacen que parezca un abreviado cielo; no sólo por la copia de efigies de santos que en el cielo de la capilla se veneran, sino por la belleza y variedad que de se adorna. El suelo o pavimento de la capilla tiene debajo una soterrana bóveda y entierro, que consignó el convento a la estirpe generación de los Medranos, Solórzanos y Alvarez de la Vega, no sólo por premio de la donación que hicieron al convento de tan peregrina imagen [la imagen de la Virgen de Loreto venerada en la capilla], sino por haber sido tan singulares bienhechores de la capilla.[67]

The first general reconstruction of the conventual quarters since the 1540s was carried out between 1612 and 1625. The new convent had two stories, and had a tile roof.[68] Further reforms to the conventual block were carried out between 1625 and 1637, including a separate noviciate, perhaps to the south of the main convent building; a vaulted *portería*; and new quarters for the kitchen and refectory and the *De profundis*. The friars themselves provided the manpower, 'cargando lodo y piedra'.[69]

During the 1630s new construction also took place on two new lateral chapels to the church. From this period date the chapels of San Benito de Palermo and the chapel of the Tercera Orden.[70] Lightning struck the south tower of the church in 1634, killing the friar who lived above the Loreto chapel and damaging the chapel itself. Repairs were carried out with Royal assistance in 1636.[71]

During the next 37 years no essential alterations were made. By the early 1670s, however, it was realized that the century-old timbers of the church roof were in need of replacement. Beginning in 1673 'the finest woods' – cedar, pine, and cypress – were brought from distances of up to 20 leagues from the city. In November 1674, after the rainy season had ended, the old roof was removed, and by February of 1675 the new roof was in place, a 'primoroso trabazón de lacería y artesón, remates de tirantes pintados y dorados, perfiles plateados de la forma del cordón de San Francisco'.[72] The repairs of 1674-1675 only affected the roof; nothing was done to change the church structure or walls.

Either in the late 1670s or early 1680s, the beams supporting the floors and ceilings of the infirmary were also replaced. The renovated infirmary was evidently still not satisfactory, because between 1684 and 1689 a new one was made, at the same time that a whole series of additions were made to the south side of the existing convent block:

> Sacose de cimientos un hermoso cuarto de tres viviendas, continuado por el sur a la obra antigua de la enfermería, que era solamente por donde se podía alargar; con tal disposición, que, siendo el inferior espacio todo de arquería y de bóvedas, se trazaron en él seis celdas, tres de cada parte, y su dormitorio que las divide, todas de bernegales de cal y canto; así para seguridad y conveniencia de alguno o algunos religiosos dementados, como para otros menesteres monásticos, en casos de corrección y castigo de quien lo mereciere; las unas miran sus ventanas al oriente y las otras al ocaso, todas con rejas de fierro fuertes y seguras, si bien muy humanas, porque tienen luz suficiente, y vista lago divertible a la huerta del convento y a la botica.
>
>   En el segundo espacio, vivienda o entresuelo se dispusieron a la misma traza, seis celdas de muy capaz habitación para los enfermos, con sus azoteas de arquería, para la mayor limpieza y conveniencia de ellas y para sacar al sol la ropa de cama, o túnicas y tener un brasero y otros menesteres de curación y necesidad. En el cuarto, o vivienda superior, se trazaron solas cuatro celdas, en el espacio y distancia que ocupan las seis referidas, sobre ellas mismas. Pero estas cuatro son grandes, espaciosas y de muy linda disposición, para religiosos graves, que actual, o habitualmente enferman, con sus hermosas y alegres azoteas, para servicio, que descuellan, hasta la vista de los campos y montes, para recreo religioso de sus habitadores. Toda esta obra termina en otra más excelente toda la bóveda en sus tres espacios; en el superior, se trazó

y dispuso una capilla, cuyo titular es nuestro padre San Antonio y cuya hermosura no es fácil delinear y sólo diré que echó el esmero el arte en sus bernegales, en imaginería y alcorzados, y que su longitud es de oriente a poniente, todo el espacio de las celdas, y dormitorio y aún más; que viene a estar como atravesada y su puerta en el un costado que hace remate y frente al dormitorio; con hermoso ventanaje, y sacristía muy decente y capaz. Debajo de esta capilla, en todo el distrito que ella ocupa se dispuso un salón muy espacioso para botica, con sus claraboyas que la hermosean, donde en desahogada disposición, caben en sus estantes todos los botes y cajones que oficina tan esencial necesita, para la curación de los religiosos y socorro de muchos pobres, que frecuentemente acuden a pedir ...

No es menos útil y aun esencial la bóveda inferior a la botica, que forma un espacioso salón, aseado, blanqueado y enladrillado, con dos ventanas en los extremos, una al oriente y al ocaso otra. Es pieza muy esencial y lucida, y lo es toda la obra que se ha insinuado, muy digna de ser agradecida y contada con las más buenas, que tiene el convento de nuestro Padre San Francisco de Guatemala.[73]

Needless to say, the Franciscan convent of Guatemala had by the seventeenth century gone far beyond the simple architectural program stipulated by the Province's statutes. And no sooner were the luxurious additions to the convent completed, than the great earthquake of 1689 brought them down again. The damages were estimated at 30,000 pesos, and 'not a cell' remained habitable.[74]

Unfazed by the projected cost of rebuilding, repairs were begun at once, beginning with the vault of the stairwell, which was now replaced with a wooden *artesón* for safety's sake. By 1691 the cells had been repaired, and a new kitchen built, 'toda la bóveda con su chimenea, fogones, alacenas y pilas corrientes en todas la partes convenientes: que es una de las magníficas obras del convento'.[75] The barrel vaults of the lower cloisters were completed in 1694-1697. Between 1697 and 1700 the convent received an aula Magna for holding its scholastic functions, and the fountain was built in the main patio. Between 1700 and 1702 the library was built above the sacristy, and roofed with a series of three vaults.[76]

The church had also been damaged beyond repair in the earthquake, and was rebuilt from the foundations up beginning in 1692. The work in the church proceeded from east to west, the *capilla mayor,* sacristy, crossing and transepts – all vaulted – being constructed between 1692 and 1697. Between 1697 and 1700 the old wooden roof of the nave was replaced, following the style of the crossing, with a series of six masonry vaults, the last two of which covered the choir above the main entrance. A new floor was also built, 'con fuertes bóvedas de entierro'. It was not until 1702 that the church was completely finished, and all the centers removed.[77]

Notes to Chapter 2

1   Fr. Antonio de Remesal, *Historia general de las Indias Occidentales y particular de la gobernación de Chiapa y Guatemala* (Guatemala, 1930); Francisco de Fuentes y Guzmán, *Recordación florida ... del Reyno de Guatemala* (Madrid, 1882-83); *Isagoge histórica apologética de las Indias Occidentales y especial de la provincia de San Vicente de Chiapa y Guatemala de la Orden de Predicadores* (Guatemala, 1935); Fr. Francisco Ximénez, *Historia de la provincia de San Vicente de Chiapa y Guatemala de la Orden de Predicadores* (Guatemamala 1965); Fr. José García de la Concepción, *Historia belemítica* (Guatemala 1956); Pedro de Cortés y Larraz, *Descripción geográfico-moral de la diócesis de Goathemala* (Guatemala 1958); and Domingo Juarros, *Compendio de la historia de la ciudad de Guatemala* (Guatemala 1936).

2   For a description of the first edition see: José Toribio Medina, *La imprenta en Guatemala* (1660-1821) (Santiago de Chile 1910), pp. 52-53, and 59. I have used the second edition published in four volumes by the Tipografía Nacional, Guatemala, 1937-1944, and edited by Fr. Lázaro Lamadrid, O.F.M.

3   Lamadrid, in his introduction to Vol. 1 of Vázquez, pp. VIII-XV; Juarros, *Compendio*, 1, p. 245; Ramón A. Salazar, *Historia del desenvolvimiento intelectual de Guatemala* (Guatemala 1897), pp. 137-139.

4   Vázquez, Lib. 1, pp. 38-39.

5   Quoted in Francisco de Paula García Peláez, *Memorias para la historia del antiguo Reino de Guatemala*, 3rd. ed., Vol. 2 (Guatemala 1971), p. 218.

6   Lib. 1 p. 171.

7   Lib. 1, p. 154; Lib. IV, p. 15; Lib. V pp. 220, 252-253, 309.

8   Lib. V, pp. 350-351.

9   Lib. 1, pp. 158-159. My italics.

10   Lib. V, p. 289.

11   Lib. 1, pp. 40-41.

12   Lib. V, p. 246.

13   Lib. V, pp. 342-346.

14   Lib. 11, p. 236.

15   Lib. 11, p. 289; Lib. V, p. 313.

16   Lib. V, p. 311.

17   Lib. V, p. 344.

18   Lib. V, pp. 279-284.

19   Lib. 11, pp. 179-183 and 255.

20   Lib. V, p. 330.

21   Lib. III, pp. 99, 237, 281-282, 291; Lib. IV, pp. 79, 92, 110, 156, 170-173, 179, 262.

22   Lib. III, 343-346; Lib. IV, pp. 56-60.

23   Lib. 1, p. 150.

24   Lib. III, pp. 317-318.

25   Lib. 11, p. 257.

26   Lib. 11, pp. 42-243, 249.

27   Lib. 11, pp. 219-220, 245-246.

28 Lib. II, p. 217.

29 Lib. II p. 244.

30 Lib. II pp. 291-292; Lib. V, pp. 222-223.

31 Lib. II, p. 279.

32 Supplemented by the *Tablas Capitulares* of 1574 and 1581 (see editor's notes to Lib. II p. 219 and 254) and a 'Nomina y lista y relación jurada del número de religiosos que tiene esta santa Provincia del Santísimo Nombre de Jesús de Guatemala ... hecha este año de 1690', conserved in the manuscript collection of the University of Texas Library, and reproduced in Vázquez, Vol. IV, pp. 12-13.

33 A.C. van Oss, 'Mendicant Expansion in New Spain and the Extent of the Colony', *Boletín de Estudios Latinoamericanos y del Caribe*, 21 (1976), pp. 32-56, see this volume, Chapter five.

34 Robert Ricard, *The Spiritual Conquest of Mexico*, trans. L.B. Simpson (Berkley 1966), p. 23; Vázquez, Lib. I, pp. 134, 137; Lib. II, pp. 176-179.

35 Lib. I, pp. 98-99, 134; Lib. II, pp. 177, 213, 217.

36 Lib. I, pp. 62-64, 99-100, 102, 105; Lib. II, pp. 215, 293; Lib. III, pp. 308, 342; Lib. IV, p. 11.

37 Lib. II, pp. 220-223, 278-282, 294-295.

38 Lib. IV, pp. 161, 279; Lib. V, p. 105.

39 Lib. V, p. 351.

40 Lib. III, pp. 8, 9, 19, 89, 93, 105, 113, 140.

41 Lib. III, pp. 221, 224, 321; Lib. IV, p. 10.

42 Lib. II, pp. 177-179.

43 'Nómina y lista y relación jurada', Vol. IV, pp. 12-33.

44 Lib. I, p. 113.

45 Lib. II, p. 181.

46 Lib. I, p. 65.

47 Lib. I, p. 99.

48 Lib. V, p. 245.

49 Lib. V, p. 273.

50 Lib. V, pp. 273-274.

51 Lib. V, p. 351.

52 Lib. V, p. 360.

53 Lib. III, p. 40.

54 Lib. I, pp. 154-155; Lib. II, pp. 245-246.

55 Lib. II, p. 226.

56 Lib. II, pp. 261-263.

57 Lib. II, p. 220.

58 Lib. II, pp. 221-222, 294-295.

59 Lib. II, pp. 263-265.

60 Lib. IV, pp. 133-134.

61 Lib. I, pp. 98-99, 163-164; Lib. V, p. 384.

62 Lib. I, pp. 164-166.

63 Lib. I, p. 115.

64 Lib. i, pp. 154, 183; Lib. ii, pp. 215, 217-218, 227.
65 Lib. ii, pp. 244-245.
66 Lib. ii, pp. 296-305; Lib. iv, p. 169; Lib. v, pp. 219-222.
67 Lib. v, pp. 222-223.
68 Lib. v, pp. 243, 247-248, 272.
69 Lib. iv, pp. 96-97, 235.
70 Lib. iv, p. 157.
71 Lib. ii, pp. 296-305; Lib. iv, p. 308; Lib. v, pp. 234, 271.
72 Lib. v, p. 329.
73 Lib. v, pp. 329-331.
74 Lib. v, pp. 331-332.
75 Lib. v, p. 332.
76 Lib. v, pp. 307-308, 390-392.
77 Lib. ii, pp. 244-245; Lib. v, pp. 307-308, 390-391.

3

Where mountains met the sea: a primitive geography of Venezuela (ca. 1580)

As a consequence of the 1577 royal questionnaire aimed at gathering more exact knowledge of the American territories, local authorities in a number of Venezuelan towns completed elaborate forms dealing with the demographic, economic, religious, and other peculiarities of the regions under their jurisdiction. Responses dating from 1578 and 1579 are known for Caracas, Tocuyo, Trujillo, Barquisimeto and Zamora. Collectively, they are known as the *Relaciones geográficas de Felipe II*. Other *relaciones* were probably compiled at Coro, and Nirgua, but they have been lost to us.[1]

The respondents to the questionnaire answered its fifty questions point by point, and the answers make a candid and reliable impression. They make it possible to draw a portrait of late sixteenth-century Venezuela in greater detail than is possible on the basis of the more universal geographical descriptions of López Velasco and Vázquez de Espinosa.[2]

The area under consideration corresponds to that of the bishopric of Coro, whose seat was later transferred to Caracas. During the colonial period, we may speak of a 'third-rate' diocese in many respects.[3] Economically and culturally, Venezuela was relatively obscure throughout most of the colonial period. Like that of Buenos Aires, its importance within the American continent dawned late. During the early period it was a marginal zone, with a somewhat schizophrenic character. Culturally as well as economically, colonial Venezuela was caught between two larger forces: by sea it looked towards Spain via the Caribbean islands of Santo Domingo, Margarita, and Puerto Rico. By land it was bound to New Granada at its west.

The immigrants

If Spaniards migrated from the Old World to the New in the expectation of El Dorado, they were sure to be disappointed if chance carried them to Venezuela. Where the northernmost spur of the Andes fell into the sea, little frontier settlements awaited them with mud huts and muddy streets; Santiago de León (Caracas), with its 24 blocks separated by unpaved streets 32 feet wide, its single plaza, and its humble church and houses,[4] could in 1578 not begin to compete with any one of dozens of Andalusion towns from which many settlers came. Out of the pot and into the fire, so it must have seemed to many who paid the one-way fare to the Indies.

By 1580, the principal Spanish settlements in Venezuela were: Coro (founded 1527), El Tocuyo (1545), Nueva Segovia de Barquisimeto (= Barquisimeto) (1552), San Pedro de Nirgua (= Nirgua) (1554), Nueva Valencia (= Valencia) (1555), Trujillo (La Paz) (1557), Santiago de León de Caracas (= Caracas) (1567), Nuestra Señora de Caraballeda (= Caraballeda) (1568), Ciudad Rodrigo de Maracaibo (1568) in 1574 renamed Nueva Zamora de Maracaibo (= Zamora), El Portillo de Carora (= Carora) (1569). More to the west were founded: Mérida (1558), San Cristóbal (1561), El Espíritu Santo de la Grita (= Grita) (1576), and Altamira de Cáceres o Barinas (1577).[5]

Most of the Spanish *vecinos* had Indians in encomienda, although we are repeatedly told that the Indians were too poor to be of much profit to their encomenderos. The size of the encomiendas never exceeded 300 Indians, and many included fewer than 100. Slicher says that large proportions of encomenderos among the vecinos are characteristic of frontier areas, still in the process of being settled.[6]

For eight of the Spanish pueblos, numbers of vecinos are given: Caracas, 40 vecinos encomenderos and 20 without encomienda; Tocuyo, 38 vecinos encomenderos (in 1581, 28-30 encomenderos); Barquisimeto, 32 vecinos (in 1581, 30 encomenderos); Zamora, 30 vecinos; Valencia, 25 vecinos encomenderos; Caraballeda, 20 vecinos encomenderos (in 1581, 10-12 vecinos); Coro, 15 or 16 vecinos encomenderos.[7]

So the total number of vecinos probably lay in the region of 300, given a few more or less. The largest individual concentration was Caracas, with 60 Spanish vecinos, or 80 if the port population of Caraballeda is counted. With what other Spanish American bishoprics is this total comparable? We may refer to the figures supplied by López de Velasco around 1574.[8]

South American Bishoprics*	Estimated number of vecinos 1574
Lima	2,115
Bogotá	1,425
Cuzco	900
Quito	859
Trujillo	670
Huamanga	600
Arequipa	425
Paraguay (Asunción)	380
Cartagena	308
Popayán	298
Tucumán	200
Santa Marta	137

* Buenos Aires, Santiago, Concepción, Charcas, Santa Cruz and La Paz lack comparable data.

As far as total vecino population is concerned, the Venezuelan diocese may be best compared with the dioceses of Cartagena and Popayán.

When we look at the distribution of the vecinos, however, Cartagena turns out to have had a different character: 250 of its vecinos lived in the port city itself: the city of Cartagena accounted for more than 80 percent of the total Spanish population. In Venezuela the Spanish population was spread more or less evenly over a number of centers, with vecino populations mainly ranging from 30 to 60 in each town. This was also the case in the diocese of Popayán, where the four largest Spanish concentrations were of about equal size (Cali, 36 vecinos; Almaguer, 33; Popayán, 30; Anserma, 30). Whereas the Spanish population of Cartagena was highly centralized, those of Venezuela and Popayán were more decentralized.

The Indian population

During the sixteenth century, the Venezuelan Indians were excused from the obligation, enforced in most Spanish American regions, to pay tribute. This explains the lack of statistics on the number of Venezuelan tributaries which are necessary for reconstructing the size and distribution of the native population. Some of the *Relaciones geográficas* do, however, include broad estimates of the Indian populations of the different jurisdictions.[9]

In 1578, the district of Caracas was thus estimated to have and Indian population of 7,000 to 8,000. The jurisdiction of Trujillo was said to count some 5,000 –6,000 Indians males (*indios varones*), and Barquisimeto, 3,200. In the case of Barquisimeto we are told explicitly, and in those of Caracas and Trujillo we may suppose, that the figures refer to adult males, and are thus comparable to the numbers of tributaries noted for other regions, where the Indians did pay tribute. Insofar as can be judged from these fragmentary estimates, the Indian population concentrations of Venezuela were comparable to those of the diocese of Popayán recorded by López de Velasco ca. 1574 (Popayán, 9,000 tributaries; Anserma, 5,000; Cali, 3,000). We may also say that the Venezuelan Indian population never knew concentrations such as those found in the neighboring Nuevo Reino de Granada, where Bogotá and Tunja alone had tributary populations ca. 1574 of 40,000 and 52,000-53,000 respectively.[10]

As elsewhere in Spanish America, the indigenous populations of Venezuela had shrunk depressingly from their original levels. This is the universal complaint of the *relaciones*. In Trujillo the depopulation among the Indians amounted to more than 50 percent (originally 14,000 or 15,000, down to 5,000 or 6,000 in 1579);[11] for the other jurisdictions no estimates are to be found in the *relaciones*, but a decline is invariably noted. The causes given for the decline in Indian population are:
1 Epidemics of viruela, sarampión, cámaras (de sangre), romadizo and catarros (Caracas, Tocuyo, Trujillo, Barquisimeto);

2   Wars and rebellions against the Spaniards (Caracas, Trujillo, Barquisimeto);
3   Other dislocations caused by the arrival of Europeans (Zamora, Caracas, Trujillo). In Trujillo, a great cause of sickness and death was that Indians fled their original lands, some leaving the hot lowlands for the sierra, and others abandoning the cool highland for *tierra caliente*; the change of climate in both directions proved deadly;
4   The use of Indians as slaves and beasts of burden (Barquisimeto); by 1577 we are told that both of these abuses had ended.

Except around Zamora, the Indians led a primitive agrarian existence, cultivating some small plots, and supplementing a rudimentary diet with wild game. The introduction of urban life was a Spanish innovation. Outside the Spanish centers there were no permanent settlements. The common pattern was that of groups of three to six houses, separated by interspaces ranging from 'shooting distance' to a few kilometers. These miniscule communities were largely self-sufficient: in the vicinity of Caracas, there was no trade whatsoever among the Indians, if not in salt and fish. In the jurisdiction of Trujillo every family constructed its house on the plot of land it worked. In Tocuyo the Indians lived in tiny huts, and slept on the ground, 'in much misery'. There was a great profusion of dialects, and there was no common language in which all could make themselves understood.

The Spanish view of Indian life and the level of Indian intelligence was on the pessimistic side: 'Son rudos y de muy torpe disposición. No son inclinados a ningún género de policía, y toda su manera de vivir se funda sobre la pereza. Son prontos para lo malo y nada hábiles para lo bueno' (Caracas).[12] 'Son de bajo entendimiento y de malas inclinaciones. Siempre andan necesitados y faltos de bastimientos por ser haraganes' (Tocuyo).[13] 'Es gente muy holgazana, y de muy bajo entendimiento e inclinaciones, sin que se les conozca codicia de poseer ningunos bienes, ni tienen ningunas granjerías, excepto comer y beber' (Trujillo).[14] 'Es gente de poco entendimiento, bajos de inclinación y muy rudos, dados a los vicios de la carne y la bebida ... y como beben mucho se emborrachan y después de borrachos se matan unos a otros' (Barquisimeto).[15]

Only the Indians living in and near to Zamora, on the western shore of Lake Maracaibo, would seem to have reached a higher degree of civilization. Most lived on land, forming villages, but others constructed their houses on platforms above the surface of the waters of the lake. These Indians are described as being of 'delicate understanding, inclined to preserve their liberty, adept at speaking Spanish, and proud of going clothed'. Nevertheless, they are said not to like to work, 'por el gran vicio que tienen del pescado'.[16]

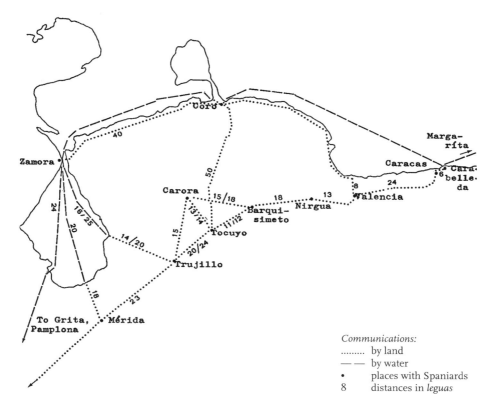

Figure 1 *Land and water communications in Venezuela, ca. 1580*
(Relaciones geográficas ..., pp. 119-120, 148, 149, 165-166, 170, 187)

Communications by land and water

First colonized form the Caribbean islands, Venezuela's earliest settlement was Coro, on the Caribbean coast. Caracas was likewise a coastal town, although removed several kilometers inland. Just as Lima had its Callao, Caracas had Caraballeda as a maritime appendage. Later Caraballeda was replaced as Caracas's port by La Guaira, a short distance down the coast.[17] Zamora was founded just inside the narrow strait separating the lake of Maracaibo from the sea. The strait was shallow enough to be forded on horseback; only small ships could enter. This was in some ways a blessing, however, as it afforded some protection from the threat of pirates.

By land, a second thrust of colonization came from New Granada, following the Andes route via Mérida, Trujillo, Tocuyo, Barquisimeto, Nirgua, Valencia, finally reaching Caracas. While Coro and Caracas continued to look seaward, by 1580 a network of roads communicated the inland towns to New Granada. From Zamora it was possible to navigate over the lake to roads leading to Trujillo and Mérida. By river it was possible to arrive very near to La Grita and Pamplona in canoes. Zamora came to have closer relations with Andean Venezuela and the New Reino than with Coro and Caracas.[18] The system of road and water communications, as described in the *relaciones*, is shown in Figure 1. By 1580, most or all of the roads were fit for use by horses and mules.

Economic activities and trade

The *Relaciones Geográficas* portray a hardly differentiated agrarian economy in which trade, even in the Spanish centers, was of limited importance. Indeed, there are indications that even the centers had only a primitive form of money economy. Non-agricultural production was limited to textiles. There is no mention of glass, ceramics, printing, or metallurgy.

Caracas imported pearls from Margarita, which were used, together with what little gold was to be found, as a medium of exchange. Salt was imported from Araya, and unspecified 'mercadurías' from Spain. All this trade went by sea. In exchange, Caracas exported agricultural products to Margarita and Santo Domingo: maize, meat and processed meat (*tocino*), cheese, lard, honey, sisal (*maguey, cocuiza, caroata*), cotton cloth, hammocks, wax, blankets, biscuit and flour. Aside from this limited commerce, Caracas had to look after its own needs. The Indians did not engage in any trade amongst themselves, but subsisted on the fruits of their own fields.[19] The Indian population was judged too poor to pay tribute; their economic contribution was limited to personal service to the *encomenderos* and occasional payments of 'some gold' which they found, and cotton goods.

Tocuyo imported salt from Coro and Borburata. It was almost impossible to procure goods from Spain, although sometimes they arrived by ship and could be bought at Coro, or they arrived by land from the Nuevo Reino. Such goods were always very expensive, since there were so few local products to exchange for them. Export products (in exchange for salt and goods from Spain) were cotton goods, livestock and some maize and sugar. The main economic activity was the raising of livestock, 'menor' as well as 'mayor', and cultivation of maize, manioc (yuca), sugar cane and some cotton. Among the Indians there was barter of foodstuffs, and there was a kind of money which they used and which consisted of 'small shells or pebbles of little value, and animal bones'. They were too poor to pay tribute, but they sometimes gave cotton goods, honey, fire-wood, personal services and fish during Lent. They raised chickens, which they sold to the Spaniards.[20]

Trujillo imported salt from Zamora, which it paid with biscuit, flour and maize. The Indians did not pay tribute, 'since they have nothing to give'. Some cotton was raised, which was woven into cloth, blankets and hammocks. Various fruits and vegetables were raised, some native, some European. Wheat and barley were grown, but not in large quantities. There were hogs, cows and horses.[21]

Barquisimeto exported cattle to New Granada. Maize and cattle were sometimes sold to ships which put in at the port (river-port?), but few ships put in. It imported salt from the coast, and wine, oil, vinegar, and clothes made in Spain, from Santo Domingo. Maize was grown in great quantities; the soil was reported to be very fertile, and it was irrigated. Also grown were all of the European vegetables, and all of the native ones as well. Little wheat was planted, and no barley. The Indians paid no tribute.[22]

Zamora exported salt to Mérida and Trujillo, and imported maize, biscuit and flour from them. No wheat or other crops were cultivated, 'por ser tierra nueva'. A variety of European vegetables were grown. The city fed itself mainly with wild game and with fish from the lake. The Indians did not pay tribute.[23]

Striking is the lack of trade among the Venezuelan towns themselves. This trade was almost exclusively limited to salt. The explanation for this lies not in the difficulty of transport, since distances were not excessive, and the road and water communications were adequate. The explanation is the lack of differentiation in economic activity. Practically everywhere, the products were the same: maize, cotton, meat and cattle. The population concentrations were not of sufficient size to generate a greater degree of economic specialization. So for trade, Venezuela had to look abroad; there again, however, the possibilities were highly limited. The only products which were interesting for export over any distance at all were cattle, cotton, and certain foodstuffs (maize, honey). Cattle could be driven to New Granada; the foodstuffs could be sold to ships which passed by one of the ports, and to the Caribbean islands. There was also a certain market for textiles, but it appears to have been limited.

It is possible to be more precise about the degree of economic differentiation of the various Venezuelan centers, by referring to Slicher's system of economic criteria, at least to those which are applicable in the case of Venezuela.[24] This is done in the table below.

Caracas had the greatest variety of economic activities, and was especially important as a trade center. Tocuyo and Barquisimeto formed a kind of middle group; there areal farming was relatively important. Trujillo and Zamora formed the periphery, specialized in cattle (Trujillo), and in mineral and natural resources (Zamora – salt, fish, wild game). Reliance on cattle-raising, mineral and natural resources are characteristic of the periphery; commerce is typical of the central districts.

Table 1   *Degree of economic differentiation*

Criterion	Caracas	Tocuyo	Trujillo	Barqui-simeto	Zamora	Total
Trade						
Import from outside Venezuela	X	X		X		3
Export to markets outside Venezuela	X					2
Trade in grain and grain products	X		X			3
Trade in sugar		X				1
Trade in meat	X					1
Trade in cheese	X					1
Trade in cattle		X				2
Trade in cattle products (lard)	X					1
Trade in textiles	X	X				2
Trade in salt	X	X	X	X	X	5
Trade in wine						1
Ports	X					1
Trade within Venezuela		X	X	X	X	4
Trade in unspecified mercadurías	X					1
Trade in maize	X	X	X	X	X	5
Trade in honey	X					1
Trade in pearls	X					1
Trade in sisal	X					1
Trade in wax	X					1
Total number of criteria relating to trade	15	7	4	7	4	37
Areal farming						
Irrigation				X		1
Fertile soil				X		1
Wheat, barley	X		X			2
Sugar cane		X				1
Cotton	X	X	X			3
Manioc		X				1
Maize	X	X	X	X		4
Maguey	X					1
Total criteria relating to areal farming	4	4	3	3	0	14
'Nature'						
Fish					X	1
Honey, wax	X					1
Wild game					X	1
Deer					X	1
Wild birds					X	1
Total criteria relating to 'nature'	1	0	0	0	4	5
Total all criteria	20	11	7	10	8	56

As one moves westward form Caracas, one leaves the center, passes through the middle group (Barquisimeto, Tocuyo) and arrives finally at the periphery (Trujillo, Zamora). Coro, with its weak ties to the center, and a small vecino population, probably also belonged to the periphery. Nirgua, Valencia and Carora, between Caracas and Trujillo and with respectable vecino populations, belonged to the middle group. The resulting pattern is one of concentric layers, distorted – in this case elongated towards the West – by the road system (see Figure 2).

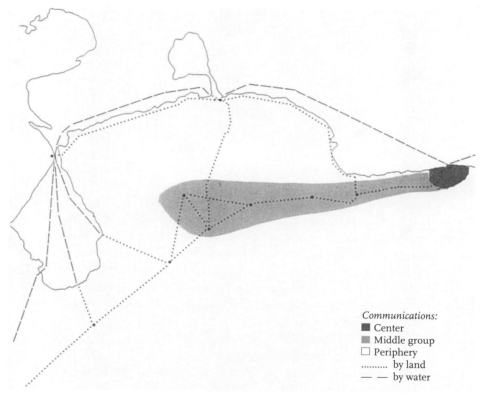

Communications:
■ Center
▨ Middle group
☐ Periphery
.... by land
— — by water

Figure 2 *Economic differentiation in Venezuela, 1578/1579*

We may also compare the degree of economic differentiation and of economic importance of the entire Venezuelan diocese with those of other South American dioceses. This has been done by Slicher van Bath on the basis of data from López de Velasco and Vázquez de Espinosa; the two are expressed in terms of a percentage index.[25]

In economic importance, Venezuela was comparable to Trujillo, in economic differentiation, to Popayán. In the context of entire Spanish America, Venezuela was thus a member of the 'middle group' in economic importance and differentiation.

South American Bishoprics	Economic importance	Economic differentiation
Lima	9.5	4.3
Bogotá	4.6	3.5
Cuzco	3.4	3.5
Quito	7.2	4.8
Trujillo	3.0	3.3
Huamanga	1.9	2.7
Arequipa	4.2	3.2
Paraguay (Asunción)	1.3	2.6
Popayán	3.7	3.0
Venezuela	3.0	3.0
Cartagena	1.9	2.8
Tucumán	2.7	2.8
Santa Marta	1.6	2.6

(Buenos Aires, Santiago, Concepción, Charcas, Santa Cruz, La Paz, lack comparable data.)

The towns

We have plans of Barquisimeto (middle group) and Caracas (center).[26] They both follow the checkerboard pattern normal to Spanish American cities. Caracas had 24 blocks (*manzanas*) and a plaza (i.e. five blocks east-west by five blocks north-south). Barquisimeto had eight blocks and a plaza (three blocks by three blocks). In Barquisimeto three new terrains outside the 3x3 gridiron had been opened. The map of Barquisimeto shows 31 lots; this agrees almost precisely with the number of vecinos given in the questionnaire (32). Caracas's plan shows 65 lots marked with the word 'casa'; Caracas is said to have had 60 vecinos in 1578 (the maps are attached to the questionnaires, and date therefore from the same years).

One may distinguish four different types among the sixteenth-century colonial houses, according to the materials used in construction, and whether or not there is a second storey:

1   Stone, brick or adobe (tapería), with or without lime, roofed with tiles; two stories.
2   Tapería, thatched roof; two stories.
3   Tapería, thatched roof, one storey.
4   Wood frame, covered by reed mats (*bejucos*), thatched roof, one storey.

Housing needs depended upon climate, different from place to place, and on the availability of building materials. Still, two-storey houses were only to be found in towns with a certain economic importance (Caracas and Tocuyo). One-storey houses dominate the periphery. Similarly, roof-tiles, and stone and brick masonry are only found in the more important towns, while thatch, earth and cane are the only building materials to be found outside them.

Town	House type			
	1	*2*	*3*	*4*
Caracas	3 houses	-	most	some
Tocuyo	2 houses	4 houses	-	most
Trujillo	-	-	all	-
Barquisimeto	-	-	-	all
Zamora	-	-	-	all

In Trujillo, Barquisimeto and Zamora, the lack of masonry houses, of brick or stone, and of roof-tiles, was not due to lack of building materials nearby: Trujillo had stone, and brick and roof-tiles were beginning to be made; in Barquisimeto stone and lime had been found; in Zamora there was stone, and clay for bricks and tiles.[27] It must have been for economic reasons that poorer building materials were used.

Religious institutions

Although Caracas already represented the most important economic and demographic center in Venezuela around 1580, the cathedral had been erected much earlier in Coro, and was not transferred to Caracas until 1637. It was a case in which the site of the cathedral had been chosen much too early, in fact, at a time when Coro was the only Spanish settlement in Venezuela.

Caracas, about 1580, had already more religious buildings than had Coro. There was a parish church with two priests, and a Franciscan convent, 'de tapias no durables' with four or five resident friars and three or four friars outside the convent walls who worked in the eight or nine *doctrinas de indios* on the outskirts of the city.[28]

Coro's cathedral had three prebends: a dean, an archdeacon and a cantor. The church was a poor construction of wood and thatch, plastered on the outside, and from inside painful to see. The sacraments had to be carried out with care, for fear of fire. Three *doctrinas de indios* were attended by two secular clergy and one Dominican friar.[29]

Caraballeda had a parish church with one priest; the roof was thatched and the walls were of wood, covered by plaster on the outside.[30]

Tocuyo's parish church was attended by two priests. There was also a Franciscan monastery with one or two resident friars, and another three *doctrineros*. Having been founded about 1575, in 1578 it was being rebuilt. A second monastery, of the

Dominican order, had also been founded towards 1575; it had one resident friar. But neither friars nor secular clergy stayed long in Tocuyo's *doctrinas*, 'por no tener con qué sustentarse, y así pasan luego delante al Nuevo Reino de Granada'.[31]

The parish church of Barquisimeto had two priests; the church building itself was of 'muy grande pobreza'. Although there were technically five or six *doctrinas de indios*, there were neither friars nor clergy to serve them, for lack of any means of material support. Instead, two or three 'mozos estudiantes' attended to the Indians, 'doing their work very well'. There was a small hospital (San Lázaro) founded by a secular priest.[32]

Trujillo had one secular priest and a Franciscan convent, founded ca. 1576, the church of which had not yet been built in 1579, 'por la mucha pobreza de la tierra'. In the convent four or five friars lived, and attended to the six doctrinas. There existed a great desire to obtain more clergy for the doctrinas, but the poverty of the region made it impossible to attract them.[33]

Valencia had one priest and one *doctrina de indios* under care of a priest. Zamora, Carora, and Nirgua had but one priest apiece; there were no doctrinas about 1580.[34]

Table 2 *Summary of religious institutions ca. 1580, by place and economic category (center – middle group – periphery)*

Place	Secular parishes	Conventos		Hospitals	Total religious	Total religious criteria
		OFM	OP			
Center						
Caracas/Caraballeda	2	1			11	14
Middle group						
Tocuyo	1	1	1		7 or 8	10 or 11
Barquisimeto	1			1	4 or 5	6 or 7
Valencia	1				2	3
Nirgua	1				1	2
Carora	1				1	2
Periphery						
Coro	1	(cathedral)			6	7
Trujillo	1	1			5 or 6	7 or 8
Zamora	1				1	2
Total	10	3	1	1	38 or 41	53 or 56

The evangelization of Venezuela during the sixteenth century proceeded with considerably less fervor than in New Spain. In New Spain the mendicant orders sought out the centers of Indian population during the early decades and founded their monasteries there.[35] They tried to discourage Spanish civil settlement in their monastic *pueblos de indios*. In sixteenth-century New Spain the Augustinians, Franciscans and Dominicans succeeded in establishing a 'special relationship' with the Indians under their care, and showed a protective attitude towards the Indians. Some dreamed of an ideal republic of Indians and friars, to the exclusion of non-religious Spanish colonists. In Venezuela this pattern was not followed: the convents of the religious orders, and the parishes and doctrinas of the secular church were to be found in the Spanish population centers. To some extent, this may be explained by the primitive nature of the Indian population of Venezuela: they stood at a much lower level of civilization at the time of the Conquest than the Indians of New Spain.

But a second factor was certainly the attitude of the religious themselves. In Venezuela the constant complaint is that there are no material means of support for the necessary friars and priests; in the literature dealing with the 'spiritual conquest' of New Spain, there is no mention of lack of economic means as an obstacle to evangelization, although poor regions also existed there: in the evangelization of Mexico, idealistic motives played a greater role than in that of Venezuela. In part, this may be a result of the decades separating the start of the Mexican from that of the Venezuelan religious campaigns; by the 1570s, the fervor of the Mexican effort had already dissipated to a large degree: it was clear by then that a new republic of religious and Indians was not within the realm of possibility.

A third characteristic of the Mexican evangelization not to be found in Venezuela is the heated competition among the religious orders, and between the orders and the secular church, for the loyalty of the local Indian populations. In New Spain it was highly unusual during the sixteenth century to find more than one order in one place. There were even entire regional monopolies. In Venezuela, by contrast, parish churches, and monasteries of the Dominican and Franciscan orders are found together in the same places. This peaceful coexistence among the different church branches leads us to suspect that in Venezuela the 'special relationship' between religious and Indians never existed, and that the convents and churches were meant more for the Spanish than for the Indian population. This also accounts, perhaps in part, for the poverty-stricken and abject condition of the Indians in Venezuela around 1580; in contrast to their Mexican brothers, the Venezuelan missionaries had not been especially diligent in their educative task.

A comparative study of the colonial South American bishoprics shows that the Venezuelan dioceses may again be compared profitably with that of Popayán.[36]

Conclusions

The above considerations above lead to the following conclusions for Venezuela ca. 1580.

1   Sixteenth-century Venezuela had relatively small numbers of Spanish settlers, and a dispersed and primitive Indian population. Demographically it may best be compared with a diocese such as that of Popayán.

2   Economically, Venezuela was twice peripheral. Lacking internal markets and export products of interest for long-distance trade, a weak agrarian economy developed, based on labor-extensive agriculture (cattle and cotton). Cotton could be sold to the Caribbean islands (in this respect Venezuela was dependent upon the island economies), and cattle could be driven up to Pamplona and Tunja (in this respect Venezuela can be seen as a satellite of New Granada). With respect to the economic criteria, Venezuela may again be compared to sixteenth-century Popayán.

3   Within Venezuela we may distinguish three zones on the basis of their relative degree of economic differentiation. A central zone (Caracas) had the most highly developed economy; trade was especially important to colonial Caracas. A less differentiated economy is characteristic of a 'middle group' (Barquisimeto, Tocuyo and probably Valencia, Nirgua and Carora). In the middle group areal farming was relatively important. Zamora, Trujillo and probably Coro belonged to the economic periphery. Their economies were the least differentiated of all, and were especially reliant upon natural and mineral resources, and upon cattle-raising.

4   The three zones of economic complexity describe a system of concentric circles, deformed by the system of roads. The center is Caracas. Moving westward towards New Granada one crosses first the zone of the middle group, and later enters the periphery.

5   The building materials used in the construction of houses, and the number of stories, reflects the degree of economic differentiation at a given place.

6   The size (number of houses and blocks) of the towns reflect the size of the Spanish *vecino* population.

7   The distribution of religious institutions and of secular and regular clergy tend to reflect the distribution of the Spanish population and the degree of economic differentiation, although the religious criteria are more evenly than the economic criteria (i.e. more priests and friars in the periphery than would be expected on the basis of the economic criteria; the spread of the religious institutions was conform to the economic criteria). Ecclesiastically, the Venezuelan diocese may be conveniently compared with that of Popayán.

Notes to Chapter 3

1 *Relaciones geográficas de Venezuela*, ed. Antonio Arellano Moreno, Biblioteca de la Academia Nacional de la Historia, Vol. 70 (Caracas: Academia Nacional de la Historia, 1964).

2 Juan López de Velasco, *Geografía y descripción universal de las Indias*, ed. Marcos Jiménez de la Espeda, Biblioteca de autores españoles, t. 248 (Madrid: Atlas, 1971); Antonio Vázquez de Espinosa, *Compendio y descripción de las Indias Occidentales*, ed. B. Velasco Bayón, Biblioteca de autores españoles, t. 231 (Madrid: Atlas, 1969).

3 Adriaan C. van Oss, 'Comparing colonial bishoprics in Spanish South America', see this volume.

4 *Relaciones geográficas*, p. 114.

5 Antonio Arellano Moreno, *Orígenes de la economía Venezolana* (Caracas-Madrid: Ed. Edime, 1960, 2a ed.) pp. 118-119: Federico Brito Figueroa, *Historia económica y social de Venezuela* (Caracas: Dirección de cultura, Universidad Central de Venezuela, 1966) t. I, 124.

6 Bernard Slicher van Bath, *Spaans Amerika omstreeks 1600* (Utrecht-Antwerpen 1979), p. 32.

7 *Relaciones geográficas*, pp. 120, 150, 166, 188, 206, 224-225, 228.

8 Slicher, *Spaans Amerika*, p. 26.

9 *Relaciones Geográficas*, pp. 118-119, 148, 164-165, 185-186, 205.

10 López de Velasco, *Geografía y descripción*, pp. 181, 185, 206, 207, 210.

11 *Relaciones Geográficas*, pp. 164-165.

12 Ibid., pp. 118-119.

13 Ibid., p. 148.

14 Ibid., pp. 164-165.

15 Ibid., pp. 185-186.

16 Ibid., p. 205.

17 Ibid., p. 217.

18 Ibid., pp. 119-120, 148-149, 165-166, 170, 187.

19 Ibid., p. 134.

20 Ibid., pp. 157-158.

21 Ibid., pp. 169-170.

22 Ibid., pp. 195-196.

23 Ibid., pp.209-210.

24 Slicher, *Spaans Amerika*, pp. 70-86; Bernard Slicher van Bath, 'Economic diversification in Spanish America around 1600: Centers, intermediate zones and peripheries', *Jahrbuch für Geschichte von Staat, Wirtschaft und Gesellschaft Lateinamerikas*, 16 (1979) pp. 53-96.

25 Slicher, *Spaans Amerika*, p. 88; idem, 'Economic diversification', p. 65.

26 *Relaciones geográficas*, pp. 114, 173.
27 Ibid., pp. 133-134, 157-158, 169, 196-197, 210.
28 Ibid., pp. 134-135.
29 Ibid., pp. 224-225.
30 Ibid., pp. 134, 228.
31 Ibid., pp. 159, 225-226.
32 Ibid., pp. 197, 227.
33 Ibid., pp. 170, 226-227.
34 Ibid., pp. 210, 227-228.
35 Adriaan C. van Oss, 'Mendicant expansion in New Spain and the extent of the colony (sixteenth century)', see this Volume, Chapter 5.
36 Adriaan C. van Oss, 'Comparing colonial bishoprics', see this Volume, Chapter 4.

4

COMPARING COLONIAL BISHOPRICS IN SPANISH SOUTH AMERICA*

Far from the mother country, the Spanish empire in America was in many ways a world unto itself. Thinly strewn across vast stretches of the continent, a number of relatively isolated centers of Spanish culture took form: the Spanish American world resembled an archipelago of weakly intercommunicated islands. To the colonial mind, the unifying element was the Catholic faith. Of all the titles of the Laws of the Indies compiled in 1681, the first is 'De la Santa Fe Católica.' The immigration of large numbers of Spaniards and the baptism of Indians led to the introduction of Christian practices. But the Church itself was composed of a variety of semi-autonomous bodies, which were sometimes at odds with one another. Just as in Europe, there was a division between the secular and the regular clergy. Within the secular Church, bishops struggled to assert themselves, sometimes against the efforts of the cathedral chapters and lower clergy.

Above all, however, the island-like character of the Spanish American empire imposed itself upon the activities of the Church. There were ecclesiastical centers, which coincided largely with those of demographic, economic and administrative importance. Between them were sparsely populated interspaces where little cultural activity could unfold.

This article is aimed at the comparative study of certain aspects of the secular branch of the Church. The bishoprics are the islands: facing commonly shared structural limitations, some bishoprics overcame them better than others. An important question becomes, to what extent do ecclesiastical developments mirror other historical trends?

The secular church

Beginning in 1514, the South American continent was divided into archbishoprics, bishoprics and parishes. The chronology of the founding of the parishes is obscure. The founding of the dioceses proceeded with great, in some cases excessive, expediency. The first South American diocese was founded at Antigua, in the inhospitable rain forests of Darién (to this day no road crosses this part of the isthmus of Panamá). The history of Antigua is short enough. In 1514 Antigua's first and only bishop arrived with seventeen secular clergy and six Franciscans to find a town of 200 wooden houses populated by 500 Spaniards and 1500 'indios de servicio'. By 1515 there was a cathedral, a Franciscan convent and a hospital, but only four priests and three friars remained. In 1518 bishop Quevedo returned to Spain, and by 1524 Antigua had been completely abandoned.

Far from the mother country, the Spanish empire in America was in many ways a world unto itself. Thinly strewn across vast stretches of the continent, a number of relatively isolated centers of Spanish culture took form: the Spanish American world resembled an archipelago of weakly intercommunicated islands. To the colonial mind, the unifying element was the Catholic faith. Of all the titles of the Laws of the Indies compiled in 1681, the first is 'De la Santa Fe Católica.' The immigration of large numbers of Spaniards and the baptism of Indians led to the introduction of Christian practices. But the Church itself was composed of a variety of semi-autonomous bodies, which were sometimes at odds with one another. Just as in Europe, there was a division between the secular and the regular clergy. Within the secular Church, bishops struggled to assert themselves, sometimes against the efforts of the cathedral chapters and lower clergy.

Above all, however, the island-like character of the Spanish American empire imposed itself upon the activities of the Church. There were ecclesiastical centers, which coincided largely with those of demographic, economic and administrative importance. Between them were sparsely populated interspaces where little cultural activity could unfold.

This article is aimed at the comparative study of certain aspects of the secular branch of the Church. The bishoprics are the islands: facing commonly shared structural limitations, some bishoprics overcame them better than others. An important question becomes, to what extent do ecclesiastical developments mirror other historical trends?

The secular church

Beginning in 1514, the South American continent was divided into archbishoprics, bishoprics and parishes. The chronology of the founding of the parishes is obscure. The founding of the dioceses proceeded with great, in some cases excessive, expediency. The first South American diocese was founded at Antigua, in the inhospitable rain forests of Darién (to this day no road crosses this part of the isthmus of Panamá). The history of Antigua is short enough. In 1514 Antigua's first and only bishop arrived with seventeen secular clergy and six Franciscans to find a town of 200 wooden houses populated by 500 Spaniards and 1500 'indios de servicio'. By 1515 there was a cathedral, a Franciscan convent and a hospital, but only four priests and three friars remained. In 1518 bishop Quevedo returned to Spain, and by 1524 Antigua had been completely abandoned.[1]

The other South American bishoprics were more durable, although the existence of some of them during the early years was fragile. The diocese of Coro (Venezuela) was erected in 1530, and its first bishop was appointed the next year. He did not arrive in Coro, however, before 1536. Little missionary work was accomplished.[2] By 1613 it was recognized that the selection of Coro as the episcopal seat had been a mistake, and that Caracas was destined to surpass it in population and importance. The seat was officially transferred in 1637/1638.[3]

The first cathedral at Santa Marta was built in 1531; it had a thatched roof. In 1548, not Santa Marta, but Riohacha, with its pearl-beds, was judged to be the best place in the jurisdiction. In 1554, the churches of the diocese were 'poor, of thatch, and some of them have burned down'.[4] In 1562 the episcopal seat was transferred to Bogotá, and Santa Marta was degraded temporarily to the status of abbacy. Its restoration to the level of diocese in 1573 amounted to a cosmetic change: in 1580 the diocese possessed 'neither churches nor missions'.[5] Towards the close of the sixteenth century, English and French pirates sacked both Santa Marta and Riohacha. The English robbed the church at Santa Marta: Bishop Ocando repaired it as well as he could ('dos veces la reparé como pude').[6]

In the south of Chile, danger also threatened, not from pirates, but from hostile Araucan Indians. The episcopal seat of La Imperial seemed, nevertheless, at first to flourish. A seminary was founded early in the 1580s. Around 1583 the first catechism was translated into the Araucan language (printed Lima 1606). About 1571 the cathedral had two priests; by 1590 there was a bishop, a canon and a cantor. The diocese boasted eight cities with at least one parish priest, and 27 missions.[7] But the Araucan rebellion of 1598 forced the abandonment of Imperial, as well as all other settlements to the South of the Biobío river.[8] The episcopal seat was transferred northwards, to Concepción, about 1605, although it is not certain that the new seat was actually occupied as early as that, for in 1607 or 1608 the entire diocese was incorporated within that of Santiago. In 1620 Concepción regained its autonomy, but remained impoverished. In 1610 the city only counted 76 houses (36 were of thatch). The reduced number of families did not, however, preclude what may appear to our eyes to be a large number of religious institutions: a parish church and three 'convents' (Franciscan, three friars; Dominican, two friars; Mercedarian, three friars). But all, religious and civil alike, were poor and weary as a result of the wars.[9] A pessimistic account of the diocese in 1659 states: 'No hay ciudades, ni hay iglesias, ni rentas para ellas ...'.[10]

Santiago del Estero, with fewer than fifty Spanish *vecinos*, was the largest settlement in present-day northern Argentina, and was thus chosen as episcopal seat for the new diocese of Tucumán in 1570. The first bishop only deigned to take up his miter eleven years later. In 1583 the diocese consisted of five cities with a total population of 153 vecinos and about 35,000 Indians.[11] As in Venezuela and southern

Chile, the wrong place had been chosen for the erection of the cathedral. As early as 1599, when the Jesuit colegio of Córdoba was founded, it was apparent that this city was bound to usurp the primacy of Santiago del Estero within the diocese. In 1621 the University of Córdoba was founded by papal decree.[12] By 1613, the Jesuits had already begun their '*convictorio de San Francisco Javier*' in Córdoba, with thirty students. A similar attempt to organize a school for children in Santiago del Estero in 1609, by contrast, had failed for economic reasons. Nevertheless, the episcopal seat was not officially transferred until 1699.[13]

Erected in 1605, at the same time as that of La Paz, the diocese of Santa Cruz de la Sierra (Bolivia) was to remain one of the most primitive in South America throughout the colonial period. In 1587, it is claimed, a number of Jesuits arrived in Santa Cruz to preach 'the first sermon ever heard in this city.' Although a hospital was founded towards 1612, its existence seems to have been ephemeral, since it was 'restored' and given its name (Santa Bárbara) only in 1648. In 1793 the city was still in its beginnings. Its most noteworthy feature was the *plaza*, 'de mucha extensión y cuadrada.' On the other hand, the cathedral was small and 'indecent'.[14]

Reasons for the abject poverty of some of the South American dioceses, and the inevitable transfer of others, were the haste with which the ecclesiastical organization of the continent was carried out, and the desire on the part of the Spaniards to place cathedrals in even the most remote corners of the colony.

A simple example will illustrate the point. As is known, the Spanish colonization was characterized by a quite rapid urbanization.[15] The greatest numbers of cities and towns were founded during the sixteenth century. Of 191 towns and cities founded by 1620, 110 (57 percent) had been founded by 1550, and only 81 thereafter. There are two peak decades, those of 1530-1540 and 1550-1560.[16] By comparison, of the 37 dioceses founded in Spanish America up until 1620 – and no more new ones were founded until 1777 – 23 (62 percent) were founded before 1550. The two peak decades are 1510-1520 and 1530-1540.[17] If anything, therefore, the Spanish American bishoprics were founded more rapidly than the towns, at least during the early period. Many of those bishoprics were thus founded on future expectations, in anticipation of the actual settlement of the areas they were to serve. A better illustration of the formalistic character of Spanish colonialism could hardly be asked for.

Although Spain's ecclesiastical expansion in South America proceeded, *grosso modo*, from the Caribbean shores southward, it was more like a game of hopscotch than the slow, even spread of an oil stain. Geographically, we can distinguish three main theatres; chronologically there are three phases. The founding of dioceses in *Greater Colombia* (present-day Ecuador-Colombia-Venezuela) began in 1514 (Antigua), and ended in 1564 (Bogotá). In *Greater Peru* (Peru-Bolivia), the same process only began in 1537 (Cuzco), and ended in 1609 (Huamanga). Dioceses were founded in the *Southern provinces* (Chile-Argentina-Paraguay) between 1547 (Asunción) and 1620 (Buenos Aires).

In all three theaters, a number of early dioceses were founded which correspond to an initial, or opening, phase of expansion. In most cases these bishoprics are located in coastal regions, or along a navigable river (Asunción). With the exception of Cuzco, they are not located in areas with large indigenous populations.

A second phase involved the establishment of dioceses in the centers of indigenous population. Usually located between the scattered outposts of the first phase, the second-phase dioceses, with the exception of Lima, are all located in the Andean highlands. In the Southern provinces, where few concentrations of Indian population existed, this phase did not take place.

The third phase was one of readjustment, or of partition, of already existing dioceses. Some of the first and second-phase dioceses were too large and/or populous to be conserved intact. Thus Tucumán was broken off from Santiago, and Buenos Aires from Asunción. In these thinly populated regions, the problem was one of excessive distances. In the dioceses of Quito, Lima, Charcas and Cuzco, large distances were compounded by high population levels. Thus in the third phase, Arequipa and Huamanga were carved out of the border areas between Lima and Cuzco, Trujillo was taken from Lima and Quito, and La Paz and Santa Cruz were shaped out of the edges of Los Charcas. In Greater Colombia, where neither distances nor population levels were intolerably large, this third phase did not take place.

Table 1   *Three phases in the foundation of the South American dioceses, 1514-1620*

Greater Colombia	Greater Peru	Southern provinces
I. Opening		
Antigua 1514	Cuzco 1537	Asunción 1547
Santa María 1529		Santiago 1561
Coro 1530		La Imperial 1563
Cartagena 1534		
II. Consolidation		
Quito 1546	Lima 1541	
Popayán 1546	Charcas 1552	
Bogotá 1564		
III. Readjustment		
	Arequipa 1577*	Tucumán 1570
	Trujillo 1577*	Buenos Aires 1620
	La Paz 1605	
	Santa Cruz 1605	
	Huamanga 1609	

* Only carried out in 1609.

After 1620 (Buenos Aires), the colonial ecclesiastical division was practically complete. No new dioceses were erected after 1620 until Cuenca was elevated to this

Map 1   *Three phases in the foundation of new dioceses, Spanish South America, 1514-1620*

rank in 1769. With the erection of the diocese of Cuenca, a final round of episcopal expansion began that incorporated the late colonial dioceses of Mérida/Maracaibo (1778), Guayana (1790), Mainas (1803) and Salta (1806). Small and poor, at least in their early years, these late colonial bishoprics only flowered, if at all, during the National Period, and cannot be considered here.

Of the colonial bishoprics, those founded during the first phase experienced the greatest problems of survival. The quick death of Antigua, mourned by no one, the *via crucis* of Santa Marta and those of Coro and Imperial have been mentioned. The richest dioceses, those of Lima, Charcas, and to a lesser extent, Bogotá and Quito, were products of the second phase. The dioceses founded during the third phase tended neither to be very rich nor very poor. With the exceptions of Buenos Aires and Tucumán, they were rather carefully engineered neither to die of poverty nor to stun by their opulence.

In the first and second phases of expansion, no one worried very much about the exact boundaries which were to separate the dioceses. The limits of the early bishoprics were vaguely defined in the *Leyes de Indias* as describing a radius of fifteen *leguas* (63 km) about the episcopal seat, and further, one-half of the distance separating one episcopal seat from the next.[18] In the third phase, this simple formula was discarded. In the cases of Arequipa, Trujillo, La Paz, Santa Cruz and Huamanga, the erection of new dioceses was preceded by careful preliminary study of how the new boundaries would affect the tithe incomes of the already existing ones.[19]

Until 1547, all of the South American bishoprics were subordinated to the archdiocese of Seville. In 1547 Lima was raised to metropolitan rank, independent of Seville. Bogotá was raised to the same status in 1564, and Los Charcas in 1609.[20]

Episcopal incomes and the cathedral chapters

To the bishops belonged the proceeds of tithes (*diezmos*) collected within their dioceses.[21] Tithes were not levied indiscriminately upon persons, but were a fixed percentage (generally ten percent) of gross economic production. Thus of all harvests of grain, garden produce, etc., one part in ten – before subtraction of seed and other costs – fell due in tithes. Products exempted from the *diezmo* were pearls, precious stones, metals, fish and wild game.[22] Royal officials were charged with the collection and notation of the annual levels of the *diezmo* income of each diocese; if the value of this income fell below the level of 500,000 maravedís (1,838 pesos), it was to be supplemented from the royal treasury to this amount.[23]

The administration of tithe incomes was left in hands of the bishop and cathedral chapter (*cabildo catedral*). But the *Leyes de Indias* stipulated a strict formula for the destination of these incomes. They were to be divided five ways, as follows: one-fourth of the revenues to the bishop, one-fourth to the *cabildo catedral*, two-ninths to the clergy, one-sixth to the building of cathedral and hospitals, and one-ninth to the Crown.[24] The activities of the secular Church were thus rather intimately bound to the economic fortunes of the areas it served. In the poor bishoprics little in the way of ecclesiastical activity could be expected.

Vázquez de Espinosa has provided a list of the South American bishoprics with their respective incomes, and the salaries of the different members of each cathedral chapter.[25] Table 2 summarizes Vázquez de Espinosa's tabulations, which may serve as an index to the relative wealth of the various bishoprics early in the seventeenth century (ca. 1615-1628). The tithe income levels are approximate, and presumably varied during the colonial period. I am unaware, however, of a similar tabulation for any other point in time. These figures compiled by Vázquez thus serve as the sole basis for comparison.

Our impression of the first-phase bishoprics as including a number of barely viable ones, is reinforced by the figures in Table 2. Taken as a group, their tithe incomes per diocese average 5,773 pesos. The phase-two dioceses, by contrast, have an average income almost five times as high: 27,968 pesos per year. The phase-three dioceses form an intermediate group, with average tithe incomes of 9,691 pesos per year.

The richest bishoprics are in Greater Peru, with average tithe incomes of 23,625 pesos; those in Greater Colombia are considerably poorer at 7,160 pesos, and the incomes of the Southern dioceses are the lowest of all, averaging 3,503 pesos.

Table 2 *Episcopal incomes (rentas), and salaries of members of the cabildo catedral South American bishoprics ca. 1628 (estimates in pesos; actual values could fluctuate; '… que no tienen punto fijo'.)*

| Bishopric | Rentas | Salaries | | | | Total | Ratio Salaries: rentas |
		Deán	Arced., Chantre ME, TES[a]	Canon	Others		
Los Charcas	60,000	5,000	4.500	4,000	3,000	16,500	.275
Lima	50,000	4,250	3,360	2,816	6,313	16,739	.334
Cuzco	20,000	2,955	2,580	1,984	1,188	8,707	.435
Bogotá	14,000	1,500	1,300	1,000	600	4,400	.314
Quito	14,000	1,858	1,610	1,240	900	5,608	.401
Trujillo	14,000	2,069	1,785	1,385	970	6,209	.444
Arequipa	14,000	2,070	1,800	1,380	1,464	6,714	.480
La Paz	14,000	1,400	1,200	1,000	700	4,300	.307
Santa Cruz	9,000	1,800	1,600	1,300	-	4,700	.522
Huamanga	8,000	1,830	1,590	1,220	-	4,640	.580
Coro/Caracas	-	-	-	-	-	-	-
Tucumán	7,000	1,600	1,400	-	-	3,000	.429

Table 2 *Continued*

Bishopric	Rentas	Salaries				Total	Ratio Salaries: rentas
		Deán	Arced., Chantre ME, TES[a]	Canon	Others		
Santiago	5,000	1,000	800	600	-	2,400	.480
Cartagena	4,125[b]	1,400	1,200	1,000	-	3,600	.873
Buenos Aires	1,838[c]	550	500	400	-	1,450	.789
Popayán	1,838[c]	700	550	-	-	1,250	.680
Santa Marta	1,838[c]	600	400	300	-	1,300	.707
Asunción	1,838[c]	550	500	400	-	1,450	.789
Imperial/ Concepción	1,838[c]	700	550	400	-	1,650	.898

[a] Arcediano, chantre, maestre escuela, tesorero.

[b] 3,000 ducados; 1 ducado = 11 reales; 1 peso = 8 reales (Vázquez de Espinosa, op. cit., pp. 540, 563).

[c] 500,000 maravedís; 1 real = 34 maravedís; 1 peso = 272 maravedis (Váquez de Espinosa. op. cit., p. 552).

The richest dioceses were those of Los Charcas and Lima, followed at some distance by Cuzco, Bogotá, Quito, Trujillo, Arequipa and La Paz. Buenos Aires, Popayán, Santa Marta, Asunción and Imperial/Concepción were the poorest South American dioceses: their incomes were – thanks to the royal guarantee of minimum stipend – identical at 500,000 maravedís. The *rentas* of the richest bishopric, Los Charcas, were about 33 times as high as those of the poorest.

A structural drag upon the ecclesiastical development of all but the very richest dioceses was the existence of the *cabildo catedral* (cathedral chapter). The institution of the church cabildo served two purposes: (a) to increase the splendor of divine worship in the cathedral, and (b) to assist the bishop in the administration of the diocese. In view of the bucolic nature of most South American dioceses, these aims, however laudable in themselves, would seem to deserve a low priority. But entirely true to the already mentioned formalistic tendency of Spanish colonial policy in general the *Concordia de Burgos*, signed in 1512, two years before the founding of the first (failed) South American diocese, stipulated that each cathedral chapter should ideally consist of five dignitaries (*deán, chantre, maestre escuela, tesorero, arcediano*), ten canons, twelve prebendaries (six *raciones* and six *media raciones*), six acolytes and six choir chaplains.[26] The execution of this program would depend upon the resources available to each diocese, but in practice, the number of clergy called for were unrealistic, even for such wealthy American dioceses as Charcas and Lima, let alone the poorer ones. Nevertheless, no diocese failed to do its best, and more than its best, to approach the official precept as closely as possible.

Table 3   *Cabildos catedral, South American bishoprics ca. 1628*[27]

Bishopric	Dignitaries	Canons	Prebendaries	Others	Total
Los Charcas	5	5	6	-	16
Lima	5	8	12	12	37
Cuzco	5	6	3	-	14
Bogotá	5	4	2	-	11
Quito	5	5	4	-	14
Trujillo	3	4	2	-	9
Arequipa	5	5	4	-	14
La Paz	3	5	2	-	10
Santa Cruz	2	2	-	-	4
Huamanga	3	2	-	-	5
Coro/Caracas	-	-	-	-	-
Tucumán	5	-	-	-	5
Santiago	5	4	-	-	9
Cartagena	5	2	-	-	7
Buenos Aires	2	2	-	-	4
Popayán	5		-	-	5
Santa Marta	4	1	-	-	5
Asunción	3	2	-	-	5
Imperial/ Concepción	2	2	-	-	4
Total	72	59	35	12	178

Although the poorer dioceses had smaller *cabildos*, they were still too large to be af-forded: the size of the cabildo was less elastic than episcopal income. There was a minimum size attached to the existence of a *cabildo*, which seems to have been four persons. The largest *cabildo* (Lima) had 37 members. Thus, while the income differ-ential between the richest and the poorest bishopric was on the order of 33:1 (see Table 2), the greatest differential in the size of the *cabildo* was only about 9:1. The highest-paid position in the *cabildo* were the most rigid: Popayán and Lima both had the same number of dignitaries. In the poorer dioceses the lowest-paid clergy were the first to be sacrificed. Every diocese was well stocked with dignitaries (not to men-tion bishops – one apiece). The true sign of a rich diocese was to have quantities of prebendaries, and only Lima afforded itself the luxury of a notary, an organist or a sacristan in 1628.

Salaries in the poorer dioceses were, in all fairness, lower than in the richer, but not enough so to compensate for their very existence. The pay differentials between the richest and poorest dioceses were on the order of 10:1 (i.e. the Dean of Los Char-cas's cathedral had a salary roughly ten times as high as that of his colleague in

Asunción). Salaries had a lower limit, presumably near the subsistence level, of about 400 pesos *per annum*.

Table 4 *Tithe income after* cabildo catedral *expenses; amounts left over for other purposes (in pesos), ca. 1628 (see Table 2)*

Bishopric	Tithes minus salaries cabildo catedral	Salary bishop (one-fourth of tithes, where possible)	Remainder (king's ninth, salaries clergy, construction of hospitals and churches)
Los Charcas	43,500	15,000	28,500
Lima	33,261	12,500	20,761
Cuzco	11,293	5,000	6,293
Bogotá	9,600	3,500	6,100
Quito	8,392	3,500	4,892
Trujillo	7,791	3,500	4,291
Arequipa	7,286	3,500	3,786
La Paz	9,700	3,500	6,200
Santa Cruz	4,300	2,250	2,050
Huamanga	3,360	2,000	1,360
Coro/Caracas	-	-	-
Tucumán	4,000	1,750	2,250
Santiago	2,600	1,250	1,350
Cartagena	525	525	0
Buenos Aires	388	388	0
Popayán	588	460	128
Santa Marta	538	460	78
Asunción	388	388	0
Imperial/Concepción	188	188	0

The total salary expenses attached to the maintenance of the cathedral chapters of eighteen South American bishoprics are given in the second to last column of Table 2. In the last column, these are compared with tithe incomes. It will be remembered that one-fourth of these incomes were supposed to go to the chapters, as stipulated by the *Leyes de Indias*. Nevertheless, this precept was invariably violated in America, and most seriously in those dioceses, which were least able to afford it. Whereas the richest dioceses kept relatively close to the guideline (Charcas, Lima, Bogotá, La Paz spent between 27.5 percent and 33.4 percent of their tithe incomes on *cabildo* salaries), the medium-level dioceses were spending most of their incomes within the walls of their modest cathedrals. In the poorest bishoprics, the payroll of the *cabildo* members alone, however few their number, and however low their salaries, was devouring up to 80 percent or 90 percent of *diezmo* revenues. What was to become, in these dioceses, of the salaries of the bishop and other clergy, and the building of churches and hospitals? Table 4 makes clear that in most dioceses, and especially in the poorer ones, the unfolding of other church activities would depend in large part, or wholly, on gifts and irregular revenues of other, sometimes corrupt nature.

The bishops and clergy

Although both of the theoretical justifications for the existence of the *cabildo catedral* would seem to make it the bishop's natural partner and aid in the new and difficult American dioceses, more mundane considerations disturbed this hoped-for harmony.

Although little is known about the careers of individual *cabildo* members – except in those cases where they were promoted to the rank of bishop, always in another diocese – as a group they formed a stationary ecclesiastical bureaucracy which went along with each diocese. The bishops, by contrast, were quite mobile, either through promotion, or more often, through death. Of 347 South American bishops during the whole colonial period whose careers are comparable, actual possession of the miter lasted an average of only 7.4 years. Sixteen comparable bishoprics were vacant (*sede vacante*) during about 1,270 out of total combined period of 3,951 diocese-years (32 percent).[28] Many of the South American bishops were born in, and had to be brought from, Spain. The naming of new bishops was a bureaucratic process in which the Spanish sovereign proposed a candidate who then had to be ratified by the Pope.[29] Most of the bishops named were not young. Some died *en route* or shortly upon arrival at their sees. The delays caused by the rigid method of choosing new bishops resulted in the inordinately long *sede vacantes* suffered by the American bishoprics, and contributed to the exaggerated influence within the dioceses of the cathedral chapters. The rapid turnover of bishops, accompanied by sometimes long intervening periods of *sedevacancia* created a situation in which the cathedral chapters formed the main element of stability within the American secular Church. This situation was only aggravated by the – otherwise desirable – prolonged visitations of the outposts of the dilated American dioceses (often lasting more than a year), required of the bishops by the *Leyes de Indias*,[30] and the frequent synods and councils called for by the Council of Trent. It need not surprise us that the bishop was often seen within his own cathedral as an outsider, a stranger.

The point need not be belabored that the bishop, for his own income, was often in conflict with the chapter (see Table 4). Entering his new diocese for the first time, the colonial South American bishop was not always pleased at what he found. While the *Concilio III Limense* had fixed at 200-300 the ideal number of communicants for each parish,[31] the tithe incomes were patently insufficient to provide for sufficient numbers of parish priests. In 1653, bishop Francisco de Godoy of Huamanga complained bitterly of the state of his diocese, and especially of the neglect of spiritual care for his Indians.[32] He related, that on the high road connecting Lima and Cuzco, and spanning the heart of his diocese, there was not a single priest in the 24 *leguas* (more than 100 km) separating Huanta and Sintihuailas.[33] Where priests were to be found among the Indians, they sometimes supplemented their meager legitimate incomes through their own entrepreneurial talents. In 1626 in the archdiocese of Lima, the case of a *doctrinero* came to light who had managed to stockpile 20,000 *varas* (about 17,000 meters) of rough woolen cloth, woven for him by Indians.[34] Needless to say, such commercial pre-occupations distracted individual clergy from their spiritual responsibilities, and were prohibited by law. Bishop Juan de Almoguera, of Arequipa denounced clerical venality with such vigor in his *Instrucción de sacerdotes* (published in Madrid in 1671), that the work was sanctioned by the Inquisition: whereas the legitimate income of a parish priest could ascend to some 900 pesos in that diocese, some were reported to have incomes of 4,000 to 5,000 pesos, 'cantidad que no alcanzan algunos obispos'.[35] The illegitimate incomes of some clergy led to a further abuse, that of the outright sale of parishes: San Blas in Quito is reported to have commanded a price of 5,000 pesos towards the end of the seventeenth century.[36]

The bishop who tried to correct such abuses all too often met with an intransigent attitude not only on the part of the civil authorities, but also in the person of his own *cabildo catedral* which was often compromised in such practices. Such was the case in Arequipa, when the new bishop Pedro Perea entered his diocese in 1619 after a *sede vacante* of six years. His examination of the financial accounts of the cabildo disclosed fraud, which the responsible members of the cabildo were not prepared to restitute. The ensuing prosecution exhausted the entire period of Perea's stay in Arequipa, but never led to restitution or punishment.[37] In fairness it must be said that the formal demands made on the American Church, such as defined by the *Leyes de Indias,* the *Concordia de Burgos* and the *Concilio III Limense,* took too little account of the actual resources available to the dioceses; within the bounds of the tithe incomes very little was possible. In practice, a certain amount of corruption was tolerated in order to keep the American dioceses intact. The dilemma, all too often, was a corrupt church or no church at all.

Parish churches

Great numbers of Spanish American Christians attended their services in churches of adobe and thatch, hardly larger or more elaborate than their own simple houses. To this extent, the stereotype of the colonial church as a sumptuous repository of gilded altars encrusted with precious stones surrounded by seas of human misery is inaccurate. Especially in the rural areas the history of the parish churches evades us. Colonial writers paid little attention to them. Sometimes mentioned, they are never described. Exceptions are the sometimes opulent parishes of the largest cities, where, especially in the eighteenth century, churches arose whose façades and treasuries rivalled and surpassed those of some cathedrals. Still the chronologies of most of the colonial parish churches are too uncertain to follow.

Table 5 *Net tithe incomes (minus salaries* cabildo catedral*) and numbers of parishes per diocese, ca. 1628*

Diocese	Net tithe income (see Table 4), in pesos	Number of parishes, excluding cathedral	Income/parish, in pesos
Los Charcas	43,500	18	2,417
Lima	33,261	15	2,217
Cuzco	11,293	7	1,613
Bogotá	9,600	9	1,066
Quito	8,392	16	525
Trujillo	7,791	4	1,947
Arequipa	7,286	3	2,429
La Paz	9,700	0	-
Santa Cruz	4,300	1	4,300
Huamanga	3,360	6	560
Coro/Caracas	-	6	-
Tucumán	4,000	4	1,000
Santiago	2,600	3	867
Cartagena	525	1	525
Buenos Aires	388	2	194
Popayán	588	6	98
Santa Marta	538	2	269
Asunción	388	2	194
Imperial/Concepción	188	1	188
Total	147,698	106	1,393

In his *Compendio* Vázquez de Espinosa mentions some 106 parishes in Spanish South America for the first quarter of the seventeenth century.[38] Grouped according to diocese, they give an impression of the relative level of established secular Church activity in different regions (Table 5). In general, the number of parishes in a given diocese corresponds to the level of its tithe incomes. The amount of money available to be spent on each parish is, however, much lower in the poorer bishoprics than in the richer. The exceptions to the rule are interesting. Considered in the light of tithe incomes the dioceses of Bogotá, Quito, Huamanga and Popayán have more than the usual numbers of parishes while Trujillo, Arequipa, Santa Cruz and La Paz have too few. While the former bishoprics were all either more than a half-century old

(Bogotá, Quito, Popayán) or in a region which was evangelized early (Huamanga), all of the latter were of very recent creation around 1628. This shows that the formation of parishes was still underway in the newer bishoprics towards 1628.

Cathedrals

Every bishopric had a cathedral but the size and quality of the South American cathedrals varied widely. We know the chronologies and characteristics of most of the colonial cathedrals. Their histories shed light on the histories of the dioceses of which they were the focal points. The richest cathedrals were the longest in building, and the most elaborate. Some dioceses saw the coming and going of a number of different temples.

Such was the case in Lima, where a first small church was built in 1535-1538, inaugurated in 1540 and raised to the rank of cathedral in 1543. A second church was built to replace the first in only two years, from 1549 to 1551. It was of a single nave without transept. Its adobe walls and wooden roof covered an area of about 75 x 15 meters. The sanctuary boasted a rare vault of stone masonry. A more ambitious plan was that presented by Alonso Beltrán in 1565 for a huge basilical church; although the first stone was laid between 1569 and 1575, very little progress was made until about 1598 and then on new plans made by Francisco de Becerra, who also designed the plans for Cuzco cathedral (both plans from 1598). The cathedral of Jaén (Spain) was his model both in the rectangular plan and in assigning equal heights to central and lateral naves. Becerra's cathedral would have a length of about 101 m (120 *varas*) and a width including lateral chapels of about 44 m (52.5 *varas*). By 1604 half of the new cathedral was ready for use, but earthquake damage in 1606 and 1609 retarded its completion. Finally its vaults were closed in the years 1613-1622. During the earthquake of 1687 the stone-masonry vaults of the sanctuary and neighboring bays collapsed. These were replaced by wood-and-stucco vaults imitating the appearance of stone masonry in the period 1687-1697. In spite of the lightness of the new *ersatz* construction, damage from the great earthquake of 1746 was so complete that only the outside walls of the church could be utilized in the reconstruction which began in 1751 and ended (except for the façade) in 1758.[39]

Wethey believes that the original cathedral at Cuzco (second quarter of the sixteenth century) was long and narrow with a single nave presumably roofed on a wooden armature. Although the first stone of the cathedral we know today was laid in 1560, little construction took place before 1598, when Becerra presented his plans. As at Lima they included three naves and recessed lateral chapels. The main campaign of construction lasted from 1644 to 1654. The belfries date from 1657. Completely rib-vaulted, the structure is somewhat smaller than Lima cathedral (about 81 m long by 42 wide).[40]

The early church at La Plata (Los Charcas), begun in 1551 and completed before 1561, was of notoriously poor construction 'falsa y peligrosa'. Nevertheless, in 1583, 1586 and 1599, additions and modifications to the same basic structure were being carried out. About 1608 it consisted of a single rib-vaulted nave and four lateral chapels (two to a side). In 1622 a new crossing was under construction which still survives. The large *capilla de Guadalupe* seems to have been added between 1616 and 1625. The vaults of the crossing, capilla mayor and sacristy date from 1633. In the period 1689 to 1693 vaulted side aisles replaced the lateral chapels, converting the church into a spacious basilica. But the construction had always remained defective, and in 1712 the vaults had to be revised anew. According to Egaña, the tower dates from 1725.[41]

A parish church was begun in La Paz in 1556, and continued under construction in 1561. About 1653, now a cathedral, it seems to have conserved its original form: a single nave with two lateral chapels. In 1653-1682 the church was enlarged to include two lateral naves (total length 60 *varas* = about 50 m) and matching towers. The nave was vaulted at this time as well. In 1826 this structure was demolished to make way for a more modern one.[42]

In 1560, Quito's cathedral was small, with earthen walls and a roof of thatch. A new three-aisled church of stone, brick and adobe, with a wooden roof, was built from 1565 to 1572. There was a tower, and the *capilla mayor* had a masonry vault. Enlarged and partially reconstructed after the earthquake of 1755, the present cathedral conserves some sixteenth-century elements, notably the pointed arcades on squared pillars separating the nave from the side aisles.[43]

Bogota's first cathedral collapsed spontaneously in 1565. Its replacement, begun in 1572, shared the same basic plan as the cathedral of Quito: three naves separated by arcades supporting a wooden roof. According to Duque Gómez, building activity was especially intensive about 1610. The towers and interior decoration were from about 1678. Damage from the 1785 earthquake was repaired towards 1792, but continued fear of possible collapse caused the cathedral to be closed in 1806. The present neo-classical edifice dates from 1806-1814.[44]

In Cartagena the primitive cathedral (1537) burned down in 1552. Although a new one was begun in 1554, the definitive construction took place during the years 1577 and 1578. After the roof collapsed in 1600, it took twelve years before it could be replaced. The church was similar to those of Bogotá and Quito, i.e. three naves separated by arcades sustaining a wooden roof.[45]

Begun in 1583 and finished in 1632 or 1633, the cathedral of Coro has three naves separated by arcades and a wooden roof. It is 51 m long and 23.4 m wide. It has a tower. Soon after its completion, an ungrateful bishop transferred the episcopal seat to Caracas (official transfer 1637), where the new cathedral was only built from 1655 to 1674. It had five naves separated by arcades, and wooden roof. The *capilla de la Trinidad*, also with a wooden roof, was added in 1698. The façade of stuccoed brick dates from 1710-1713.[46]

To the family of wooden-roofed basilicas also belong the colonial cathedrals of Popayán, Santiago del Estero (1618), Santa Marta and Santa Cruz. The walls of Popayán's cathedral (begun 1595) were made of brick with 'a little lime and a lot of stamped earth'. After having threatened to collapse for more than a half a century, it was finally dismantled in 1786. Sixty *varas* long by about 18 wide, it seems not to have enchanted by its beauty: '... desagradable a la vista, no está sujeta a alguno de los órdenes de arquitectura que enseñan a edificar con proporción, hermosura y fortaleza'. A new cathedral was not begun until 1819, and not finished until 1906.[47]

The first, presumably extremely modest cathedral at Santiago del Estero (Tucumán), burned down in 1615. The second (ca. 1618) was destroyed by floods in 1627 or 1628. A third cathedral met its end in the decade of the 1660s or '70s. From 1675 to 1685, a fourth cathedral, this time with two towers, was built. In 1699 the episcopal seat was transferred to Córdoba.[48]

The colonial cathedral at Santa Marta does not survive. Begun about 1668, it was not completed until 1711.[49] Poor and unsightly, the early cathedral of Santa Cruz was ruined a number of times before 1770, when a more or less definitive construction arose (perhaps the wrong term: the walls were only about four meters high), which lasted until about 1838. Three naves separated by wooden colonnades were covered by a wooden roof whose maximum height was about 7.5 m (9 *varas*) above the central nave. A reasonable guess is that this was one of the darkest of the colonial cathedrals.[50]

Arequipa's original parish church (1544) was destroyed in the earthquake of 1604, and thus missed by a few years the arrival of the first bishop of that city. Towards 1621 construction began on a new building. By 1656 the cathedral stood: three naves, 15 vaults of brick and a tower. The sanctuary was enlarged in 1745-1752. Until it was consumed by fire in 1834, the cathedral is reputed to have been Arequipa's finest seventeenth-century monument.[51]

In Huamanga an older church was replaced by the present one beginning in 1632. Financial difficulties paralyzed construction for a quarter of a century (1636-1662), but barrel-vaulting, two towers and a dome were in place by 1669-1672. The rectangular basilical plan of this cathedral follows those of Lima and Cuzco.[52] Earthquakes in 1619 and 1635 damaged or ruined Trujillo's first cathedral. A new and larger building was proposed in 1643, and built from 1647 to 1666. Damage from the earthquake of 1687 was only repaired in 1721-1740. The last great earthquake was that of 1759 (restoration 1768-1771; reconsecration 1781). New towers were added in 1782-1784. The basilical floor plan resembled those of Lima and Cuzco. The sanctuary was domed. The materials of construction were brick and stucco.[53]

Cordoba's original wooden-roofed parish church, built in 1620, collapsed in 1677. Towards 1687 a new church was begun, which was to consist of a single nave with transept and two towers. The transfer of the episcopal seat to Córdoba from Santiago del Estero in 1699, and the partial collapse of the walls in 1723 may have occasioned the modification of the plans to include the three naves which characterize the present structure. The barrel-vaulting and main portal seem to have been completed by 1729. The dome was probably finished in 1757 or 1758, when the cathedral was inaugurated. The completion of at least one of the towers was only realized at a later date.[54]

In Buenos Aires, the first cathedral of which we have notice was built in 1668-1671, but so badly that it was torn down by 1692, in which year plans were presented for a basilical church with two towers. Work did not begin, however, until 1727. Still under construction in 1750, it collapsed under its own weight in 1752, except for the façade and towers. The body of the present church thus dates from the second half of the eighteenth century (finished 1791). In the meanwhile, it had been decided to replace the old façade, with towers, with the neo-classical colonnade which we see today. The old façade was demolished in 1778; the new one was finished in 1822.[55]

Santiago de Chile's primitive parish church of adobe with a thatched roof (ca. 1545), was probably replaced by a more elaborate structure when it was raised to the status of cathedral in 1561. But earthquakes in 1647 and 1730 erased whatever church there may have been. The present basilical, vaulted, neo-classical structure was only begun in 1782, although the foundations seem to have existed before that date. It has two towers.[56]

Egaña tells us that the primitive church of Asunción was built of wood and earth about 1540. Its cost: 15 *quintales* of cassava flour and 10 *fanegas* of maize.[57] We know less about the cathedral at Concepción, only that one was built around 1744.[58] Its predecessor at Imperial has left no trace.

Building on the colonial cathedrals thus continued throughout the colonial period. Styles, techniques and materials changed. Table 6 is an attempt to schematically compare the different colonial cathedrals as they were in the first half of the seventeenth century.

Table 6 *Characteristics of the South American cathedrals, ca. 1600/1650*

Diocese	Material walls	Roofing	Plan	Size	Towers	Tithe income ca. 1628*
Lima	stone masonry	fully vaulted	3 naves	101 x 44	2	33,261
Cuzco	stone masonry	fully vaulted	3 naves	ca.81 x ca.42	2	11,293
Los Charcas	stone masonry?	fully vaulted	single nave			43,500
Quito	stone brick adobe	wood; vault in *capilla mayor*	3 naves		1	8,392
Bogotá		wood	3 naves			9,600
Arequipa	adobe?	wood				7,286

Table 6   *Continued*

Diocese	Material walls	Roofing	Plan	Size	Towers	Tithe income ca. 1628 *
La Paz	adobe	wood	single nave			9,700
Coro	adobe? brick	wood	3 naves	51 x 23.40	1	
Santiago del Estero	adobe?	wood	3 naves			4,000
Cartagena	adobe?	wood	3 naves			525
Popayán	brick and earth	wood	3 naves	50 x 15		588
Asunción	earth	wood	3 naves			388

* Net tithe income in pesos (from Table 4).

Stone masonry walls, masonry vaulting, and two towers are characteristic of the richest cathedrals around 1600/1650. Characteristic of the poorest ones are the use of stamped earth for walls and wooden frames for the roofing system. In the intermediate cathedrals, brick and adobe predominate as wall materials, and wood for roofing; some have one tower. Logically, the poorer cathedrals are smaller in size than the richer. The richest and best-built cathedrals lie along the road Lima-Los Charcas; this road was the axis about which colonial life turned.

The basilical or three-naved plan was far and away the most popular one in the early seventeenth century. The American cathedrals were wide and rectangular, as were their Andalusian models. Only in Los Charcas and La Paz do we still find single-naved cathedrals in the seventeenth century; the other early examples of which we have knowledge, at Lima and Cuzco, had already been replaced.

By the eighteenth century all cathedrals shared the basilical plan; Caracas cathedral even had five naves (the status of Asunción and Concepción are, however, unknown).

Comparison of Tables 6 and 7 gives insight into the changes that took place in the South American dioceses in the intervening 150 years. The greatest changes are to be found in the extension of the high road from Lima to Bolivia. Whereas in the early seventeenth century the axis Lima-Cuzco-La Plata was the backbone of the colony, at the end of the eighteenth century this axis includes Trujillo to the north, Huamanga, Arequipa and La Paz in the heartland and Córdoba, Buenos Aires and Santiago de Chile to the south. The architectural expansion reflected in the introduction of stone masonry and elaborate vaulting systems towards the south is striking. Architectural expansion during this period follows exactly the well-travelled commercial route described by Concolorcorvo in his eighteenth-century guide, *El lazarillo de ciegos caminantes.*[59] In contrast to this development along the southern axis the area defined by the present-day states of Ecuador, Colombia and Venezuela would seem to have stagnated. The situation with respect to the cathedrals did not change impressively. Insofar as there are new cathedral buildings (Santa Marta, Caracas) they follow the slightly archaic pattern of the older cathedrals, i.e. barn-like three or five-aisled structures with wooden roofs.

Table 7 *Characteristics of the South American cathedrals, second half of the eighteenth century*

Cathedral	Material walls	Roofing	No. of naves	Size	Towers
Lima	stone masonry	fully vaulted	3	101 x 44	2
Cuzco	stone masonry	fully vaulted	3	81 x 42	2
Los Charcas	stone masory?	fully vaulted	single nave		
Trujillo	brick and stucco	fully vaulted	3		2
Arequipa	stone masonry	fully vaulted	3		2
La Paz	stone masonry	fully vaulted	3	50 long	2
Huamanga	stone masonry	fully vaulted	3		2
Córdoba	stone masonry	fully vaulted	3		2
Santiago de Chile	stone masonry	fully vaulted	3		2
Buenos Aires	Stone? brick?	fully vaulted	3		2
Bogotá			3		2
Quito	stone, brick and adobe	wood, one vault of stone	3		1
Santa Cruz	brick? adobe?	wood	3	15 wide	
Caracas	brick and stucco	wood	5		1
Cartagena	adobe?	wood	3		
Popayán	earth and brick	wood	3	50 x 15	
Santa Marta	adobe	wood	3		

For the period ca. 1600, Slicher van Bath distinguishes two economic complexes which correspond to Greater Colombia (including Quito and Coro/Caracas) and Greater Peru (Trujillo-Lima-Cuzco-Potosí/La Plata).[60] These complexes are easily recognized in the architectural developments as reflected in the form of the colonial cathedrals. by the eighteenth century, Tucumán, Buenos Aires and Chile had been incorporated within the Peruvian complex, while the Great Colombian complex retained its distinctive architectural flavor characterized by a certain archaic tendency. In another study we have shown that architectural activity in general depends upon certain – local and regional – economic conditions.[61] The chronology of activity on the South American cathedrals suggest that Argentina and Chile gained in relative economic importance during the seventeenth and eighteenth centuries while Greater Colombia was more static.

Architecturally we may distinguish three groups of families of colonial cathedrals. There is a chronological as well as a stylistic or technical difference.

– *Family 1 (ca. 1535 – ca. 1561)*. Although the type survives in many Spanish American parish churches, the single-naved, wooden roofed, 'shoebox-like' church held a limited number of people, and was only used for the earliest South American cathedrals (Lima I and II, Cuzco I, Los Charcas I and La Paz I). All of these churches were soon replaced by more elaborate structures.

The basilical cathedrals may be divided into two groups. In the first, roofing was provided by relatively light systems of wooden trabeation. This type of roof made little demand of strong supporting walls. These could thus be fabricated with simple materials: adobe, brick and earth. A second group employed the more expensive and technically difficult systems of stone or brick-masonry vaulting. The quality of the supporting walls not only had to be much higher, but the lateral thrust of the vaults also required buttressing at the vault intersections. Ashlar or heavy brick construction was indicated for the walls and buttresses; earth and adobe were not strong enough. The advantages or wood trabeation lay in its cheapness, and in the relative ease of construction. Its disadvantages were in the barn-like quality of the churches it enclosed, and in its vulnerability to insects, fire, bats and rot. On the other hand, vaulted churches presented an impressive appearance and relative permanence, in spite of their peril during earthquakes. The disadvantages or vaulting were in its expense and technical difficulty. The choice between the two different options was mainly one of a smaller or larger initial investment. As a group, the vaulted churches are later than the wooden ones.

– *Family 2 (ca. 1565 – ca. 1770)*. Basilical cathedrals with wooden roofs were built at Quito, Bogotá, Cartagena, Coro, Popayán, Caracas, Santa Marta, Santiago del Estero and Santa Cruz (at Quito and Coro they survive). Their grace lies in the arcades which separate their naves. Thin arches resting on slender columns or wood or brick unobtrusively articulate spacious interiors. Rectangular plans, the sometimes elaborate carpentry of their ceilings, and the sometimes pointed profiles of their arcades betray their Moorish and Medieval Spanish models.[62]

– *Family 3 (ca. 1598 – ca. 1782)*. Although the wide rectangular plans of the vaulted basilical cathedrals also reveal their Andalusian – and indirectly Moorish – extraction,[63] other aspects of their style are severe, classicizing (gothic vaults at Lima reflected fear of seismic instability and not aesthetic preference[64]), Italianesque.[65] This type of cathedral, the most elaborate and expensive known in colonial South America, was built at Trujillo, Lima, Huamanga, Arequipa, Cuzco, La Paz, Los Charcas, Córdoba, Buenos Aires and Santiago de Chile.

Map 2 traces the progress and the chronology or the three families of cathedrals. The contrast between the southern and northern colonial complexes is easily seen.

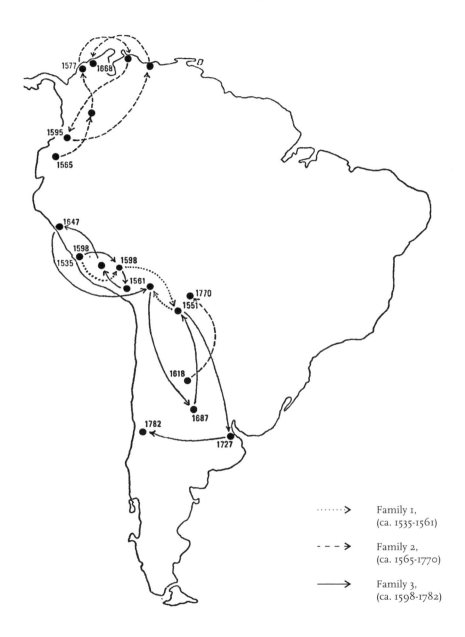

Map 2 *Three cycles in the building of the colonial cathedrals*

The bishops

The King of Spain named new bishops. His choices were thereupon ratified by the Pope. In many cases bishops were promoted from one American diocese to another. A long career could include as many as four American bishoprics. The promotions followed a predictable path in the colonial period. It was a system of one-way streets, leading from the more obscure to the more prominent cathedrals. Egaña provides us with the careers or 93 bishops who occupied more than one South American episcopal seat.[66] Their movements are summarized in Table 8.

Table 8　*Successive episcopal appointments of 93 South American bishops, 1537-1805*

Jerónimo de Loaysa, OP*	1537 Cartagena
	1540 Lima
Juan de los Barrios, ofm	1547 Asunción
	1552 Santa Marta
	1564 Bogotá
Antonio de San Miguel, OFM	1561 Imperial
	1587 Quito
Luis Zapata de Cárdenas, OFM	1570 Cartagena
	1570 Bogotá
Luis López de Solis, OSA	1592 Quito
	1605 La Paz
	1605 Charcas
Bartolomé Lobo Guerrero	1595 Bogotá
	1607 Lima
Reginaldo de Lizárraga, OP	1599 Imperial
	ca. 1608 Asunción
Diego de Guzmán Zambrana	ca. 1606 La Paz
	ca. 1607 Charcas
Lorenzo Pérez de Grado	1609/18 Asunción
	1619 Cuzco
Hernando Arias de Ugarte	1613 Quito
	1617 Bogotá
	ca. 1627 Charcas
	1628 Lima
Julián de Cortázar	1618 Tucumán
	1625 Bogotá
Tomás de Torres, OP	ca. 1621 Asunción
	1626 Tucumán
Francisco de Sotomayor, OFM	1623 Cartagena
	1623 Quito
	1630 Charcas
Ambrosio Vallejo, CD	1619 Popayán (Santo Domingo)
	1631 Trujillo

Table 8   *Continued*

Feliciano de la Vega	1628 Popayán
	ca. 1634 La Paz (Mexico)
Cristóbal de Arestí, CSB	1628 Asunción
	1635 Buenos Aires
Pedro de Oviedo, SOC	1629 Quito (Santo Domingo)
	ca. 1645 Charcas
Luis de Córdoba, OST	1630 Cartagena
	ca. 1640 Trujillo
Diego de Montoya y Mendosa	1633 Popayán
	1637 Trujillo
Pedro de Villagómez	ca.1635 Arequipa
	1640 Lima
Antonio Condorino, OSA	1630 Santa Marta
	1642 Huamanga
Francisco de la Serna, OSA	1637 Popayán
	1645 La Paz
Agustín de Ugarte y Saravia	(Chiapas) (Guatemala)
	ca. 1643 Arequipa
	ca. 1646 Quito
Gaspar de Villaroel, OSA	1637 Santiago
	ca. 1651 Arequipa
	ca. 1660 Charcas
Bernardino de Cárdenas, OFM	1640 Asunción
	1666 Santa Cruz
Juan Alonso de Ocón	(Yucatán) 1643 Cuzco
	ca. 1652 Charcas
Andrés García de Zurita	1647 Huamanga
	1650 Trujillo
Pedro de Ortega y Sotomayor	1645 Trujillo
	ca. 1646 Arequipa
	1651 Cuzco
Juan de Arguinao, OP	1646 Santa Cruz
	1659 Bogotá
Francisco Godoy Campos	1650 Huamanga
	1659 Trujillo
Vasco López de Contreras	1658 Popayán
	1666 Huamanga
Antonio Sanz Lozano	1659 Cartagena
	1680 Bogotá
Juan de Almoguera, OST	ca. 1660 Arequipa
	ca. 1674 Lima
Juan de la Calle y Heredia, OBMVM	ca. 1663 Trujillo
	1674 Arequipa

Table 8 *Continued*

Melchor de Liñán y Cisneros	1664 Santa Marta
	1668 Popayán
	ca. 1672 Charcas
	ca. 1678 Lima
Francisco de Borja	ca. 1665 Tucumán
	1679 Trujillo
Gabriel Guillestegui, OFM	1666 Asunción
	ca. 1671 La Paz
Cristóbal de Castilla	1668 Huamanga
	ca. 1679 Charcas
Francisco de Loyola y Vergara, OSA	1669 Concepción
	ca. 1677 Santa Cruz
Antonio de León	(Panamá) 1676 Trujillo
	1677 Arequipa
Diego de Baños y Sotomayor	1677 Santa Marta
	1683 Caracas
Sancho Pardo de Andrade	1679 Huamanga
	1685 Quito
Bernardo Carrasco de Saavedra, OP	ca. 1679 Santiago
	ca. 1695 La Paz
Juan Queipo de Llano	ca. 1682 La Paz
	ca. 1694 Charcas
Pedro Díez de Cienfuegos	1686 Popayán
	ca. 1697 Trujillo
Juan Vítores de Velasco, OSB	1694 Santa Marta
	1703 Trujillo
Diego Ladrón de Guevara	(Panamá) 1699 Huamanga
	1704 Quito
Luis Francisco Romero	1705 Santiago
	1717 Quito
	ca. 1726 Charcas
Diego Morcillo, OST	(Nicaragua) ca. 1709 LaPaz
	ca. 1712 Charcas
	1723 Lima
Diego Montero del Aguila	ca. 1711 Concepción
	1715 Trujillo
Francisco del Rincón, Minim	(Santo Domingo) 1712 Caracas
	1716 Bogotá
Alonso del Pozo y Silva	ca. 1715 Tucumán
	ca. 1725 Santiago
	ca. 1731 Charcas
Jaime de Mimbela, OP	1716 Santa Cruz
	1719 Trujillo

Table 8 *Continued*

Juan de Nicolalde	ca. 1716 Concepción
	ca. 1724 Charcas
Francisco Gómez Callejas	1718 Cartagena
	ca. 1722 Popayán
Alejandro Fernando de Rojas	1718 Santiago
	ca. 1724 La Paz
Juan Cavero de Toledo	ca. 1720 Santa Cruz
	1725 Arequipa
Juan Gómez Frías	(after 1716) Popayán
	1726 Quito
Antonio Escandón, Theatine	ca. 1724 Concepción
	1730 Quito
	ca. 1731 Lima
Juan Manuel de Sarricolea	1724 Tucumán
	1731 Santiago
José Antonio Gutiérrez	1731 Tucumán
	ca. 1742 Lima
Diego Fermín de Vergara, osa	ca. 1732 Popayán
	1740 Bogotá
Agustín Rodríguez Delgado	ca. 1732 La Paz
	ca. 1742 Charcas
	1746 Lima
Juan Bravo del Rivero	1734 Santiago
	ca. 1743 Arequipa
Salvador Bermúdez Becerra	ca. 1734 Concepción
	ca. 1743 La Paz
	ca. 1746 Charcas
José Peralta, op	1736 Buenos Aires
	ca. 1746 La Paz
Gregorio Molleda	(after 1722) Cartagena
	1741 Trujillo
	ca. 1749 Charcas
Pedro Felipe de Azúa	1743 Concepción
	1744 Bogotá
Juan González Melgarejo	1743 Santiago
	ca. 1754 Arequipa
Juan Nieto Polo del Aquila	ca. 1745 Santa Marta
	1748 Quito
José Javier de Arauz	1746 Santa Marta
	1754 Bogotá
Bernardo de Arbiza	1747 Cartagena
	1751 Trujillo
	ca. 1756 Charcas
Fernando José Pérez de Oblitas	1747 Asunción
	ca. 1757 Santa Cruz

Table 8 *Continued*

Pedro Miguel de Argandoña	ca. 1747 Tucumán
	ca. 1762 Charcas
Cayetano Marcellano	1749 Buenos Aires
	ca. 1759 Charcas
Diego del Corro	? Popayán
	1758 Lima
Jacinto Aguado	ca. 1754 Cartagena
	1755 Arequipa (Osma, Spain)
Diego Antonio de Parada	ca. 1754 La Paz
	ca. 1762 Lima
Manuel Antonio de la Torre	1756 Asunción
	1762 Buenos Aires
Francisco Ramón Herboso	ca. 1761 Santa Cruz
	ca. 1777 Charcas
Manuel Abad e Illana, Premonstratensian	1762 Tucurnán
	ca. 1772 Arequipa
Agustín Manuel Camacho, OP	ca. 1765 Santa Marta
	1770 Bogotá
Juan Manuel Moscoso y Peralta	ca. 1770 Tucumán
	ca. 1778 Cuzco (Granada, Spain)
Agustín de Alvarado	1772 Cartagena
	ca. 1775 Bogotá (Ciudad Rodrigo, Spain)
Blas Sobrino	ca. 1775 Cartagena
	ca. 1775 Quito
	1788 Santiago
	1794 Trujillo
José Fernández Díaz de la Madrid, OFM	ca. 1776 Cartagena
	ca. 1792 Quito
Juan Domingo González de la Reguera	1777 Santa Cruz
	1780 Lima
José Antonio de San Alberto, CD	1778 Tucumán
	ca. 1785 Charcas
Baltasar Martínez de Compañón	1778 Trujillo
	1788 Bogotá
Francisco José Marán	ca. 1780 Concepción
	1794 Santiago
Alejandro José de Ochoa	ca. 1782 Santa Cruz
	ca. 1791 La Paz
Bartolomé Maria de las Heras	1789 Cuzco
	1805 Lima
Miguel Agustín Alvarez Cortés	ca. 1793 Cartagena
	1795 Quito

* Membership in one of the monastic orders is indicated, where applicable, according to the following set or abbreviations: Dominican, OP; Franciscan, OFM; Augustinian, OSA; Discalced Carmelite, CD; Benedictine, OSB; Cistercian, SOC; Trinitarian, OST; Mercedarian, OBMVM.

Map 3 *Frequent promotion routes followed by the colonial bishops (three or more)*

Theoretically there are 171 exchange possibilities among the 19 South American dioceses, or 342 possible moves (171 x 2; e.g. Lima to Cuzco, or Cuzco to Lima). Table 9 enumerates the 112 moves which actually took place. It can be shown that between any two given dioceses, movement only took place in one direction (in the example of Lima and Cuzco, *from* Cuzco *to* Lima). The most frequent moves were from Charcas to Lima, from La Paz and Quito to Charcas, from Cartagena to Quito, Trujillo and Bogotá, from Santa Marta to Bogotá, from Popayán to Trujillo and from Trujillo and Santiago to Arequipa (see Map 3). Within Greater Colombia, bishops are promoted towards Bogotá and Quito, and away from Santa Marta and Cartagena. In Peru, Lima and Charcas are the most important dioceses. In general, the colonial bishops gravitated towards Peru, southwards from Greater Colombia, and northwards from Chile.

When the episcopal promotions are grouped according to diocese, a certain hierarchy can be observed.

Table 9 *Pattern of episcopal promotions among 19 South American dioceses, 1540-1805, per diocese*

Diocese	Bishops are recruited from:	Bishops are promoted to:
Lima	Arequipa, Cartagena, Quito, Bogotá, Charcas, Tucumán, Popayán, La Paz, Santa Cruz, Cuzco	-
Charcas	La Paz, Bogotá, Quito, Arequipa, Cuzco, Popayán, Huamanga, Santiago, Trujillo, Imperial/ Concepción, Santa Cruz, Tucumán, Buenos Aires	Lima
Bogotá	Santa Marta, Cartagena, Quito, Tucumán, Santa Cruz, Coro/Caracas, Popayán, Trujillo	Lima, Charcas
Cuzco	Asunción, Arequipa, Tucumán	Lima, Charcas
La Paz	Quito, Popayán, Asunción, Santiago, Imperial/Concepción, Buenos Aires, Santa Cruz	Lima, Charcas
Quito	Santiago, Imperial/Concepción, Cartagena, Arequipa, Huamanga, Popayán, Santa Marta	La Paz, Bogotá, Lima, Charcas
Arequipa	Santiago, Trujillo, Santa Cruz, Cartagena, Tucumán	Lima, Quito, Charcas, Cuzco
Trujillo	Imperial/Concepción, Santa Marta, Popayán, Santa Cruz, Cartagena, Huamanga, Tucumán	Arequipa, Charcas, Bogotá

Table 9 *Continued*

Diocese	Bishops are recruited from:	Bishops are promoted to:
Huamanga	Santa Marta, Popayán	Trujillo, Charcas, Quito
Coro/Caracas	Santa Marta	Bogotá
Popayán	Santa Marta, Cartagena	Trujillo, La Paz, Huamanga, Charcas, Quito, Bogotá, Lima
Buenos Aires	Asunción	La Paz, Charcas
Santiago	Tucumán, Imperial/Concepción	Quito, La Paz, Arequipa, Charcas
Tucumán	Asunción	Santiago, Bogotá, Trujillo, Lima, Charcas, Arequipa, Cuzco
Santa Cruz	Asunción, Imperial/Concepción	Bogotá, Trujillo, Arequipa, Charcas, Lima, La Paz
Santa Marta	Asunción	Trujillo, Bogotá, Coro/Caracas, Huamanga, Popayán, Quito
Cartagena	-	Lima, Bogotá, Quito, Trujillo, Popayán, Arequipa
Asunción	Imperial/Concepción	Cuzco, Tucumán, Santa Marta, La Paz, Buenos Aires, Santa Cruz
Imperial/Concepción	-	Asunción, Trujillo, Quito, Santa Cruz, Charcas, Quito, La Paz, Santiago

Imperial/Concepción gives to Asunción, Asunción to Santa Marta, Santa Marta to Popayán, and so forth up to Lima. From Lima there is no promotion possibility within South America (Pedro Antonio Barroeta, bishop of Lima from 1751 to 1758, was promoted to Granada, Spain). In descending order, the line of promotion is as follows: (1) Lima, (2) Charcas, (3) Bogotá-Cuzco-La Paz, (6) Quito, (7) Arequipa, (8) Trujillo, (9) Huamanga, (10) Popayán, (11) Santa Marta, (12) Asunción, (13) Imperial/Concepción. Coro/Caracas falls somewhere between (3) and (11), Buenos Aires between (5) and (12), Santiago and Tucumán between (7) and (12), Santa Cruz between (8) and (12) and Cartagena between (10) and (14). The order of promotion corresponds to the level of tithe incomes of each diocese.

There are certain exceptions to the correspondence between promotional rank and tithe incomes: the incomes of Los Charcas are higher than those of Lima, yet bishops are promoted in the other direction, from Charcas to Lima. Other incomes which seem on the high side are those of Cuzco, Tucumán and Santa Cruz. Coincidentally, these four dioceses adjoin one another.

Table 10 *The South American dioceses ranked according to episcopal promotions, and comparison with the net tithe incomes (from Table 4)*

Diocese and promotion rank (in decending order)	Net tithe income, ca. 1628 (in pesos)
1. Lima	33,261
2. Charcas	43,500
3. Bogotá	9,600
4. Cuzco	11,293
5. La Paz	9,700
6. Quito	8,392
7. Arequipa	7,286
8. Trujillo	7,791
9. Huamanga	3,360
10. Popayán	588
11. Santa Marta	538
12. Asunción	388
13. Imperial/Concepción	188
Between (3) and (11) Coro/Caracas	-
Between (5) and (12) Buenos Aires	388
Between (7) and (12) Santiago; Tucumán	2,600; 4,000
Between (8) and (12) Santa Cruz	4,300
Between (10) and (14) Cartagena	525

Several recent articles revise the older view that creoles were systematically excluded from the highest colonial offices, and that these were almost exclusively reserved for Spaniards born in Spain (peninsulars).[67] It has now been shown that at certain times in the eighteenth century, creoles held majorities of the positions in the audiencias of Lima, México and Santiago de Chile. In Lima, at least 40 percent of the total number of appointments to the audiencia between 1701 and 1750 went to creoles. The high percentage of Americans named is, however, misleading in its implication that there was little discrimination against creoles, since nearly two-thirds of the creoles appointed had to purchase their appointments: their purchases formed a disproportionate share of 81 percent of the total sales made.[68] In fact, the increased eighteenth-century participation of creoles in the audiencias is explained by the different authors mainly in terms of the royal policy of selling audiencia judgeships, especially during the 1740s. After 1775 Crown policy towards the creoles would seem to have changed, and a larger proportion of peninsulars were appointed. In part this is seen as the result of alleged non-impartiality and vested interests on the part of the locally-bred creole judges.[69]

Of some 464 South American bishops named during the colonial period, Egaña provides the birthplaces of 350. Almost 40 percent were born in America. Arranged according to bishopric, there is a tendency towards higher percentages of peninsular bishops in the richer dioceses, and higher percentages of creoles in the poorer. This finding supports the view that creoles were discriminated against at the highest level of ecclesiastical appointment. On the other hand, there are important exceptions. At least 30 percent, and perhaps even a majority of the arch-bishops of Los Charcas were American-born. Distance from Spain may have played a role: in general, those dioceses closer to Spain (Lima, Bogotá, Popayán, Coro/Caracas, Cartagena, Santa Marta) have higher numbers of peninsular bishops than would be suggested by their relative income levels, while the more distant bishoprics of Cuzco, Los Charcas, La Paz, Santa Cruz and Huamanga have higher numbers of creoles than might be expected.

Table 11   *Place of birth, Spanish South American bishops, ca. 1530 – ca. 1820, per diocese*

Diocese	Place of Birth			
	Spain*	America	Unknown	Total
Lima	16	1	1	18
Bogotá	23	5	1	29
Quito	17	7	1	25
Popayán	9	2	7	18
Arequipa	13	7	0	20
Trujillo	15	8	3	26
Coro/Caracas	10	3	14	27
Cuzco	14	8	2	24
Cartagena	15	6	17	38
Los Charcas	15	10	8	33
Santa Marta	9	4	20	33
Asunción	7	4	11	22
Buenos Aires	7	6	0	13
Tucumán	9	8	1	18
Santiago	9	10	1	20
Imperial/ Concepción	9	11	0	20
La Paz	5	8	13	26
Santa Cruz	6	10	12	28
Huamanga	10	14	2	26
Total	218	132	114	464

* Including Portugal (one instance) and Gran Canaria (one instance).

Arranged chronologically, the data suggest that the rate of appointment of creole bishops increased gradually during most of the colonial period, and reached its peak around the middle of the eighteenth century, when more creoles than peninsulars were being appointed. In other words, the same trend is observed as in the case of the audiencia appointments.

Although the rise and fall in creole participation in the colonial bishoprics follows the same chronology as that observed for the audiencias, neither the 'sale-of colonial-offices' explanation for the rise, nor the 'local-vested-interest', i.e. reform theory of the fall, are applicable in the case of the bishoprics. Miters, in contrast to audiencia positions, were not sold, and American-born bishops almost never served in their native dioceses.

The explanation is probably simpler and has two components. One is the mere fact of an advancing creole population: in the early period there was no question of American-born bishops since so few schooled Christians had been born there. By the eighteenth century this had ceased to be an obstacle. The second factor was the gradual establishment of the *seminarios, diocesanos, colegios* and/or universities in most of the American dioceses. This process took place very slowly in many places, however.

Table 12 *Place of birth, Spanish South American bishops, nineteen dioceses, according to year of appointment, (grouped by 40-year periods)*

| | Place of Birth | | | | | | | |
| | Spain[*] | | America | | Unknown | | Total | |
Appointed	No.	%	No.	%	No.	%	No.	%
ca.1530-1579	38	93	0	0	3	7	41	100
1580-1619	31	53	9	16	18	31	58	100
1620-1659	33	43	26	34	18	23	77	100
1660-1699	30	45	16	24	20	30	66	99
1700-1739	31	47	22	33	13	20	66	100
1740-1779	29	32	40	43	23	25	92	100
1780-ca.1820	26	41	19	30	19	30	64	101
Total	218		132		114		464	

[*] Including Portugal (one instance) and Gran Canaria (one instance).

These developments led to a growing home-bred ecclesiastical 'class' in America. Nevertheless, there remained a preference for bishops trained in Spain, logical to the extent that although the American provinces developed their own seminaries, these remained weak reflections of their Spanish counterparts, just as the American cathedrals always suffered by comparison with those of Spain. It seems that Spain could not, or chose not to, supply unlimited numbers of episcopal candidates. Peninsulars were nominated at a relatively steady rate of about 30 every 40 years throughout the colonial period. The creole nominations show heavier fluctuations. The creole share depended, in effect, on the rate of turnover among the bishops. When the rate of turnover was especially high, creoles stood a greater chance of obtaining episcopal appointments. This was the case in the mid-eighteenth century. When fewer ap-pointments were available, creoles took a lower percentage of the total, since the peninsular nominations remained at about the same level. The creoles were more dependent on the fluctuations in demand than were the peninsulars. Since the rate of turnover was determined to a large extent by the number of dioceses in existence and rate of mortality among the bishops themselves, it is not possible to attribute fluctuations in the naming of creole bishops to changes in royal policy towards creoles.

Throughout Spanish America the monastic orders played an important role in the implantation of Christian practices. In many areas their presence overshadowed that of the secular Church, especially during the early decades, when convents of the Dominican, Franciscan, Augustinian, Mercedarian and Jesuit orders sprang up more rapidly than the cathedrals and parish churches. Many disputes took place be-tween the religious orders and the secular church; usually they had to do with in-comes (tithes), parochial jurisdiction (the right to administer sacraments), and the supposed independence of the orders from episcopal supervision. In general, the process of the colonial Church was one of bringing the – at first –highly independ-ent monastic orders within the ambit of the secular Church, under supervision of the bishops.

Table 13   *Regular and secular bishops, nineteen dioceses, according to year of appointment (grouped by 40-year periods)*

	Regular		Secular or uncertain		Total	
Appointed	No.	%	No.	%	No.	%
ca.1530-1579	29	71	12	29	41	100
1580-1619	34	59	24	41	58	100
1620-1659	34	44	43	56	77	100
1660-1699	27	41	39	59	66	100
1700-1739	23	35	43	65	66	100
1740-1779	13	14	79	86	92	100
1780-ca.1820	17	27	47	73	64	100
Total	177*		287		464	

* 56 Dominicans, 39 Franciscans, 27 Augustinians, 8 Mercedarians, 8 Trinitarians, 7 Discalced Carmelites, 6 Benedictines, 5 Jeronymites, 4 Cistercians, 4 Premonstratensians, 3 Minims, 3 Theatines, 3 *basilios*, 1 of the Order of St. Philip Neri, 1 Jesuit, 1 Capuchin and one of uncertain order, referred to only as 'fray'.

An indication of the strength of the regular orders resides in the large number of regulars who stepped out of their cloisters to take up a bishop's miter. Of the 464 bishops mentioned by Egaña for nineteen South American dioceses, at least 177 (38 percent) were members of a monastic order. The monastic share in episcopal appointments was very large at first, but declined steadily: whereas two-thirds of the sixteenth-century appointments went to friars, less than a quarter of the late eighteenth-century appointments fell to regulars. This development runs parallel to the progressive secularisation of the colonial church observed in many regions.[70]

The regular orders supplied the most bishops in the more marginal dioceses: in Coro/Caracas, Santa Marta and Cartagena to the North, and in Asunción, Tucumán, Buenos Aires and Imperial/Concepción to the South. In Peru their contribution was the weakest. Large numbers or monastic bishops are characteristic of the weaker bishoprics (Table 14).

Table 14 *Regular and secular bishops, ca.1530-ca.1820, per diocese*

Diocese	Regular	Secular*	Total	% Regular of total
Lima	4	14	18	22
Trujillo	7	19	26	27
Huamanga	7	19	26	27
Popayán	5	13	18	28
La Paz	8	18	26	31
Charcas	11	22	33	33
Cuzco	8	16	24	33
Santiago	7	13	20	35
Quito	9	16	25	36
Santa Cruz	11	17	28	39
Arequipa	8	12	20	40
Bogotá	12	17	29	41
Cartagena	16	22	38	42
Santa Marta	14	19	33	42
Coro/Caracas	12	15	27	44
Tucumán	9	9	18	50
Imperial/Concepción	10	20	20	50
Buenos Aires	7	6	13	54
Asunción	12	10	22	55
Total	177	287	464	

* Includes 'unknown'.

Table 15 *Statistical comparison, and approximate ranking, of the Spanish South American bishoprics*

	Diocese	Ca. 1628			Ca. 1530-ca.1820			Ca. 1600	
		Income[a]	Cabildo[b]	Parishes[c]	Promotions[d]	Creoles[e]	Regulars[f]	Economic importance[g]	Economic Differentiation[h]
I	Lima	33,261	37	15	1	8%	22%	9.5%	4.3%
	Charcas	43,500	16	18	2	(42%)?	33%	-[i]	-[i]
II	Cuzco	11,293	14	7	3	38%	33%	3.4%	3.5%
	Quito	8,392	14	16	6	30%	36%	7.2%	4.8%
	Bogotá	9,600	11	9	3	19%	41%	4.6%	3.5%
	Arequipa	7,286	14	3	7	35%	40%	4.2%	3.2%
	Trujillo	7,791	9	4	8	37%	27%	3.0%	3.3%
	La Paz	9,700	10	0	3	(56%)?	31%	-[i]	-[i]
III	Santiago	2,600	9	3	8/11	52%	35%	-[i]	-[i]
	Coro/ Caracas	-	-	6	4/10	(37%)?	44%	3.0%	3.0%
	Popayán	588	5	6	10	(31%)?	28%	3.7%	3.0%
	Tucumán	4,000	5	4	8/11	47%	50%	2.7%	2.8%
	Santa Cruz	4,300	4	1	9/11	(57%)?	39%	-[i]	-[i]
	Huamanga	3,360	5	6	9	58%	27%	1.9%	2.7%
	Cartagena	525	7	1	11/13	(39%)?	42%	1.9%	2.8%
IV	Buenos Aires	388	4	2	6/11	46%	54%	1.3%	2.1%
	Santa Marta	538	5	2	11	(42%)?	42%	1.6%	2.6%
	Asunción	388	5	2	12	(43%)?	55%	1.3%	2.6%
	Imperial/ Concepción	188	4	1	13	55%	50%	-[i]	-[i]

Table 15 *Continued*

ᵃ Net tithe income, ca. 1628 (minus salaries *cabildo catedral*) from Table 4.
ᵇ Size of *cabildo catedral,* ca. 1628, from Table 3.
ᶜ Number of parishes mentioned by Vázquez de Espinosa, excluding cathedral, from Table 5.
ᵈ Rank in episcopal promotion hierarchy, see *supra,* pp. 23-29.
ᵉ Percentage of creole bishops in total number per diocese; the percentages marked with a '?'
are very uncertain; see *supra,* pp. 29-31.
ᶠ Percentage of bishops belonging to one of the monastic orders in total number of bishops
per diocese; see *supra,* pp. 33-35.
ᵍ,ʰ Slicher van Bath, op. cit.
ⁱ Not comparable: Slicher has included the bishoprics of Santa Cruz and La Paz under the
region 'Charcas'.
ʲ Not comparable: Slicher has treated the bishoprics of Santiago and Imperial/Concepción
under the single heading 'Chile'.

Conclusions

On the basis of the above comparisons made among the various dioceses, a number
of generalizations suggest themselves, which may be summarized as follows.

1   The first South American bishoprics were founded too hastily, and often in the
wrong places. Many experienced difficulties in surviving, and remained among the
poorest or the colonial dioceses. In a second phase or expansion, the richest dioceses
were founded and the axis joining the port or Lima/Callao and the mining center or
Potosí was defined. During the colonial period, Greater Peru constituted the ecclesiastical heart of the Spanish South American empire. In a third phase, a number of
new dioceses were created out of border areas of already existing ones; on the whole,
the third-phase dioceses were less rich than the second-phase, but less poor than the
first-phase dioceses.
2   Tithe incomes were too low in the South American dioceses to support churches
of the scale and magnificence known in Spain. Of the tithe incomes, a disproportionate share went to the members of the cathedral chapters. The remaining incomes were too low, in some cases, to even support an 'honest' Church: there were
cases of illegal commercial activity on the part of priests, and some parishes were
sold. Financial difficulties were disproportionately large in those bishoprics where
tithe incomes were lowest.
3   The richest dioceses had the largest cathedral chapters, i.e. the greatest differentiation of secular ecclesiastical offices.
4   The richest bishoprics had the greatest numbers of parishes around 1628. In the
newer bishoprics, the process of erecting new parishes was still underway.
5   The income levels of the different dioceses are reflected in the roofing systems,
the building materials, the sizes, and the numbers of towers of their cathedrals.

6   The rate of cathedral-building suggests that the southern bishoprics (Tucumán, Buenos Aires and Santiago) increased in relative importance during the eighteenth century, while those in the north (Quito, Popayán, Bogotá, Santa Marta, Cartagena and Coro/Caracas) stagnated.

7   The careers of the South American bishops followed lines of promotion which took them from the poorer towards the richer dioceses.

8   American-born ecclesiastics were more readily appointed bishop in the poorer dioceses, while peninsular Spaniards dominated the richer ones.

9   Although the number of creole bishops rose during the colonial period, peninsulars continued to be preferred.

10 Members of the monastic orders stood a better chance of being appointed bishop in the poorer dioceses than in the richer.

11 During the colonial period the proportion of bishops belonging to one of the monastic orders declined steadily.

It is now possible to attempt a schematic comparison of all the dioceses, on the combined basis of six criteria that can be statistically expressed. According to tithe income levels, cathedral-chapter size, number of parishes, percentage of American-born bishops, percentage of bishops belonging to one of the regular orders, and the careers of the individual bishops, it is possible to distinguish roughly four categories of dioceses which correspond to a kind of ecclesiastical 'pecking order' for the colonial period (Table 15: groups I-IV, in descending order of importance). From the point of view of the secular Church, Lima and Charcas were the most central dioceses; those of Asunción and Southern Chile were indubitably the most peripheral.

For the early seventeenth century, Slicher van Bath has tried to establish the relative economic importance of each of 36 colonial American regions or 'districts'. Fourteen of these districts correspond more or less exactly to fourteen of our South American bishoprics. On the basis of 85 different economic criteria (the presence or absence within each district of each of 85 different economic activities), he has developed two indexes, expressed as percentages, which make a global comparison possible. The first, 'economic importance', refers to the percentual share of each district in the total economic activity of Spanish America, calculated on the basis of all the separate places where a given economic activity took place. The second index, 'economic differentiation,' refers to the diversity of economic activity within each district.[71] Both indexes are given for the respective dioceses in Table 15. It will be seen that there is a close correspondence between the level of economic importance or diversity (the two run parallel to each other), and the level of secular ecclesiastical activity.

The secular Church, while pointing the way to another, better world, had to make its own way in this one, just as any other *poblador de Indias*. Just as many other immigrants, the Church encountered its greatest opportunities in the most important demographic and economic concentrations. In the poorer regions the Church enjoyed no special advantage. On the whole, the Church fared not much better and not much worse in the different regions than the other settlers. Levels of ecclesiastical development among the South American bishoprics seem a fair reflection of the corresponding levels of economic development.

Notes to Chapter 4

* Published in *Boletín de Estudios Latinoamericanos y del Caribe* 24 (1978) pp. 27-66.

1 Antonio de Egaña, S.I., *Historia de la iglesia en la América Española, desde el descubrimiento hasta comienzos del siglo XIX: Hemisferio sur* (Madrid: Editorial Católica, 1966), pp. 9-12.

2 Ibid., pp. 22-24.

3 Ibid, pp. 558-560.

4 Ibid., pp. 13, 17, 21.

5 Ibid., pp. 22, 470-471.

6 Ibid., p. 472.

7 Ibid, pp. 221, 224.

8 Except for the island of Chiloe. Antonio Vázquez de Espinosa, O. Carm., *Compendio y descripción de las Indias Occidentales*, edición de B. Velasco Bayón, O. Carm., *Biblioteca de Autores Españoles* 231 (Madrid: Atlas, 1969), pp. 489, 485-492.

9 Egaña, op. cit., pp. 251-252.

10 Ibid., p. 254.

11 Ibid., pp. 111-113, 116.

12 A.M. Rodríguez Cruz, O.P., *Historia de las universidades hispanoamericanas: Período hispánico*, 2 vols. (Bogotá: Instituto Caro y Cuervo, 1973), Vol. II, p. 227.

13 Egaña, op. cit., pp. 121, 123-124, 142.

14 Ibid., pp. 380-385.

15 Mauro, 'Prééminence urbaine et réseau urbain dans l'Amérique coloniale', *Des produits et des hommes: essais historiques Latino-Americaines XVIe-XXe siecles* (Paris et Le Haye: Mouton, 1972).

16 B.H. Slicher van Bath 'Spaans Amerika omstreeks 1600' (Utrecht, 1979), based upon data compiled from Juan López de Velasco, *Geografía universal de las Indias*, ed. de M. Jiménez de la Espada, Biblioteca de Autores Españoles 248 (Madrid: Atlas, 1971) and Antonio Vázquez de Espinosa, op. cit.

17 There is slight disagreement about some of the exact dates. Compare León Lopetegui, S.I. and Félix Zubillaga, *Historia de la iglesia en la America española, desde el descubrimiento hasta comienzos del siglo XIX: México, América Central, Antillas* (Madrid: Editorial Católica, 1965), pp. 178-179, and Egaña, op. cit., who gives the details surrounding the foundation of each diocese separately.

18 *Recopilación de leyes de los Reynos de las Indias*, facsimile edition (Madrid: Ediciones Cultura Hispánica, 1973), tomo I, título VII, ley iii.

19 Fernando de Armas Medina, 'La jerarquía eclesiástica peruana en la primera mitad del siglo XVII', *Estudios sobre historia de América* (Sevilla: Excmo. Cabildo Insular de Gran Canaria, 1973), pp. 59-63, 72, 78-79.

20 Lopetegui y Zubillaga, op. cit., pp. 178-179.

21 *Recopilación de leyes*, tomo I, título VII, ley ii.

22 Ibid., tomo I, título XVI, leyes ii-xix.

23 Ibid., tomo I, título VII ley xxxiiii.

24 Ibid., tomo I, título XVI, ley xxiii.

25 Vázquez de Espinosa, op. cit., pp. 510-512.

26 Rafael Gómez de Hoyos, Pbro., *La iglesia de América en las leyes de Indias* (Madrid: Instituto Gonzalo Fernández de Oviedo, Instituto de Cultura Hispánica de Bogotá, 1961), pp. 187-188.

27 Vázquez de Espinosa, op. cit., pp. 510-512.

28 My own calculation based on data compiled from Egaña, op. cit.

29 Gómez de Hoyos, op. cit., pp. 179-181, *Recopilación de leyes*, tomo I, título VI, ley iii.

30 *Recopilación de leyes*, tomo I, título VII, ley xxiiii.

31 Egaña, op. cit., pp. 271.

32 Letter to His Majesty, 30 August 1653: 'No se puede decir, señor, sin grandes lágrimas el estado en que se halla este obispado, en especial en lo que toca a los indios, así en lo espiritual como en lo temporal, porque desde la primera doctrina en que entré confirmando, e hallado están los indios muy faltos en el conocimiento de los misterios de nuestra santa fe'. Ibid., p. 344.

33 Ibid., p. 345.

34 Ibid., p. 289.

35 Ibid., p. 325

36 Ibid., p. 455.

37 Ibid., pp. 320-321.

38 This number only includes the parishes of the secular branch of the Church. Located in the towns they are usually referred to by Vázquez de Espinosa as 'iglesia mayor'. Left out of consideration are the many parishes attached to monasteries of the regular orders. Also left out of consideration are the large numbers of doctrinas de indios served by both secular and regular clergy. Although Vázquez gives numbers of doctrinas for many of the dioceses, the totals given in different passages of his work are contradictory and thus practically useless.

39 E. Marco Dorta, *La arquitectura barroca en el Perú* (Madrid: Consejo Superior de Investigaciones Científicas, 1957), pp. 9, 16, 43; E. Marco Dorta, *Arte en América y Filipinas, Ars Hispaniae XXI* (Madrid: Plus Ultra, 1973) pp. 72, 85, 86, 97, 98, 104, 221, 222, 233, 251, 252, 260, 267, 329, 384; J. Bernales Ballesteros, *Lima, la ciudad y sus monumentos* (Sevilla: Escuela de Estudios Hispano-Americanos, 1972) pp. 38-40, 77-81, 114-119, 222-225, 316-320; H.E. Wethey, *Colonial Architecture and Sculpture in Peru* (Westport: Greenwood Press, 1971, reprint; originally published 1949); George Kubler and Martin Soria, *Art and Architecture in Spain and Portugal and their American Dominions 1500-1800* (Harmondsworth: Penguin, 1969), pp. 90, 95.

40 E. Marco Dorta, op. cit., (1957), pp. 19-21; Egaña, op. cit., pp. 315; Marco Dorta, op. cit., (1973), pp. 72, 85, 86, 97, 98, 99, 235, 267, 268, 290, 330, 335, 367, 368, 373, 374, 384; Kubler and Soria, op. cit., pp. 90. 92; Wethey, op. cit., 29, 39-46, 56.

41 Egaña, op. cit., p. 637; Kubler and Soria, op. cit., pp.90, 94; Marco Dorta, op. cit., (1973), pp. 82, 283, 285; J. De Mesa y T. Gisbert, Bolivia; *Monumentos históricos y arqueológicos* (México: Instituto Panamericano de Geografía e Historia, 1970) pp. 69-70.

42 Marco Dorta, op. cit., (1973), p. 385; Mesa y Gisbert, op. cit. p. 26; A. Camponova, *La catedral de La Paz* (La Paz: Ministerio de Gobierno y Fomento, 1900).

43 Marco Dorta, op. cit., (1973), pp. 67, 68, 327, 328; J.M. Vargas, O.P., *Ecuador: monumentos históricos y arqueológicos* (México: Instituto Panamericano de Geografía e Historia, 1953) pp. 30-33; P. Rodríguez de Aguayo, 'Descripción de la ciudad de Quito y vecindad de ella, por el arcediano de su Iglesia', D. Marcos Jiménez de la Espada, *Relaciones geográficas de Indias – Perú*, 3 tomos, Biblioteca de Autores Españoles 183, 184 (Madrid: Atlas, 1965) III, p. 203; 'La ciudad de San Francisco del Quito – 1573'. Ibid, p. 221.

44 Marco Dorta, op. cit., (1973), pp. 361, 384; E. Marco Dorta, *Viaje a Colombia y Venezuela: impresiones histórico-artísticas* (Madrid: Maestre, 1948) pp. 21-23 Figs. 11, 12; L. Duque Gómez, *Colombia: monumentos históricos y arqueológicos* (México: Instituto Panamericano de Geografía e Historia, 1955) pp. 156-165

45 Duque Gómez, op. cit., pp. 88-90; Marco Dorta op. cit., (1973), pp. 60-61; Egaña, op. cit., p. 480; Kubler and Soria, op. cit., p. 66

46 Marco Dorta, op. cit., (1973), pp. 60, 61, 226, 227, 356; G. Gasparini, *Venezuela, Monumentos históricos y arqueológicos* (México: Instituto Panamericano de Geografía e Historia, 1966) pp. 31-34, 43-44; G. Gasparini, *La arquitectura colonial en Venezuela* (Caracas: Armitano, 1965) pp. 169-184, 254-255.

47 Duque Gómez, op. cit., pp. 201-202; E. Marco Dorta, *Fuentes para la historia del arte hispanoamericano*, 2 tomos (Sevilla: Consejo Superior de Investigaciones Científicas, 1960), pp. 26-33, documentos 7-15 (p. 131-152).

48 Egaña, op. cit., pp. 124, 136,137, 139, 638; M.J. Buschiazzo, *Argentina: monumentos históricos y arqueológicos* (México: Instituto Panamericano de Geografía e Historia, 1959) p. 152.

49 Duque Gómez, op. cit., pp. 99-101; Egaña, op. cit., pp. 474, 964. On the latter page Egaña refers to a church under construction in 1771; it is possible that he means 1671.

50 Mesa y Gisbert, op. cit., p. 86.

51 Marco Dorta, op. cit., (1960), 67-71, documentos 37-40 (pp. 207-215); Egaña, op. cit., pp. 324, 869; Wethey, op. cit., pp. 140-141; J. Bernales Ballesteros, 'Informes de los daños sufridos en la ciudad de Arequipa con el terremoto de 1784', *Anuario de Estudios Americanos* 29(1972), pp. 301, 308.

52 Kubler and Soria, op. cit., p. 91, Wethey, op. cit., pp. 99-101; Egaña, op. cit., pp. 341, 346.

53 Wethey, op. cit. pp. 112-114; Egaña, op. cit., pp. 335, 876; Marco Dorta, op. cit. (1973), p. 260.

54 Buschiazzo, op. cit., pp. 49-51; Marco Dorta, op. cit., pp. 285, 302; G. Furlong, S.J., *Historia social y cultural del Río de la Plata, 1536-1810. El trasplante cultural: arte* (Buenos Aires: Tipográfica, 1969), p. 485.

55 Egaña, op. cit., pp. 694, 699, 716; Furlong, op. cit., 480-482; Marco Dorta, op. cit., (1973), pp. 300, 336, 386.

56 Egaña, op. cit., pp. 205, 630, 780; Marco Dorta op. cit., (1973), pp. 336, 385.

57 Egaña, op. cit., pp. 84-85.

58 Marco Dorta, op. cit., p. 296.

59 Alonso Carrió de la Vandera (Concolorcorvo), *El lazarillo de ciegos caminantes*, many editions.

60 B.H. Slicher van Bath, 'De veelvormige wereld van Spaans Amerika' (Leiden: Universitaire pers Leiden, 1978) pp. 7-9.

61 A.C. van Oss, 'Architectural activity, demography and economic diversification: regional economies of colonial Mexico', *Jahrbuch für Geschichte von Staat, Wirtschaft und Gesellschaft Lateinamerikas* 16 (1979), pp. 97-145, also in this volume, see Chapter 6.

62 See Manuel Toussaint, *Arte mudéjar in América* (México; Porrúa, 1946) pp. 64-79 on Venezuela, Colombia and Ecuador.

63 The plans of the cathedrals at Lima and Cuzco are modeled upon those of the cathedral at Jaén, according to Kubler and Soria, op. cit., p. 90. The rectangular plan of Jaén, in turn, follows that of the Seville cathedral, which owes its plan to its erection on the site of a mosque. Ibid., p10; L. Torres Balbás, *Arquitectura gótica, Ars Hispaniae VII* (Madrid: Plus, Ultra, 1952) pp. 281-288.

64 Wethey, op. cit., pp. 72-73.

65 Kubler and Soria, op. cit., p. 90.

66 Compiled following the text. Egaña, (op. cit.) has organized his history per diocese; the history of each diocese is subdivided according to the lives of its bishops.

67 D.A. Brading, 'Government and Elite in Late Colonial Mexico', *Hispanic American Historical Review (HAHR)*, 53(1973) pp. 389-414; L.G. Campbell, 'A Colonial Establishment: Creole Domination of the Audienca of Lima during the Late Eighteenth Century', *HAHR* 52 (1972), pp. 1-25; M.A. Burckholder and D.S. Chandler, 'Creole Appointments and the Sale of Audienca Positions in the Spanish Empire under the early Bourbons, 1701-1750', *Journal of Latin America Studies* 4, no. 2 (1972), pp. 187-206; M.A. Burckholder, 'From Creole to Peninsular: The Transformation of the Audiencia of Lima', *HAHR* 52 (1972), pp. 395-415.

68 Burckholder and Chandler op. cit, pp. 191-192.

69 Burckholder, op. cit., p. 413.

70 Although the two observed chronological trends, rising numbers or secular and creole bishops, and a declining proportion of regulars and peninsulars, run roughly parallel to each other, there is no clear correlation between place or birth and membership in one or the religious orders. The two trends are thus unconnected.

71 B.H. Slicher van Bath, 'Spaans Amerika omstreeks 1600', op. cit., An English version of the relevant part of this study appeared in the *Jahrbuch fur Geschichte von Staat, Wirtschaft und Gesellschaft Lateinamerikas* 16 (1979), pp. 53-6.

5

MENDICANT EXPANSION IN NEW SPAIN AND THE EXTENT OF THE COLONY (SIXTEENTH CENTURY)[*]

Spanish missionary work in the New World was not executed in a well-organized way by a single unified body; the young American Church was a patchwork of diverse elements working in tenuous cooperation. In sixteenth-century New Spain, the fundamental ecclesiastical division was between the secular branch, headed by an archbishop and bishops, and the regular branch, composed of the monastic orders. The secular branch was the more centralized of the two, both in its organization and in its geographical distribution.

Spanish missionary work in the New World was not executed in a well-organized way by a single unified body; the young American Church was a patchwork of diverse elements working in tenuous cooperation. In sixteenth-century New Spain, the fundamental ecclesiastical division was between the secular branch, headed by an archbishop and bishops, and the regular branch, composed of the monastic orders. The secular branch was the more centralized of the two, both in its organization and in its geographical distribution.[1] The regular branch, on the other hand, was composed of various orders, independent of one another as well as of the bishops, and indeed, relatively independent of any central control. Each order had its own province (or provinces), which only partly overlapped the provinces of the other orders. The evangelical authority of the mendicant orders, the principal components of the regular branch in New Spain, was derived from the Pope indirectly, by way of the Spanish Crown, under the peculiar institution of *patronato real*.[2] Under it, the Pope delegated radical privileges to the king of Spain, who became the spiritual guardian as well as the political one, of the new pagan subjects. The Spanish king, now responsible for the evangelization of the American territories, proceeded to elect the mendicant orders – Franciscans, Dominicans and Augustinians – and not, in the first instance, the secular clergy, as his agents in this vast work.[3] Under the provisions of *patronato real*, friars might serve as parish priests, and might administer sacraments normally reserved to the authority of the secular church. The secular church was thus temporarily circumvented by this arrangement, and the mendicant orders were able to realize an extraordinary degree of local autonomy, not only in the carrying out of their daily missionary task, but also in the establishment of new monasteries.

The first of the regular orders to arrive in New Spain was that of Saint Francis *(Ordo Fratrum Minorum* = OFM). From 1523 onwards, Franciscans were in New Spain;

two of the first three died shortly after arrival. A contingent of twelve friars arrived in México in 1524. By 1559 the number of Franciscan friars had risen to about 380.[4] In 1526 the first Dominicans (*Ordo Praedicatorum* = OP) followed, also with twelve friars. Although five of these died in the first year, and four others returned sick to Spain in 1527, the remaining three were reinforced by an additional 28 in 1528, and another 34 in 1534.[5] By 1559 there were an estimated 210 Dominicans in New Spain.[6] The Augustinians (*Ordo Eremitarum S. Augustini* = OSA) came as third, and last, among the important evangelizing orders: they were seven in the first year (1533), but their number grew to some 212 by 1559.[7]

Much later in the century, when there would seem to have been relatively little demand for them, other religious orders joined these three, but never engaged in parochial work on anything resembling the same scale. Among these later arrivals were the Jesuits (1572), the Carmelites (1585) and the Mercedarians (1594). In his classic study of the mendicant crusade,[8] Robert Ricard described the 'Spiritual Conquest' of New Spain, but left a number of questions open which are of crucial importance to the study of any conquest, even a spiritual one: why did the 'conquerors' go where they did, and what led them to some places instead of others? How rapid was their advance? Where did they stop along the way, and where did they finally stop? Another way to ask the last question is to inquire into the limits to the lands to be overwon: what were the limits inherent in the conquest from the outset? At what point could the original objectives be said to have been reached, and the conquest over?

In all conquests the point at which success can be claimed is also the point at which the original engineers of that success, whether they be soldiers or missionaries, become superfluous, a burden to the larger society, leading to conflicts with more settled groups. In the literature on the mendicant expansion in New Spain, the decline of the regular orders towards the end of the sixteenth century is a commonplace. But the explanations of this decline are sought in the area of civil and secular religious opposition to the orders, without a satisfactory explanation of why this opposition only became effective towards the end of the sixteenth century. One school of thought (eventually traceable to the writings of the Franciscan Mendieta) has it that, in the words of John McAndrew:

> towards the end of the century the character of the brothers themselves would appear to have changed, and some mendicant writers had to admit that the high standards of earlier times had been relaxed … Compassion and persuasion seem to have given way to authoritarianism …[9]

Whether it is true or not that the quality of individual friars was generally on the wane, the opponents of the orders had often enough made the same complaint earlier in the century, even during the 'golden age' of the 1550s and 1560s, when the orders were accused of cruel oppression and exploitation of the native populations in their ambitious church-building programs. In 1561, for instance, Archbishop

Montúfar joined Michoacán bishop Quiroga in bringing suit against all three orders for alleged abuse of Indians 'the religious have inflicted and are now inflicting many mistreatments upon the Indians, with great haughtiness and cruelty, for when the Indians do not obey them, they insult and strike them, tear out their hair, have them stripped and cruelly flogged, and then throw them into prison in chains and cruel irons, a thing most pitiable to hear about and much more pitiable to see'.[10] The potential arguments, and the political enemies of the mendicants had always been there; there is no reason to believe that they became more eloquent towards 1570 or 1580. There was another reason in the background.

That reason was in the demographic limits to the colony. The mendicant orders were attracted to, and were commanded to seek out the centers of Indian population. Our suggestion is that the mendicant orders were able to justify and maintain their privileged position with respect to episcopal and civil authority as long as there remained important pockets of Indian population that could not be brought within the European sphere of influence except by the mendicant orders. The secular church had an organization that was not suited to the bringing under control of disperse populations. Their task, at first, was more in ministering to the needs of the European settlements, a task for which they had the necessary experience. For the more revolutionary work of ministering to the Indians, and pacifying them, a different approach was needed. The mendicant orders mastered a new approach, measured to the need.[11]

But the need was of a temporary nature. With the passing of time, the colony acquired a shape, an economy, a settled population. Continued European presence became more assured. There were ever fewer frontiers to be explored, reduced and evangelized by the mendicant missionaries. With the limits to the colony in sight, the challenge to the special privileges of the legions of Ricard's spiritual conquest therefore became stronger.[12]

The limits to the colony were not topographical. An ocean, a mountain range and difficult rivers had not prevented the arrival of the Spaniards in the Aztec capital; plans existed to continue the spiritual conquest westward from Mexico right across the Pacific, to the mainland of China itself.[13] The limits to New Spain were demographic. The sixteenth-century mendicant expansion directed itself towards the concentrations of Indian population, as we shall see. The geographical limits to these concentrations were early reached. The number of souls to be reduced and converted was large, but not unlimited, and the number decreased continually during the entire period of mendicant expansion.[14]

As the limits to expansion began to make themselves felt, the colony acquired a shape and a maximum extent, which ceased to change significantly. The orders, in their new establishments, ceased to extend themselves further, and chose instead to fill in the spaces between their existing outposts, areas at first skipped over in favor of more remote settlements. A rule of diminishing returns set in. Ever less emphasis came to bear on what the mendicants, with their decentralized organization, had shown themselves best able to do: open up, pacify and carry out the initial conversion of the Indians. Since the secular church was the body that by tradition must care for the parochial needs of the congregations thus formed, the mendicants became the victims of their own success in a demographically limited field. The bishops were always in the background waiting for the chance to reclaim the privileges temporarily usurped by the mendicants under *patronato real*. They were able to do this as the exceptional situation of a territorially expanding colony came slowly to a close. The approach of a point of relative saturation sharpened the already existing competition among the orders themselves, and between the orders on the one hand, and the civil and secular religious authorities on the other. This competition proved fatal to the continued prosperity of the mendicant orders as all successful 'armies', they became a nuisance once their primary objectives – those of occupation and initial conversion – had been reached. When did a situation of relative saturation show signs of appearing?

Ricard, writing in 1932, gave admittedly short shrift to the problem of the chronology and cumulative distribution of the orders in New Spain, saying '... it has been very difficult to fix the chronology of the monastic foundations of New Spain. The documents ... are niggardly in precise information. At times they ignore chronology entirely at others they give only round and very approximate figures'.[15] The problem, although an important one, since the approach of the demographic limits of the colony would necessarily be reflected in the pattern of settlements of the orders, has been more or less left at that.

But data published by George Kubler[16] and Peter Gerhard[17] provide a basis upon which to reconstruct tentatively the expansion of the mendicant orders (the new foundations) in New Spain, and allows us to map that expansion. A picture emerges of one aspect, one of the most important ones, of the European penetration of the area that was to become Spain's most important colony in America.

A difficulty in tracing the chronology of mendicant expansion in New Spain is in determining when friars of a given order came to a place to stay; since they did not isolate themselves behind cloister walls, a date of 'foundation' is difficult to arrive at in most cases. The friars' usual procedure was to go into an area in very small groups – of perhaps two or three – to preach to the Indian communities. After a while a temporary church might be built, and temporary housing for the friars. Only later could more permanent church and monastery buildings be constructed. Most mendicant establishments thus developed gradually over a period of years.

In this article, a new mendicant establishment is taken to mean one where more or less permanent evangelical work is begun by resident friars of one or another order for the first time. This mayor may not coincide with the official date of foundation of a monastery. Kubler and Gerhard have, where possible, recorded the date of foundation, although this might follow by as much as a few years the actual taking up of residence. The reverse situation – foundation preceding residence – is also not inconceivable, in view of the heavily competitive atmosphere which surrounded some new establishments. Still, the year of foundation as the preferred indication of the start of permanent residence has the practical advantage of being relatively often available in the documentary sources. Where it is not, Kubler and Gerhard often provide some alternative indication, such as the introduction of the Most Holy Sacrament, 'initial conversion', or some other indication of the start of substantial activity at a site. Despite Ricard's complaint, it is almost always possible to arrive at a decade in which a settlement most probably came under control of one or another order.

Interestingly, Kubler and Gerhard each tend to emphasize a different set of sources. Kubler relies heavily on early religious writers, in particular the chroniclers of the orders themselves;[18] Gerhard, on the other hand, has made more extensive use of the records of Spanish civil authorities for many of his data (the *Relaciones geográficas,* the *Suma de visitas.* and Juan López de Velasco's *Geografía y descripción universal de las Indias).* On the whole, the data collected by Kubler and Gerhard complement and tend to confirm one another. Comparison of the information in both Kubler and Gerhard provides dates for 144 establishments. Initial dates for another 109 are to be found in one or the other work, but not in both; here comparison is impossible. Seventeen establishments are without any useable dates at all. These combined with four cases about which there is substantial disagreement, leave twentyone establishments about whose beginnings we can only guess. This gives a working total of 274 establishments, distributed among the orders as follows: OFM, 141; OP, 50; OSA, 83. Seven establishments changed hands among the orders during the sixteenth century, and thus appear twice in the totals. In a recent book, R. J. Mullen has published data taken from the unpublished *Actas provinciales de la provincia de Santiago de México del Orden de Predicadores* (1540-1589) relating to the acceptance of new Dominican establishments.[19] Acceptance of a new monastery usually came, if at all, a few years after the actual establishment of residence. These data are thus only useful, in this context, as a check against the dates presented by Kubler and/or Gerhard. Such a check has been possible for thirty-four Dominican establishments.

In an appendix at the end of this article a list of the establishments is arranged according to the decades in which they seem to have been founded. The Franciscan, the Dominican and the Augustinian orders chose to expand in different directions, as if trying to avoid contact with one another, while maintaining a concentration of houses in the heavily populated central region surrounding México. Map 1 shows the approximate maximum boundaries within which the settlements of each of the orders were confined.

The Franciscans, having established themselves in and around the capital, set out towards the west: by 1525 they were already in Pátzcuaro, and by 1527 in Etzatlan, on the far side of Guadalajara. The Dominicans went southeast: by 1529 they were in Oaxaca. Arriving in 1533, the first Augustinians fit themselves in between the estab-

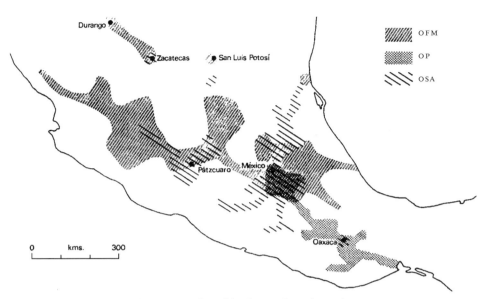

Map 1   *Approximate maximum extension of the three orders, sixteenth century*

lishments of the other two orders. Augustinian houses sprang up in the Central Valley between those of the Franciscans and Dominicans, and along with those of the
Franciscans in Michoacán, but their most important expansion was aimed to the
north from the Central Valley, towards Hidalgo, where neither of the other orders
had established itself.

The three orders thus set out in different directions. The explanation lies in the
competitive and even combative relations among the orders. Indeed, they often
seem to have been one another's worst enemies. The literature gives many incidents
of internecine disputes over towns, rights, practices, of accusations back and forth,
and even of physical violence. Later we shall return to this point. Whatever the immediate causes of such struggles, the underlying competition was for the loyalty of
the local indigenous populations. And in such an atmosphere, the most prudent policy was to avoid these conflicts by seeking new regions in which to settle, to establish
regional monopolies wherever possible. The orders were therefore governed in their
selection of a direction in which to expand, by two principles: (a) to occupy regions
with high concentrations of Indian population, and (b) wherever possible, to avoid
areas already colonized by a competing order, establishing regional monopolies.

In order to substantiate this claim, which has to do with the direction taken by
each order, and the sequence in which the choices of direction were made, we should
like to know something about the distribution of the Indian population during the sixteenth century. This is a difficult problem in view of the sketchy data at our disposal.
The documentary sources are fragmentary and confusing: 'There are wide differences

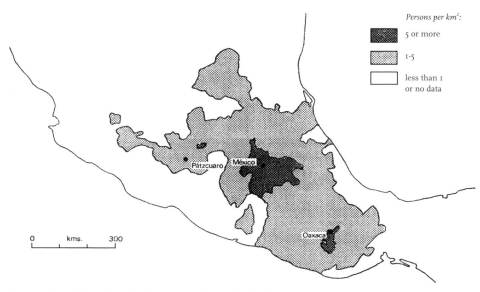

Map 2 *Population density 1620, according to Gerhard*

of opinion as to the reliability of estimates, the interpretation of data, the extent of *mestizaje*, and other factors ... Data are given in a bewildering variety of units, and some of the terms changed with time. Large segments of the population ... are often omitted in the data available. A further source of confusion is the variety of jurisdictions with dissimilar boundaries from which the population is reported'.[20]

One should like to have data on the distribution of Indian settlements, including their populations and density on the ground. Unfortunately, the settlements prove to be evasive entities: in the first place, the number of dependent Indians 'belonging' to one or another settlement was not the same as the number living within the confines of the settlement itself. Generally the Indians lived at contact in a great many scattered *rancherías*, often without any one clearly identifiable center. The coming of the missionaries might also drastically affect local living patterns. When the original Indian settlements were disperse, a first task of the Europeans was to create a center of community life as a basis for conversion and assimilation. Moreover, such a center was sometimes moved from its original location. In the sixteenth century, for instance, Tehuacán occupied two sites. The first stood on the pre-Conquest site, several miles from the present city. In 1567 the Indians were persuaded to move from the original location, which was 'pestilential, torrid, and moist,' to the 'more healthful' present site.[21] This example was repeated in many places in the sixteenth century. The second problem in dealing with the settlements is that there is a lack of comparable data per settlement, as Gerhard has been cited as saying: there is no uniformity in the districts from which population is reported.

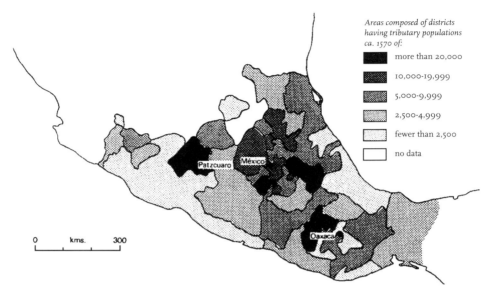

Areas composed of districts
having tributary populations
ca. 1570 of:

■ more than 20,000

■ 10,000-19,999

▨ 5,000-9,999

▨ 2,500-4,999

☐ fewer than 2,500

☐ no data

0   kms.   300

Map 3   *Population concentration ca. 1570, according to Slicher van Bath*

A number of attempts have been made at estimating populations living within larger areas. Cook and Borah and others, have done this on the basis of the various documentary sources. MacNeish has studied pre-Conquest agricultural remains in the Tehuacán valley. His estimates of population density are made for an area of 7200 km². Parsons has sketched the pre-Conquest demographic fluctuations in the Texcoco region on the basis of the area of the settlements and the area of land under cultivation during different periods. Aerial-photographic techniques have been applied in the Teotihuacan area. But these techniques are only applicable in areas of dense population, and in any case studies are not available for most areas of New Spain.[22]

The studies based on documentary sources, and therefore limited to the consideration of districts of varying size, give the only information on population distribution for all of New Spain in the sixteenth century. Gerhard has utilized in his work of 1972[23] the existing demographic studies. Since 1972 no new studies of significance for this paper have been published. In a study, Slicher van Bath has elaborated on the data collected by Gerhard.[24] This article relies on these two authors for the part dealing with the historical demography.

Gerhard has mapped population density in New Spain ca. 1620.[25] Since Europeans formed a small minority at the time, the map shows the distribution of the Indian population. A simplified version of this map is reproduced here (Map 2). There are three islands of high concentration of population (here defined as having a population density of more than 5 persons per km²): México and surroundings, Oaxaca, and a part of Michoacán. The last two are much smaller than the first. In 1620 the population of New Spain was still declining; the nadir was not reached in most areas until fifteen to 25 years later.[26] We do not have a map of population density from the sixteenth century. It is a safe assumption, however, that the area with a density of more than five persons per km[2] towards the middle of the sixteenth century would have been much larger. Slicher van Bath, using data from Gerhard, and the same division of New Spain into 129 districts used for the map of 1620, has reconstructed the situation as it may have been in ca. 1570 (Map 3).[27] In this map, a distinction is made between districts[28] having (a) 20,000 tributaries or more, (b) 10,000-19,999 tributaries, (c) 5,000-9,999 tributaries, (d) 2,500-4,999 tributaries, and (e) fewer than 2,500 tributaries. Since the districts are of varying size, this is not the same as population density; the map does, however, provide a guide to relative concentration of population in different parts of New Spain.

In a time of drastic depopulation, there is a large degree of continuity between the two maps: with some shifts, the islands of population concentration of 1620 are the heartlands of the relatively populous areas of 1570. What we know of the history of the period just before the Conquest confirms the possibility of three demographic centers: the Tarascans of Michoacán were populous and strong enough to attract and resist repeated military advances from Tenochtitlán; Oaxaca was an economically and demographically important region under Aztec domination. While Borah and Cook were of the opinion that the coastal regions were densely populated at the time of the Conquest, this judgment is based on extrapolation from later population levels and rates of depopulation observed in other areas.[29] Slicher van Bath, on the other hand, has found a large degree of continuity among the 129 districts with respect to their positions of *relative* demographic importance, over the period ca. 1570-1800. His opinion is that at the time of the Conquest, as afterwards, the demographic importance of the coastal regions was slight (Yucatán being left out of consideration).[30] We shall assume that the centers of population of 1570/1620 were approximately those of 1520, and therefore also those of the period of mendicant expansion.

The map of 1570 also holds out the possibility that Hidalgo, agriculturally and minerally rich, while not offering a separate concentration comparable to those of México, Oaxaca or Michoacán, may have been as close as anything else to a fourth center of Indian population. Comparison of the maps of population distribution with those of the sites chosen by the mendicants shows that these were located in areas of concentration of Indian population. In 1620 the heavily populated areas are the areas intensely colonized by the regulars, as Table 1 shows.

Here 129 districts are grouped according to their demographic importance. The districts are of varying size. As we have already noted, we can only relate the intensity of mendicant activity with population concentration indirectly, by way of these districts. The resulting average number of establishments per district provides an index which is not precise, but which does clearly show that the most heavily populated districts are the best supplied with religious establishments.

Table 1 *Number of mendicant establishments in districts of varying population density in 1620*

Population density (in persons/km²)	Number of districts	Number of establishments	Average per district
More than 5	29	102	3.5
1-5	70	124	1.8
Less than 1	30	26	0.9
No data	-	22	-

Table 2, based on the reconstruction of the situation ca. 1570, confirms the pattern, and is more interesting, since it represents the earlier situation: if anything, the concentration of establishments in the more heavily populated districts is clearer. The most populous districts are located in what we have described as the three demographic islands (see Map 2).

Table 2 *Numbers of establishments in districts with varying numbers of tributaries in 1570*

Tributaries per district	Number of districts	Number of establishments	Establishments per district (average)	Tributaries per establishment (average)
20,000 or more	6	53	8.8	3,151
10,000-19,999	12	50	4.2	3,189
5,000-9,999	32	78	2.4	2,745
2,500-4,999	32	38	1.2	2,993
Fewer than 2,500	39	28	0.7	1,805
No data	(8)	27	-	-

Since we are working here with absolute numbers of tributaries, it is possible to correlate population with the number of establishments in each district. The resulting figures (expressed in tributaries per mendicant establishment) are sensitive to any number of local factors, and vary widely from district to district (the highest ratio is 12,000; the lowest is 453). It is impossible to go into an analysis of the reasons for all the individual deviations from the norm. But the average number of tributaries (in 1570) per sixteenth-century mendicant establishment is in the neighborhood of 3,000. This average holds surprisingly steady for districts of varying population size (Table 2, last column), suggesting again that if we leave other purely local factors out of consideration, the distribution of the mendicant establishments closely followed that of the Indian population.

The shape of the colony, insofar as it is reflected in missionary activity, is therefore determined by the three 'islands' of Indian population concentration: the heart of the colony stretches from Oaxaca in the southeast over México to Michoacán in the northwest (see Map 1). Hidalgo, to the north of México, seems to have formed an appendage rich agriculturally and demographically, but lacking the kind of concentration found in the other three areas.

As has already been remarked, relations among the different orders were highly competitive. Motivated to seek out the most heavily populated areas, each order also tried to avoid contact with competing orders by establishing regional monopolies. When we compare the maps of population concentration (Maps 2 and 3) with that of the total distribution of the orders (Map 1) we see that the areas where more than one order are simultaneously active are exactly the three demographic islands (and Zacatecas, where the Franciscans as well as the Augustinians had small, late houses). The only area where all three orders are simultaneously present is practically identical with the area around México and Puebla with a population density of more than 5 persons per km^2 in 1620. Here we have the spectacle of three religious orders, each trying to carve out a niche of its own, and at the same time maintaining outposts in the heartlands of the territories settled by other orders.

What of the sequence of the different directions taken by each of the orders upon arrival in New Spain? The port of entry was Veracruz; the center of the colony was México. All three orders settled first in the Central region surrounding the capital, the most populous of the three demographic islands. The Franciscans, at first alone, wasted no time in settling in such primary centers as México, Texcoco, Tlaxcala and Huejotzingo, but also set out almost immediately towards the west; in 1525 they founded in Pátzcuaro, in the center of the second of the population islands, Michoacán. The Dominicans, meanwhile, also founded several early houses in and near México, but did not delay in setting out for more remote areas. The direction they took was towards the Southeast: they founded in 1529 in Oaxa-ca, at the center of the third island of population concentration. The speed and certainty with which both orders arrived at their principal targets leads to the suspicion that the choice of direction taken was a conscious one in each case. As to the sequence of the choices made, which suggests that Michoacán may have seemed somehow the more attractive area of the two, part of the explanation may lite in the distances which had to be covered: Michoacán is closer to México than is Oaxaca, and thus perhaps more attractive for rapid colonization.[31] Moreover, Borah and Cook find it probable that an urban complex smaller than, but similar to that of México existed at Pátzcuaro at the time of the Conquest; no such affirmation is made for Oaxaca.[32] Perhaps a combination of the two factors tended to favor Michoacán above Oaxaca in the eyes of the early Franciscans.

By the time the Augustinians arrived, nine years after the first Franciscans, all three of the population islands were already to some extent occupied. There was no fourth center of Indian population to compare with the México-Puebla region, Michoacán or Oaxaca. They founded houses in the area near to the capital, arranging themselves between the towns of the other two orders, then expanded in three direc-

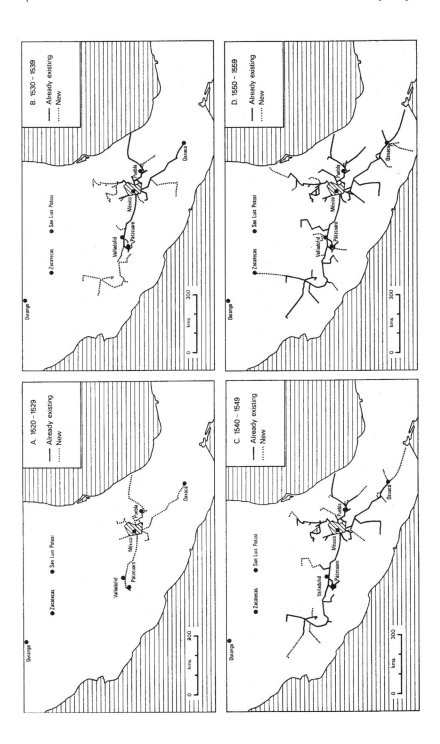

Map 4a *Reconstruction of routes of mendicant expansion, sixteenth century, per decade (A-D)*

Map 4b *Reconstruction of routes of mendicant expansion, sixteenth century, per decade (E–H)*

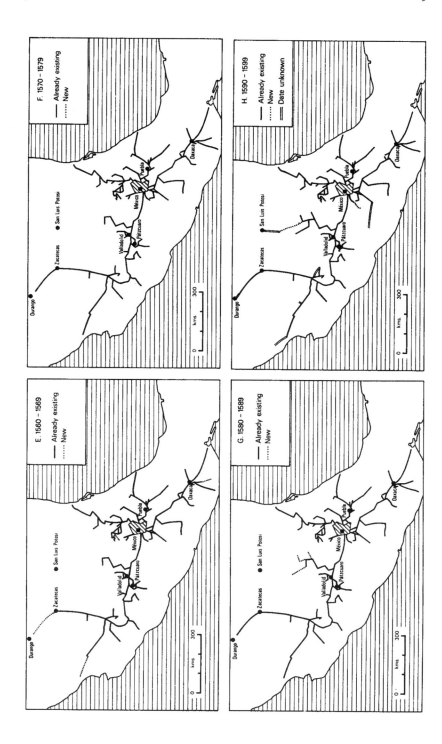

tions at once: to the west behind the thinly-spread Franciscans, to the southwest (rather avoiding the Dominicans), but especially to the north (Hidalgo), which may have been the most attractive region still unoccupied by either of the other two orders. One cannot help noticing a certain vacillation on the part of the Augustinians in moving out from México. Of the three orders, they were perhaps the least successful in carving out a regional monopoly. The explanation may well be sought in their position as late corners to the field.

The sequence of new foundations can be taken as a basis for reconstructing provisionally the routes[33] approximately followed by the orders in reaching their various destinations. A modern road atlas[34] has been consulted for the reconstruction, since no adequate description exists of the sixteenth-century paths actually followed. The overwhelming majority of the establishments lie on or very near to present-day roads. The reconstruction follows the shortest route connecting the establishments. The establishments are located in chains along this path. Since there are so few possibilities of interconnection outside the resulting network, which is essentially one of bifurcating spokes leading away from the capital, it is improbable that significant distortions occur by referring to the modern roads.

The reconstruction (see Map 4a and b) is made in such a way as to show the length added to these routes in each decade. During the sixteenth century, the length added to these routes each decade gradually decreased. The core of the colony, composed of the three population islands, was already opened up in the 1520s and 1530s, the peak decades of extension of the routes. Barely fifteen years after the coming of the first Franciscans, and a mere six years after the first Augustinians, the regions of greatest demographic importance had been opened up. A period of consolidation followed. The orders continued to expand slowly into the 1550s and to a limited extent even longer, but by then they would seem to have overshot their most important targets. After 1550 the main additions to the network of routes and settlements were in the thinly populated North and West, areas that remained architecturally and evangelical marginal until the eighteenth century.

Two types of new establishments can be distinguished: one type goes beyond the previous limits of the religious colony; the other is located along the way to a previously established outpost. Two phases in mendicant expansion can thus be distinguished, one of new *extension*, and one of filling in the spaces, or *intensification*. New settlements of extension go beyond the previous limits, opening up new territories. New settlements of intensification are located along previously existing routes, spaced between other already existing settlements. Table 3 shows, per decade, the total number of new establishments for all the orders, and the breakdown into the categories of extension and intensification. The ratio of extension/intensification provides an index of the relative importance of the two phases in each decade.

The table shows a trend in the pattern of mendicant expansion. An early period of exploration and extension is followed by one of filling in the spaces left along the routes taken. We know that the early period of extension covered great distances, leaving a few widely scattered outposts, and that the rate of opening up new routes decreased in terms of length added as time went on. Now we can add a complementary development: the declining rate of new extension is accompanied by an increasing number of new establishments within the existing framework.

To put it another way, the first settlers passed a long many future sites at which religious colonization would eventually take place, but rejected them as a first choice in favor of sites further removed from the center of the colony. Only later, with the boundaries to the colony more or less stabilized, did the orders return to these less attractive (less populous?) sites within the network. Is this not a sign of incipient saturation? If not, then it is in any case a recognition of the limited possibilities for further expansion.

Table 3 *New establishments per order per decade and phases of extension and intensification*

	1520-29	1530-39	1540-49	1550-59	1560-69	1570-79	1580-89	1590-99
OFM								
Total new establishments	20	22	19	26	17	10	11	2
Extension	20	13	8	5	5	2	3	0
Intensification	0	9	11	21	12	8	8	2
OP								
Total new establishments	5	7	5	20	5	3	2	0
Extension	5	0	4	6	1	0	2	0
Intensification	0	7	1	14	4	3	0	0
OSA								
Total new establishments	0	18	10	23	5	14	4	5
Extension	0	10	4	10	1	1	0	2
Intensification	0	8	6	13	4	13	4	3
All Orders								
Total new establishments	25	47	34	69	27	27	17	7
Extension	25	23	16	21	4	3	5	2
Intensification	0	24	18	48	23	24	12	5
Ratio: $\frac{\text{Extension}}{\text{Intensification}}$								
(All orders)	-	.96	.89	.44	.17	.13	.42	.40

The peak of extension is in the first five years of the colony. By 1540 the main routes had been opened up. The decade of the 1550s, when the most establishments came into being – a sort of mendicant golden age – was one in which the mendicants perhaps reached their greatest organizational strength, a period in which advantage could be taken from the groundwork already laid. But after this decade the mendicants entered a period of decline. They had reached, quite literally, the end of their road. This is shown in the last row of figures in Table 3: new extension falls steadily in relative importance; the drop is most dramatic after 1559. But this row of figures is less expressive than it might be: extension only means 'outside the previous limits' without specifying how far. Referring again to Map 4, it is clear that on the whole the later routes of extension are not only fewer, they are also shorter.

We have already mentioned the competitive and even combative relations among the orders and between them and the secular clergy and bishops. Disagreements were often over issues, such as the conditions, under which baptism might be administered, or the level and form of tithe and tribute obligations, but there was also an important territorial dimension. We have remarked that the orders chose to expand in different directions in order to avoid conflicts. In those areas where the orders worked in close proximity to one another, disputes erupted and were fought out at a local level, over the possession of specific villages, and over the loyalty of their populations. During the sixteenth century a number of mendicant establishments were transferred from one order to another, or from one order to the secular clergy. Take-over attempts were also made which were not successful. In areas where more than one order was active or where regulars and seculars worked in close proximity, altercations over any number of problems were possible. Three examples:

In 1573, jealous parish priests of the cathedral of Pátzcuaro sued the Franciscan mission there in an attempt to force them to remove the baptismal font from their church.[35] In 1536, when Archbishop Zumárraga (himself a Franciscan) evicted the Augustinians from their house at Ocuituco, the friars, furious with this decision, '... stripped the church of its bell, ornaments, locks and even the orange and other trees they had planted, and carried everything off to their convent at Totolapan ... then ... threatened to receive the Franciscans at the point of a lance, in case they should be sent to replace them.'[36] Sometimes expeditions were even armed by friars to sack and burn down competing churches:

> In the archdiocese of Mexico, the Franciscans, Fray Francisco de Ribera and Fray Juan Quijano in particular, gathered up six hundred Indians in the Toluca region, armed them with bows and shields, and one fine night demolished the [secular] church at San Pedro Calimaya, after which they burned everything that was left. In the same way they demolished the church at San Juan de Tepamachalco. One of their companions, Fray Antonio de Torrijos, confessed that he had also burned a church.[37]

If we interpret transfers and altercations between different orders as an indication of proximity and competition for jurisdiction over certain villages, then we might expect the frequency of such contacts to increase with the approach of a situation of relative saturation. If it is true that there were limited possibilities in the colony for new establishments, we might expect there to be more conflicts over already existing ones.

Although it is difficult to track them down, a preliminary check of the places and dates of transfers and altercations mentioned by Ricard or Kubler – some 40 in all – suggests that their frequency did in fact reach a high point during the decades of the 1560s and 1570s.[38] These are the very decades in which, as we have seen (Table 3), the phase of 'intensification' reaches its peak. A reading of the *Códice Franciscano* also leads to the conclusion that tensions ran very high in those years.[39] If this was, indeed, the general tendency, then whatever the merits of the speculations on the changing nature of the religious' personalities and political issues involved, quarrels within the church should be seen against the background of a colony which was becoming too small to please everyone.

The decline of the mendicant orders,[40] while the result of civil and secular opposition and internal dissention, was also the result of the limited possibilities that existed for further expansion. The competition with the secular church, and the bickering among the orders themselves, heightened in intensity as the extent of the colony stabilized. This competition was more than the mendicants could handle in the end: their opponents could correctly, and successfully, challenge their privileged position under *patronato real*. The orders slowly ceased to grow, and the relatively sedentary secular church began to spread out from the European centers to take in their places in the countryside. Having led the conquest, the mendicant orders were destined to become the victims of the spiritual taming of New Spain.

Appendix to Chapter 5

New establishments per order, per decade, sixteenth century

OFM, Province Santo Evangelio

1524-29 (18): Coatepec, Chalco, Coatlinchan, Cuautinchan, Cuautitlan, Cuernavaca, Huejotzingo (San Gabriel), Huexotla, México (San Francisco), México (San José de los Naturales), Otumba, Tepeaca, Tepeapulco, Texcoco, Tlaxcala, Toluca, Tula, Tulancingo, Veracruz.

1530-39 (12): Atotonilco, Tula, Cholula (San Gabriel), Huaquechula, Huichapan, Jilotepec, Puebla, Tehuacán, Tláhuac, Tlalmanalco, Tlatelolco, Xalapa, Xochimilco.

1540-49 (8): Calpan, Hueytlalpan, Ixtacamaxtitlán, Jalacingo, Quccholac, Tecamachalco, Teotitlan, Tlaquiltenango.

1550-59 (19): Acatzingo, Alfajayucan, Atlihuetzia, Calimaya, Chalco Atenco, Chietla, Cholula, (San Andrés), Metepec, Tampico, Tecali, Teotihuacan, Tepeji del Rio, Tepexi de la Seda, Tepeyango, Tlalnepantla, Tochimilco, Zacatlan, Zempoala, Zinacantepec.

1560-69 (10): Apam, Calpulalpan, Ecatepec, Huamantla, Milpa Alta, San Felipe Cuixtlan, Santa Ana Chiautempan, Tacuba, Totimehuacán, Tultitlan.

1570-79 (5): Atlancatepec, Natívitas, Tepetillan, Totolac, Xiutepec.

1580-89 (3): Amozoc, Chiauhtla, Tecómitl.

1590-99 (2): Huejotzingo (SanDiego), Pachuca.

Date unknown (5): Atlixco, Cholula (Capilla Real), Churubusco, Ixtacalco, Tlahuelilpa.

OFM, Province San Pedro y San Pablo

1524-29 (2): Pátzcuaro, Tzintzuntzan.

1530-39 (3): Acámbaro, Uruapan, Zacapu.

1540-49 (5): Jiquilpan, Morelia (Valladolid), Periban, San Miguel Allende, Tarecuato.

1550-59 (2): Tajimaroa, Tancítaro.

1560-69 (2): Erongarícuaro, Querétaro.

1570-79 (2): Apaseo, Celaya.

1580-89 (7): Charapan, Pichátaro. Purenchécuaro, San Felipe, Toliman, Zitácuaro. Xichú.

Date unknown (3): Chamacuero, Tarímbaro, Zinapécuaro.

OFM, Nueva Galicia

1530-39 (7): Ajijic, Amacueca, Etzatlan, Guadalajara, Teul, Tuxpa, Zapotlan.

1540-49 (6): Autlan, Chapala, Jalisco, Juchipila, Poncitlan, Tamazula. 1550-59 (5): Ahacuatlan, Colima, Tlajomulco, Zacatecas, Zacoalco.

1560-69 (5): Atoyac, Cocula, Nombre de Dios, Sayula, Sentispac.

1570-79 (3): Huaynamota, Techaluta, Zapotitlan.

1580-89 (1): Tecualtipan.

Date unknown (6): Acaponeta, Agua del Venado, Chalchihuites, Durango, Jala, Sombrerete.

OP

1526-29 (5): Coyoacán, Chimalhuacan, Chalco, México, Oaxaca, Oaxtepec.

1530-39 (7): Amecameca, Etla, Izúcar, Puebla, Tepetlaoztoc, Teposcolula, Yanhuitlan.

1540-49 (5): Coixtlahuaca, Tehuantepec, Tlaxiaco, Villa Alta, Yautépec.

1550-59 (20): Achiutla, Atzcapotzalco, Cuilapan, Chichicapa, Chila, Chimalhuacan Atenco, Ecatepec, Huitzo, Jalapa, Justlahuaca, Nejapa, Ocotlan, Tecomastlahuacan, Tenango Chalco, Tepoztlan, Tetela del Volcán, Teticpac, Tlacochahuaya, Tláhuac, Tonalá.

1560-69 (5): Coatepec Chalco, Hueyapan, Miahuatlan, Nochistlán, Xaltepec.

1570-79 (3): Tacubaya, Tilantongo, Tlaquiltenango.

1580-89 (2): Almoloyas, Juquila.

Date unknown (3): Atlixco, Mixcoac, San Angel.

OSA

1533-39 (18): Atotonilco el Grande, Chapulhuacán, Chilapa, Lolotla, Malinalco, Metztitlan, México, Mexquic, Molango, Ocuilan, Ocuituco, Santa Fe, Tacámbaro, Tiripitio, Tlapa, Totolapan, Yecapixtla, Zacualpan Amilpas.

1540-49 (10): Acolman, Actopan, Epazoyucan, Huanchinango, Huejutla, Morelia (Valladolid), Tempoal, Tepecoacuilco, Tlanchinol, Zempoala.

1550-59 (23): Acatlan, Culhuacan, Charo, Chiautla, Copándaro, Cuitzeo, Huacana, Huango, Huayacocotla, Ixmiquilpan, Jacona, Jonacatepec, Jumiltepec, Pahuatlan, Pánuco, Tantoyuca, Tezontepec, Tlayacapan, Tlazazalco, Tutotepec, Ucareo, Xilitla, Yuriria.

1560-69 (5): Ajacuba, Chapatongo, Chietla, Huatlatlauca, Jantetelco.

1570-79 (14): Alcozauca, Atlatlauca, Chucándiro, Guadalajara, Oaxaca, Ocotlan, Pátzcuaro, Puebla, San Felipe, Singuilucan, Tzirosto, Xochicoatlán, Zacatecas, Zacualtipan.

1580-89 (4): Atlixco, Ayotzingo, Tingambato, Tlacuilotepec.

1590-99 (5): Parangaricutiro, San Felipe (Los Herreros), San Luis Potosí, Undameo, Zacualpa (Minas).

Date unknown (4): Ajuchitlán, Mixquiahuala, Pungarabato, Tonalá.

Notes to Chapter 5

* Published in the *Boletín de Estudios Latinoamericanos y del Caribe*, 21 (1976), pp. 32-56.

1 The work or the secular church was concentrated within the centers or European population for most of the sixteenth century. Their role in the evangelization of Indians was very much secondary to that of the mendicant orders. See, for example, Robert Richard, *The Spiritual Conquest of Mexico*, trans. L. B. Simpson (Berkeley and Los Angeles: University of California Press, 1966; original edition Paris, 1933), p. 23; Rafael Gómez de Hoyos Pbro., *La iglesia de América en las leyes de Indias* (Madrid: Instituto Gonzalo Fernández de Oviedo, 1961), p. 195.

2 Conceded by papal bull *Universales Ecclesiae*, 1508. R. Gómez de Hoyos, op. cit., pp. 19-20.

3 The number or Indians baptized, often *en masse*, during the early years was astronomical: the Franciscan Motolinía ventured the wonderful guess that the number of Indians baptized by about 1536 was in the neighbourhood of 4, 5 or 9 million (either 4 or 5 or 4 + 5 million, depending on the reading). See F. Borgia Steck (trans., ed.), *Motolinía's History of the Indians of New Spain* (Washington, D.C.: Academy of American Fransiscan History, 1951), p. 182 note.

4 Ricard, op. cit., p. 23.

5 Robert J. Mullen, *Dominican Architecture in Sixteenth-Century Oaxaca* (Pheonix: Center for Latin American Studies and Friends of Mexican Art, 1975), p.22.

6 Ricard, op. cit., p. 23.

7 Ibid., p. 23.

8 Ibid. This book remains the basic study dealing with the mendicants in New Spain.

9 John McAndrew, *The Open-Air Churches of Sixteenth-Century Mexico* (Cambridge, Mass., 1965) pp. 88-89.

10 Ricard, op. cit., p. 244.

11 Many of the early mendicant friars were driven by an apostolic fervor inspired in that of the primitive fathers of the Christian Church. Some believed in the possibility of an ideal Christian republic in the New World peopled by Indians and friars. On Franciscan millennialism see J.L. Phelan, *El reino milenario de los franciscanos en el Nuevo Mundo* (México: Universidad Nacional Autónoma de México, 1972; original edition in English, Berkeley, 1956).

    On the methods used in the early evangelization, see among others Ricard, op. cit., and Pedro Borges, O.F.M., *Métodos misionales en la cristianización de América: siglo XVI* (Madrid: Consejo Superior de Investigaciones, 1960).

    As to the efficacy of the mendicants as agents of 'pacification', the Viceroy Antonio de Mendoza offers the following testimony in a letter to Charles V: 'certifico á V.M. que tengo hechos y fundados más presidios de los que se me han ordenado. Porque los que son y han sido necesarios para la pacificación destas nuevas gentes, según lo que yo he conocido de su condición y calidad, son conventos ó monasterios de frailes, porque con su doctrina y enseñanza los tienen más domésticos que palomas; y destos tengo fundados muchos por las provincias más principales é importantes desta Nueva España, y estos son los fuertes y presidios más necesarios que los de los soldados; porque los de los soldados son para inquietar lo que ya está pacífico y muy asentado ...; y vale más un soldado destos espirituales que los doctrinan y enseñan la fe, que todas las lanzas y armas con que los castellanos entraron á rendir la tierra'. Cited by Juan de Torquemada, *Servicios que las tres Ordenes han hecho a la Corona de Castilla* ..., J. Garcia Icazbalceta (ed.), *Nueva colección de documentos para la historia de México,* 5 vols. (Nendeln, Liechtenstein: Kraus reprint, 1971; original ed. México, 1892), V, pp. 187-188.

12 Accounts of the political and ecclesiastical disputes which surrounded the mendicant orders are given in Ricard op. cit., pp. 139-263; L. Lopetegui. S. I. y F. Zubillaga, S.I., *Historia de la Iglesia en la América española,* 2 vols. (Madrid: Editorial Católica, 1965). I; J. L. Phelan, op. cit., among others. Especially eloquent on the mendicant side is Jerónimo de Mendieta in various letters of the *Códice Francisco,* reproduced by J. Garcia Icazbalceta (ed.); op. cit., IV and V.

13 W. L. Schurz, 'The Spanish Lake', *Hispanic American Historical Review* 5 (1922), 181-194.

14 On the native depopulation or New Spain between 1520 and ca. 1620/1650, there is an abundant literature. One must take into consideration a decrease in total population of between 80 and 95 percent. Although some writers hold out the possibility of a slight recovery in the third quarter of the sixteenth century, it is probable that the sickening decline continued more or less unabated during the entire period. See Peter Gerhard, *A Guide to the Historical Geography of New Spain* (Cambridge: The University Press, 1972). pp. 22-24.

15 Ricard, op. cit., p. 61.

16 George Kubler, *Mexican Architecture of the Sixteenth Century,* 2 vols. (Westport, Conn.: Greenwood Press, 1972; original edition New Haven, 1948), 11, appendix: 'Documents for Mendicant Buildings', pp. 450-535.

17 Gerhard, op. cit.

18 Recurring names are those of Mendieta, Motolinía, Vetancurt, Torquemada, Rea, Beaumont and Tello (Franciscans); Basalenque, Grijalva, Escobar and García (Augustinians); Dávila Padilla, Méndez, Franco and Ojea (Dominicans).

19 Mullen, op. cit., Appendix 3, Table 11, pp. 234-237.

20 Gerhard, op. cit., pp. 22.

21 Kubler, op. cit., p. 473.

22 For a discussion of the possibilities, and the bibliographical references, see B.H. Slicher van Bath, 'De paleodemografie', *A.A.G. Bijdragen* 15 (1970), pp. 134-201.

23 Gerhard, op. cit.

24 B.H. Slicher van Bath, 'Tributarios en non-indios in Nieuw-Spanje, ca. 1570 – ca. 1800', unpublished manuscript, Wageningen, 1975.

25 Gerhard, op. cit., Map 14, p. 25.

26 Slicher van Bath, op. cit.

27 Ibid.

28 For descriptions of the districts meant, see Gerhard, op. cit., especially Map 8, p. 16.

29 Woodrow Borah and Sherburne F. Cook, *The Aboriginal Population of Central Mexico on the Eve of the Spanish Conquest* (Berkeley and Los Angeles: University of California Press, 1963).

30 Slicher van Bath, op. cit.

31 Over present-day roads, the distance México-Pátzcuaro is 381 km; the distance México-Oaxaca is 545 km.

32 Borah and Cook, op. cit., p. 90.

33 Not to be construed as roads for wheeled transport.

34 *Atlas Euzkadi: Caminos de México,* 2a. impressión (México: Compañía Hulera Euzkadi, 1966).

35 F. B. Warren, *Vasco de Quiroga and his Pueblo Hospitals of Santa Fe* (Washington, DC.: Academy of American Franciscan History, 1963), p. 106.

36 Ricard, op. cit., p. 250.

37 Ibid., p. 251.

38 Some 29 cases are recorded during this time span. Kubler, op. cit., pp. 450-535; Ricard, op. cit., pp. 250-251.

39 *Códice Fransiscano,* op. cit.

40 The millenial Franciscan Mendieta, who ceased writing about 1596, viewed the history of the New World as divided into two periods: an *edad dorada* lasting from the arrival of the first Franciscans in 1524 until the death of Viceroy Velasco in 1564, and a period of great calamities for the church beginning in 1564. See J. L. Phelan, op. cit., pp. 65-68.

6

Architectural activity, demography and economic diversification: regional economies of colonial Mexico[*]

This article is an attempt to interpret the data on the chronology and distribution of architectural activity compiled in an earlier publication, 'Inventory of 861 Monuments of Mexican Colonial Architecture'.[1] We believe that the colonial monuments can tell us a good deal about the demographic and economic history of the period in which they were built. Until now, only art historians have occupied themselves seriously with questions of architectural chronology; economic historians have neglected an important source. Many of the colonial monuments represent huge material investments, and it is not farfetched to imagine that the chronologies of their construction might reflect the economic climate of the time. One would expect building activity in general to be sensitive to population fluctuations: rising in times of population increase (greater demand for buildings, cheaper labor for construction), and stagnating in periods of decline. On the other hand, the means to build also depend on conjunctural circumstances: are resources available for the procuration of materials and labor? Finally, shifts in the kinds of buildings under construction may tell us of underlying changes in the composition of a population. These are some of the hypotheses of this study.

Geographical distribution of colonial monuments

In the above cited work it was possible to assemble a basic inventory of 861 colonial monuments of all kinds – churches, monasteries belonging to the men's regular orders, nuns' convents, houses, fortifications, bridges, fountains, customs houses, aqueducts, etc. – which has been subjected to a simple statistical analysis. It is first necessary to map the overall incidence of the monuments in the list. The geographical distribution of the colonial buildings can be looked at in two ways, by individual settlement, or by regions. For some purposes more can be learned by considering the distribution per town, especially in the case of the larger urban settlements. But since very many of Mexico's colonial monuments are located in small places in the countryside, a first step involves the consideration of the regional distribution. It

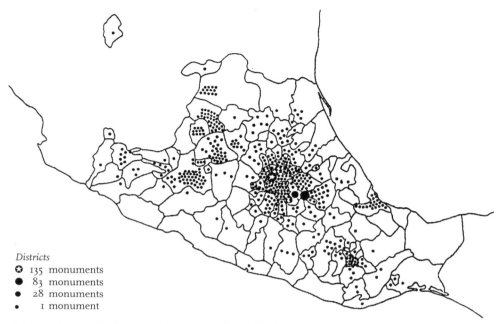

Map 1   *Overall distribution of monuments, by Gerhard*

Districts
- ✪ 135 monuments
- ●   83 monuments
- ●   28 monuments
- •   1 monument

would be possible to follow the modern political division of Mexico into states, but since the division into states is a post-colonial arrangement, and since for a number of reasons it is convenient to work with smaller areas, we have chosen to adopt as regional entities the 129 minor civil divisions which existed in 1786 for New Spain, and which have been mapped and described with precision by Peter Gerhard in his historical geography of 1972.[2]

Map 1 shows the overall distribution of the monuments per Gerhard district. They are not spread evenly, but tend to concentrate themselves in certain zones. The most densely built-up districts adjoin one another, as do the districts with the fewest monuments. The average number of monuments per district is 6.3. Only twenty-four (nineteen percent) of the districts rise above this average, while 105 (eighty-one percent) of the districts have six monuments or fewer. Two of the smallest districts geographically, Mexico and Puebla, containing the two colonial cities of the same names, are the most important in terms of their architecture. Together they account for 218 (twenty-five percent) of all monuments listed. Half (431) of the monuments are located in only eleven districts. There are islands of intensive architectural activity composed of such districts; between the islands are borderlands with fewer monuments. The largest of the islands is in central Mexico, between and surrounding Mexico City and Puebla, comprising roughly the area extending from Tula and Pachuca in the north to Cuernavaca in the south, Tlaxcala and Tepeaca in the east,

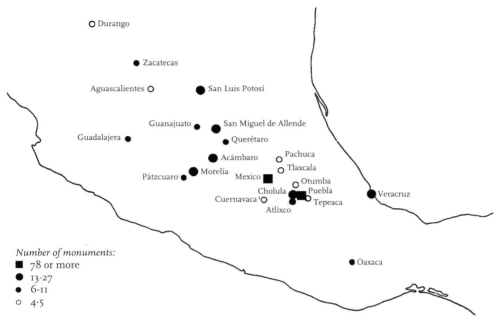

Map 2 *Twenty-four colonial urban centers*

and Toluca towards the west. A second island, much smaller than the first, consists of Oaxaca and surroundings, especially between Teposcolula and Coixtlahuaca in the northwest, and Mitla and Tlacolula to the southeast. At the other end of New Spain, Guadalajara-Sayula, Morelia-Pátzcuaro (Michoacán), Acámbaro, Querétaro, Guanajuato, San Miguel de Allende and San Luis Potosí were centers of activity.

By contrast, 21 of the districts have no monuments at all in the inventory. The districts without monuments are concentrated in the coastal regions, both Atlantic and Pacific. During the colonial period, the port of Veracruz was the only coastal settlement of architectural importance in New Spain. In Yucatán – within modern Mexico, but outside colonial New Spain – both Mérida and the port of Campeche were architecturally significant. Thus, with the exception of Yucatán, the coastal regions of Mexico are very poor in colonial architecture. The relative absence of colonial building along the coasts is in marked contrast with the situation in such countries as Peru, Chile and Brazil, where the coastal regions are generally more important than the interior.

Having distinguished the regions of greater and lesser activity, we pass to the consideration of individual cities and towns. The monuments in the inventory are spread over 410 different places; as was also the case with the districts, the monuments are unequally distributed among the towns. For 343 (eighty-four percent) of the settlements, only one monument is listed. There are thirty-eight places with two monuments, five with three, and twenty-four towns with four monuments or more. In other words, half (435) of the monuments are located in places with fewer than four monuments, and the other half (426) are located in towns with four monuments or more. Although taking the number of monuments which appear in the inventory is an arbitrary and imprecise criterion, in the remainder of this article we shall refer to urban centers as those settlements with four monuments or more, and rural settlements as those with 1-3 monuments.

The 24 urban centers have the following numbers of monuments:			
1	México, 128	13	Campeche, 8
2	Puebla, 78	14	Oaxaca, 8
3	San Miguel de Allende, 27	15	Pátzcuaro, 8
4	Cholula, 25	16	Querétaro, 8
5	Acámbaro, 21	17	Guadalajara, 7
6	Veracruz, 20	18	Mérida, 7
7	San Luis Potosí, 13	19	Zacatecas, 7
8	Morelia, 13	20	Guanajuato, 6
9	Atlixco, 11	21	Durango, 5
10	Pachuca, 5	22	Aguascalientes, 4
11	Tlaxcala, 5	23	Otumha, 4
12	Cuernavaca, 4	24	Tepeaca, 4

The distribution of the urban centers is given in Map 2. They are not located on the coast, with the exception of the ports of Veracruz and Campeche. Central Mexico has the greatest cluster of urban centers: over one-fourth of all the monuments listed are in the cities of Mexico, Puebla, Cholula or Atlixco. Agricultural and commercial towns of importance were also Oaxaca (Antequera) in the south, and Pátzcuaro, Morelia (Valladolid), Acámbaro, Querétaro, San Miguel de Allende (San Miguel el Grande) and Guadalajara in the northwest of New Spain. Beyond a line drawn between Guadalajara and San Miguel de Allende, and thus falling partly outside New Spain proper, were the mining centers, whose architecture dates largely from the late eighteenth century: Guanajuato, San Luis Potosí, Aguascalientes, Zacatecas, Durango. On the basis of the distribution of places with colonial monuments and a modern road atlas, it is possible to reconstruct a certain minimum network of overland routes of communication, which must have existed during the colonial period.[3] The road network is densest in the areas of the three islands of intensive architectural activity in central Mexico, Oaxaca and Michoacán. To the south of the line Guadalajara-San Miguel de Allende there are many rural settlements; to the north of the same line there are much fewer. In the north most architectural activity was concentrated within the relatively isolated mining centers. This fact is seen in a less dense network of roads.

Architecture and population: spatial aspect

The colonial population of Mexico drew upon three distinct racial groups, each coming from a different continent. During the colonial period these groups – Indian, European and African – tended to mix. It is necessary, however, especially for the early period, to distinguish between the subjugated Indian population (reflected in the numbers of tributaries, Indian heads of household), the European population (the Spanish *vecinos*), and the imported African slaves.

Each of the three population groups was concentrated in certain geographical areas. The African slaves (were) settled mainly in the thinly populated areas dedicated to cacao and sugar cultivation along the coasts (the plantations) and also in the mining districts. African slaves were imported to populate areas where few Indian laborers could be found, in the regions with sparse Indian populations. The greatest concentrations of black and mulatto population during the colonial period were thus located both outside the areas with high Indian population concentrations, and outside the regions with large numbers of colonial monuments.

By contrast, the Indian concentrations were to be found inland, and especially in the highlands. Although the Indian population of New Spain experienced heavy fluctuations during the period 1520-1810 – a sharp decline followed by a slow recovery in most districts – the relative population distribution over the various regions did not change much. The relatively populous districts of 1570 remained so in 1620 (and 1800, years for which there are data. Similarly, the sparsely populated districts did not gain in relative importance in most cases. There is a high degree of continuity in the relative demographic positions of the 129 districts during the entire period. For colonial New Spain then, three islands with high concentrations of Indian population can be distinguished, which maintained their basic configuration during the whole colonial period.[4] All three were islands of intensive architectural activity as well.

The largest, arranged about the urban centers of pre-Columbian central Mexico at Tenochtitlan, Texcoco, Cholula, Tepeaca, etc., corresponds roughly to the present-day states of Mexico, Morelos, Puebla, Tlaxcala and Hidalgo. A second island lies to the west, and coincides more or less with the modern state of Michoacán: this region was inhabited in the pre-Columbian period by the independent Tarascan nation. The other pole of our landlocked archipelago was in the modern state of Oaxaca. Its population consisted of the various Mixtec and Zapotec tribes. The coastal regions were sparsely populated, with the exception of Yucatán, where the descendants of the once great Maya formed a fourth area with a dense Indian population during the colonial period,[5] and the only one on or near the coast. The three islands of Indian population in New Spain are clearly visible in Map 3, which shows the distribution of the tributary population about 1570 over the 129 Gerhard districts. Comparison of Map 3 with Map 1 (overall distribution of colonial monuments) shows that the distri-

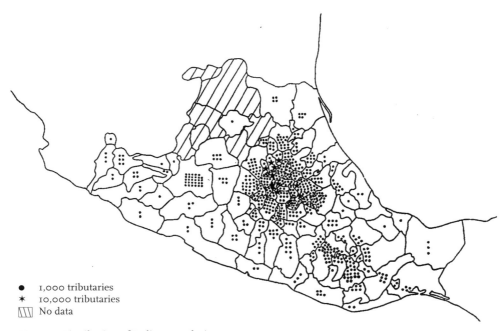

●   1,000 tributaries
✳   10,000 tributaries
⧄   No data

Map 3   *Distribution of Indian population 1570*

bution of Indian population exercised a considerable influence on the incidence of monumental architecture. Especially the monasteries of the evangelizing orders, as we have seen elsewhere, were placed with a sharp eye to the native population. It was found that on the average, districts of varying size and population tended to have a number of monastery-missions proportional to their tributary population. Expressed in terms of population figures of about 1570, the ratio of tributaries per sixteenth-century monastery centered around 3,000.[6]

Although the islands of dense Indian population are also clearly visible as islands of intense architectural activity, the number of Indians was not the only factor. In effect, the colonial monuments were more heavily concentrated within a few central districts than the tributaries. This can be illustrated by means of a table which gives the demographic profile – with respect to the number of tributaries – of the 129 districts when they are grouped as to their architectural importance (number of colonial monuments in inventory).[7]

It may be readily seen that in districts with larger numbers of monuments, the extra building activity, while accompanied by higher levels of Indian population, cannot be explained or justified on that basis alone. In these districts were the urban centers, where Spaniards, mixed-bloods and Negroes also lived. It will be noted, however, that in districts with fewer than three monuments, the average number of tributaries per monument is quite consistent with that found for the sixteenth-century mendicant establishments. In the rural areas, members of the evangelizing orders were responsible for the vast majority of the monuments in our list.

Table 1 *Average tributary population about 1570 of districts with varying numbers of colonial monuments*

Districts with	Average tributary pop. per district	Average tributary pop. per monument
0 monuments (21 districts)	2,074	–
1 monument (35 districts)	2,743	2,743
2 monuments (18 districts)	5,737	2,869
3 monuments (20 districts)	5,435	1,812
4-6 monuments (11 districts)	6,551	1,355
7-20 monuments (18 districts)	17,091	1,534
28-135 monuments (6 districts)	11,581	183

Although the available data on the Spanish population are much more fragmentary than those concerning the tributaries – Spaniards were not obliged to pay tribute, and were thus less interesting for the early head-counters – there are indications that the relation between the incidence of monumental architecture and the distribution of the European population was more intimate than that between architectural activity and the native population. The best data on the Spanish population are from the second half of the eighteenth century (ca. 1743 – ca. 1800). Slicher has assembled them in tables. The largest number of Spaniards lived in the city of Mexico: some 31 percent of those registered for New Spain at the time. Towards the end of the eighteenth century almost half (46 percent) of the population of Mexico City was Spanish. In three other cities for which data are available, the proportion of Spaniards ranged from 33 to 37 percent of the totals. Although data are lacking for most of the cities, including such large ones as Puebla and Oaxaca, one may assume that the Spanish influence was greater in the urban centers than in the countryside.[8]

Regionally speaking, the data are somewhat more complete, although even for the second half of the eighteenth century there are data on the Spanish populations of only 55 of the 129 districts. Still, this is perhaps enough to attempt a demographic profile of the districts with varying numbers of monuments, as to their Spanish residents.

Even with the fragmentary data which we have, the connection between the presence of monumental architecture and that of a sizable Spanish population is clear. There seems to be a nearly linear correlation on the average, although in the less densely settled regions somewhat more Spaniards seem to have been necessary to raise a monument than in the more densely settled ones. This is the same tendency, albeit much less pronounced, as was seen in terms of the tributary population.

Apparently, the city-dwellers either had more need of monumental buildings, or they had more resources at their disposal than their country-cousins.

Table 2 *Average Spanish population of districts with varying numbers of colonial monuments, second half of the eighteenth century (ca. 1743 – ca. 1800)*

Districts with:	Average Spanish pop. per district	Average Spanish pop. per monument
0 monuments (13 districts)	714	-
1 monument (14 districts)	578	578
2 monuments (7 districts)	1,606	803
3 monuments (6 districts)	1,669	556
4-6 monuments (4 districts)	1,175	214
7-20 monuments (8 districts)	5,919	468
28-135 monuments (3 districts)	24,094	378

To summarize the results of this part of our study, there are five provisional conclusions:

1   There are few or no monuments in the coastal regions.

2   The presence of African slaves (plantation economy in the coastal regions) may have provided the Spanish with a labor force where none previously existed, but it did not lead to any form of monumental architecture.

3   There is a correlation between the distribution of the native population and the presence of monumental architecture.

4   There is a stronger correlation between the distribution of the Spanish population and the presence of monumental architecture.

5   The architectural importance of the cities is even greater than their demographic importance; presumably the economic resources *per capita* for the purposes of building were greater in the cities than in the countryside.

Different types of buildings

Until now, the geographical distribution of the monuments has not made reference to the different types of constructions. For our purposes the following division is useful:

OFM: Convents, schools, hospitals, churches and chapels erected by the Franciscan order

OP: Convents, schools, hospitals, churches and chapels erected by the Dominican order

OSA: Convents, schools, hospitals, churches and chapels erected by the Augustinian order

Others men's: Convents, schools, hospitals, churches and chapels erected by one of the other men's regular orders, e.g. Jesuits, Mercedarians, Juaninos, Betlemitas, etc.

NUNS: Convents, schools, hospitals and churches constructed by one of the women's regular orders

SEC: Cathedrals, parish churches, schools, hospitals and chapels constructed by the secular branch of the Church

Other, rel.: Other works of religious architecture, not certain.

CIVIL: Works of civil architecture, public and private

Maps 4 and 5 show the distribution of the different types of monuments in New Spain. We have also constructed a table showing the spread of the different types over the 24 urban centers, and outside these centers.

Table 3 *Different types of buildings by location*

Place	OFM	OP	OSA	Other men's	NUNS	SEC	Other rel.	CIVIL	Total
Mexico	6	2	3	17	25	15	22	38	128
	3%	3%	3%	29%	50%	11%	35%	27%	15%
Puebla	2	2	1	10	11	27	13	12	78
	1%	3%	1%	17%	22%	19%	21%	8%	9%
San Miguel de Allende	2	1	-	5	2	2	2	13	27
	1%	1%	-	8%	4%	1%	3%	9%	3%
Cholula	4	-	-	-	-	15	1	5	25
	2%	-	-	-	-	11%	2%	3%	3%
Acámbaro	6	-	-	-	-	-	-	15	21
	3%	-	-	-	-	-	-	10%	2%
Veracruz	1	1	1	4	-	1	6	6	20
	0%	1%	1%	7%	-	1%	10%	4%	2%
Morelia	1	-	1	1	3	5	-	2	13
	0%	-	1%	2%	6%	4%	-	1%	2%
San Luis Potosí	2	-	1	2	-	3	1	4	13
	1%	-	1%	3%	-	2%	2%	3%	2%
Atlixco	2	1	1	3	1	2	-	1	11
	1%	1%	1%	5%	2%	1%	-	1%	1%
Campeche	2	-	-	2	3	-	-	1	8
	1%	-	-	3%	6%	-	-	1%	1%
Oaxaca	-	1	1	3	1	2	-	-	8
	-	1%	1%	5%	2%	1%	-	-	1%

Table 3 *Continued*

Place	OFM	OP	OSA	Other men's	NUNS	SEC	Other rel.	CIVIL	Total
Pátzcuaro	2	-	1	1	-	1	1	2	8
	1%	-	1%	2%	-	1%	2%	1%	1%
Querétaro	1	-	1	-	2	-	-	4	8
	0%	-	1%	-	4%	-	-	3%	1%
Guadalajara	1	-	1	-	1	2	1	1	7
	0%	-	1%	-	2%	1%	2%	1%	1%
Zacatecas	1	-	1	3	-	1	-	1	7
	0%	-	1%	5%	-	1%	-	1%	1%
Mérida	1	-	-	1	-	2	-	3	7
	0%	-	-	2%	-	1%	-	2%	1%
Guanajuato	1	-	-	1	-	3	-	1	6
	0%	-	-	2%	-	2%	-	1%	1%
Tlaxcala	2	-	-	-	-	2	-	1	5
	1%	-	-	-	-	1%	-	1%	1%
Pachuca	1	-	-	1	-	2	-	1	5
	1%	-	-	2%	-	1%	-	1%	1%
Durango	1	-	-	-	-	1	-	3	5
	0%	-	-	-	-	1%	-	2%	1%
Aguascalientes	-	-	-	-	-	3	-	1	4
	-	-	-	-	-	2%	-	1%	0%
Cuernavaca	3	-	-	-	-	-	-	1	4
	1%	-	-	-	-	-	-	1%	0%
Tepeaca	1	-	-	-	-	-	-	3	4
	0%	-	-	-	-	-	-	2%	0%
Otumba	2	-	-	-	-	-	-	2	4
	1%	-	-	-	-	-	-	1%	0%
Total 24 urban centers	45	8	13	54	49	89	47	121	426
	19%	10%	14%	92%	98%	64%	76%	85%	49%
Total rural settlements	191	72	78	5	1	51	15	22	435
	81%	90%	86%	8%	2%	36%	24%	15%	51%
Total	263	80	91	59	50	140	62	143	861
	100%	100%	100%	100%	100%	100%	100%	100%	100%

From Table 3 and Maps 4 and 5, a number of things become clear. In the first place, the three mendicant orders are consistently under-represented in the cities; their monasteries are mainly located in rural settings. Moreover, in any given place, there are rarely monasteries of more than one of these orders. In only six of the 410 places listed do Franciscan and Augustinian monasteries exist side by side. In only one place do we find both Dominicans and Augustinians. And in only three cities –

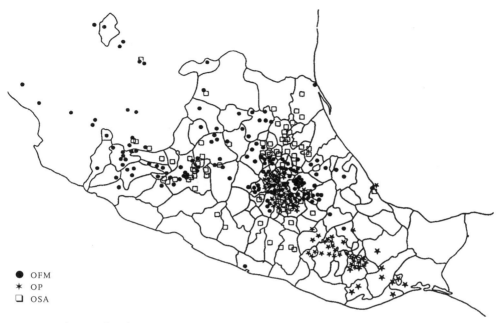

Map 4 *Places with at least one monument*

OFM
OP
OSA

Map 5 *Places with at least one monument*

Secondary men's order
Women's orders
SEC
Civil

Mexico, Puebla and Veracruz – are there monasteries of all three orders. This is in marked contrast to the situation in Ssouth America, where most towns had monasteries of a number of orders. In the countryside as well, the Mexican mendicants tended to avoid each other. Dominicans, Franciscans and Augustinians tried to establish regional monopolies: the Franciscans in the north and west and in Yucatán; the Dominicans in Chiapas and Oaxaca; the Augustinians in Hidalgo. There is much evidence of a competitive atmosphere surrounding the activities of the mendicant orders in Mexico, at least during the sixteenth century.[9]

If the monasteries of the mendicant orders are the most pronouncedly rural of Mexico's colonial monuments, the convents of the women's orders were decidedly the most urban. Especially in the largest cities – Mexico and Puebla – there are disproportionate numbers of nunneries. Nine urban centers account for 49 out of 50 women's convents in the inventory.

The convents, hospitals, etc. of the secondary men's orders are likewise located mainly in the urban centers, although not to such a degree as the women's convents. The Jesuits, for example, maintained a very large and sumptuous *colegio* at Tepotzotlán; the Mercedarians kept a house at Quecholac.

The colonial cathedrals were of course to be found in the urban centers, as were the largest numbers of parishes administered by the secular branch of the Church. There is reason to believe that activities of the secular Church in New Spain were directed mainly at the Spanish community, in contrast to those of the medicant orders, who were identified with missionary work among the Indians. Among the towns and cities, Puebla and Cholula have the greatest proportions of secular religious monuments. Such secular parishes as there were in the Mexican countryside were rather heavily concentrated within the diocese of Puebla, and especially in the immediate surroundings of the episcopal seat itself. Just four districts (Puebla, Cholula, Tlaxcala and Tecali) contain some 40 percent of the rural secular parishes listed, which points to a secular stronghold in the neighborhood of Puebla, Cholula and Tlaxcala. It was exactly in this region that many Spaniards settled. Puebla was founded as a Spanish town, and had a high percentage of non-Indian residents. In the countryside many Spanish settlers were attracted by the fertile landscape, and dedicated themselves in particular to the cultivation of wheat.[10] This can be interpreted as a confirmation of the apparent correlation between secular Church activity and Spanish population levels.

At the same time, however, the same region retained a dense native population as well, leading to the establishment of a number of large Franciscan monasteries active in the conversion to Christianity: Huejotzingo, Calpan, Tlaxcala, Cholula, Tepeaca, Tecali, Huaquechula are so many symbols of Franciscan strength during the sixteenth century. As elsewhere in Mexico where representatives of different branches of the Church worked in close proximity, jealousies and conflicts arose between the Franciscans and the secular hierarchy.

Predominantly urban were also the monuments of civil architecture. Most of the administrative buildings and private mansions listed in our inventory are to be found in the cities, along with most bridges and fountains. Outside the urban centers we find a number of aqueducts, some of them very long and well built. Generally these are found in conjunction with a monastery of one of the men's regular orders.

The fortifications are found in the ports and along the coasts. They were meant to defend against pirates and foreign invasion, and not against rebellions or civil warfare. Inland forts built at Perote and Puebla date from the late eighteenth century, and were inspired by fear of a British invasion that never came. A small *presidio* at San Felipe, Gto. was constructed to protect the road from New Spain northwards to the mining centers against Indian attack. To the first five preliminary conclusions we can now add the following:

6 The buildings of the mendicant orders are a typically rural phenomenon, found in areas with large Indian populations.

7 Typically urban monuments are the buildings of the women's regular orders, the secondary men's orders, the secular church, and the works of civil architecture.

8 The works of military architecture show little or no connection with population distribution, but are located at strategic points of trade, where there was danger of attack from outside the colonial territory (pirates and unpacified Indians).

9 There is a stronghold of secular Church activity in the vicinity of Puebla-Tlaxcala, apparently related to a high proportion of Spanish residents in the area, both in the towns and in the countryside.

Architecture and demography: temporal aspect

In the already cited inventory of colonial monuments, we have collected data on the building campaigns. We have arranged these data per decade, as Kubler has done for the mendicant orders during the sixteenth century.[11] The data can be analysed per district, per place and per type of building. In this way we can graph building activity for regions, urban centers and different types of buildings. These chronological graphs can be compared with graphs of demographic trends during the same period for comparable geographical units. The results of this comparison point strongly in the direction of a direct relation between building activity and demographic fluctuations.

Graph 1 provides the comparison of total building activity for all of present-day Mexico with the population trend observed in the districts for which we have comparable data. It shows that between 1570 and 1800, building activity at the colonial sites closely reflects the overall demographic trend. Beginning in the 1520s, building activity rose sharply until a peak was reached during the 1560s. Beginning in the 1570s, a saturation level would seem to have been reached: demand for new monumental building would seem to have collapsed, since a catastrophic decline in Indian population was taking place at the same time.[12] The dramatic rise in building activity during the period 1520s-1560s is followed by an equally rapid decline from the 1570s onwards. An absolute low in building activity is registered for the period 1630s-1650s. This coincides with the period during which the total population of New Spain reached its lowest point: the decade of the 1640s saw the culmination of the drastic depopulation of New Spain which followed the Conquest. After mid-seventeenth century a slow recovery is observed in population, which is faithfully reproduced in a gradual recovery in the level of building activity which lasts until late in the eighteenth century.

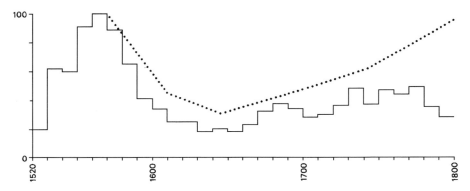

Graph 1 *Indices, population and building activity, 1520-1800 (1570 = 100; solid line is building activity per decade; dotted line is population index)*

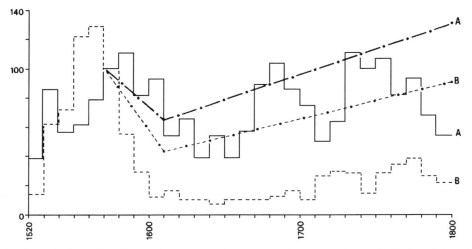

Graph 2 *Indices of building activity and total population for eight 'urbanized' districts (A) and for all other districts (B) (dotted line is population index; non-dotted line building activity; 1570 = 100)*

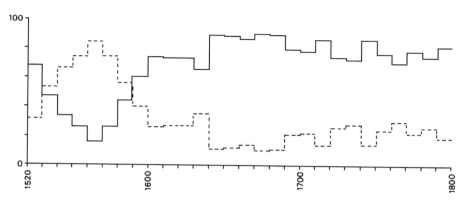

Graph 3 *Relative share in all building activity, 24 urban centers and areas outside urban centers, as a percentage of total (solid line is percentage for 24 urban centers; broken line is outside urban centers)*

We have seen that about half of the monuments in our lists were located in 24 urban centers, and about half outside them. It is possible to break total building activity per decade down into an urban and a rural component. Although it is not possible to isolate completely the urban segment of the population for comparison, we can get an idea of the population trend in the cities and in the countryside by contrasting the developments in eight districts with urban centers – Mexico, Puebla, Oaxaca, Veracruz, Cholula, Atlixco, Pátzcuaro, Morelia and Acámbaro – with the population trend outside these 'urbanized' districts. Graph 2 gives relief to the urban and rural components of the architectural and demographic trends.

The urban areas, centers of immigration from Europe and presumably the Mexican countryside, experienced a less serious net population decline during the first colonial century than the countryside. Moreover, during the period of population recovery which followed, the cities grew faster than the rural districts. Between about 1570 and 1600/1620, the urban districts lost some 35 percent of their population (net); in the rural districts the decline was considerably sharper, to less than half of the 1570 levels. While both rural and urban districts approximately doubled in population between 1600/1620 and 1800, the urban districts began their recovery from a higher base. The result was that in 1800 the population of the urban districts was about 30 percent higher than it had been in 1570, while that of the rural districts was about 10 percent lower.

The population trends are again reflected in the curves of building activity. Peak periods of building activity in the urban centers about 1580-1590 and about 1730-1780 correspond to relatively high population levels. The period of greatest architectural stagnation, about 1610-1670, corresponds to a time of demographic stagnation as well. In the non-urbanized districts, the demographic recovery was slower than in the more heavily settled ones. Levels of constructive activity also re-mained lower.

The net result of the two trends, one rural, the other urban, is an increasing im-portance of the urban centers – architecturally and demographically – at the cost of the rural areas, as the colonial period progresses. There is a clear tendency towards an ever greater concentration of monumental architecture within the cities, as may be seen in Graph 3. During the first 60 years most building activity takes place out-side the centers. For a half century (ca. 1530-1580), roughly three times as many monuments are under construction in the countryside as in the towns. The trend reaches a peak in the 1560s, when some 84 percent of the monuments under con-struction were outside the urban centers, and only 16 percent within them. In the later colonial period (seventeenth and eighteenth centuries), the roles are reversed: the share of urban building in the total hovers around 75 percent. The transition oc-curs between 1580 and 1600.

The rural-urban transition is paralleled by a contemporaneous transition in the types of buildings under construction. It will be remember that in the rural areas, the most important construction was carried out by the evangelizing mendicant or-ders, whose main activity took place during the sixteenth century. The period of mendicant expansion come to a close late in the sixteenth century, as Indian popula-tion levels declined, and the phase of conversion to Christianity exhausted itself. The phase of mendicant expansion had been characterized by animosity between the mendicant orders and the largely urban secular Church. Towards 1580, the religious conflict between the mendicants and seculars began to resolve itself clearly in favor of the seculars.[13]

This pattern also manifests itself in the graphs of building activity. Graph 4 shows that the three missionary orders experienced their period of greatest building activity between 1530 and 1590. (The curves for the orders separately run parallel). The absolute peak was reached by all three orders between 1550 and 1569. A steep decline began during the 1570s, and by 1600 few large building projects were being undertaken any more. Rock bottom would seem to have been reached during the mid-seventeenth century (ca. 1640-1670). Building activity after 1670 seems mainly to have consisted in additions and modifications to the large monastic complexes in the cities, and in some late foundations in remote or difficult-to-reach areas.

Whereas the sixteenth century, at least until the 1580s, belonged architecturally almost entirely to the mendicant orders, the secular branch of the Church only attained its greatest importance in the eighteenth century. For a century, beginning towards 1680, it entered a period of architectural productivity which outstripped that of its rivals: this is the age of the parish churches.[14] During the same period, the other urban religious bodies – the secondary men's orders and the women's or-ders – also experienced their apogee. If the graphs of building activity of the mendi-cant orders are combined and contrasted with those of the urban religious bodies, one can follow the comparative fortunes of these 'opposed' parties within the Church. This has been done in Graph 4. The two curves are in almost complete disagreement. Building activity among the mendicants shows an opposed trend to that of the urban ecclesiastical branches.

The shift in architectural production within the church, which mirrors a demographic shift as well, had consequences for the evolution of artistic styles. The most recent general style periodization for Mexican colonial architecture is that of Baird.[15] He discerns six periods between 1530 and about 1790. It is possible to re-encounter these six periods on the basis of Graph 4, which shows shifts in the relative intensity of architectural activity between the two main religious groups of which we have been speaking. The comparison is made in Table 4.

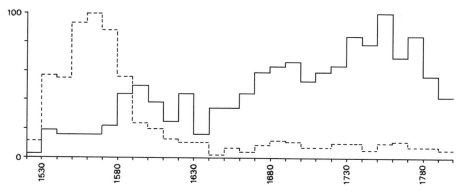

Graph 4 *Relative levels of building activity, mendicant orders as against secular Church, women's orders and secondary men's orders (indices; decade of peak activity = 100; solid line is secular Church, etc.; broken line is mendicant orders)*

Table 4 *Relative levels of building activity, mendicant orders as against secular Church, women's orders and secondary men's orders (see Graph 4), and comparison with Baird's style periodization*

Period	Relative level of building activity		Style period according to Baird
	Regular [*]	Secular [*]	
1530-1580	high	low	'Gothic survivals and plateresque'
1580-1630	moderate, falling	moderate	'Herreran and early baroque'
1630-1680	low	moderate, rising	'Assimilation of baroque'
1680-1730	low	high	'Baroque developments (*salamónica* era)'
1730-1780	low	peak	'Late baroque (*estípite* era)'
1780-1800	low	falling	'Late baroque with rococo elements'

[*] Regular = Franciscan, Dominican and Augustinian orders; Secular includes women's orders and secondary men's orders

The great stylistic transition occurs towards the end of the sixteenth century, from gothic and plateresque towards a classicizing 'baroque', the further development of which lasts for the rest of the colonial period. The great religious transition is from the mendicant orders towards the secular Church: expressed in terms of architectural production, the critical moment in this transition coincides precisely with the stylistic transition. The decline of the mendicant orders in favor of the secular Church is connected to the native depopulation which took place at the same time.[16]

Regional variants

For large areas and over long periods of time, architectural activity and population run parallel. But when we look at the smaller regions, the districts, there are marked deviations. In some districts population increase did not lead to new architectural activity, but in others building activity rose in the seventeenth or eighteenth century while population levels remained stable. Is there any pattern in these deviations?

Considered apart on the basis of building activity and population curve, the 129 districts follow a small number of characteristic patterns. With respect to building activity there are five varieties: (A) building activity during the sixteenth century only, (B) most building activity during the sixteenth century, but some activity later in the colonial period (seventeenth or eighteenth century), (C) eighteenth-century monuments only (mirror image of 'A'), (D) most construction during eighteenth century, but some earlier (mirror image of 'B'), and (E) building activity spanning all three colonial centuries.

From the demographic side, one may distinguish two families of districts. As we have seen, most areas of New Spain experienced a sharp decline in population between 1570 and 1620, as a result of the great mortality among the Indians. From the mid-seventeenth century to 1800, the population of New Spain as a whole increased. In 1800 the total population of the entire territory approached the 1570 level. This was not, however, the case in each district. In one family of districts there was substantial population recovery or even net growth (population in 1800 = 80-100 percent or more of the 1570 population). A second group of districts stabilized at substantially lower population levels in 1800 than they had had in 1570 (population in 1800 = 50 percent or less of the 1570 population).

Combining the demographic and architectural criteria there are theoretically ten possibilities, of which eight are actually found (Table 5).

Map 6 shows the distribution of the different types of districts. The G.2 districts contain the largest colonial cities: Mexico, Puebla, Veracruz. The G.2 districts are satellite towns, just outside the centers: Tacuba, Cholula, Cuautitlan. The G-districts are geographically small, but contain large numbers of monuments: they are the central districts of New Spain.

Table 5 *Eight types of districts, building activity and population curve*

Type	Building activity	Population
A	sixteenth-century only	no recovery
B	sixteenth-century only	population recovery or net growth
C	mainly sixteenth-century, but some seventeenth or eighteenth century	no recovery
D	mainly sixteenth-century, but some seventeenth or eighteenth century	population recovery or net growth
E	eighteenth century only	net growth
F	mainly eighteenth century, but some sixteenth or seventeenth century	net growth
G.1 [a]	all three centuries	no recovery
G.2 [a]	all three centuries	net growth

[a] Although the G.1 and G.2 districts are greatly different from each other demographically, they are economically and geographically inextricable, as will become apparent. With respect to chronology of building activity they are also similar. Actually, the G.1 districts turn out to be the (largely Indian) suburbs or satellite-towns of the G.2 distriscts, which are the major cities. Thus this shorthand nomenclature.

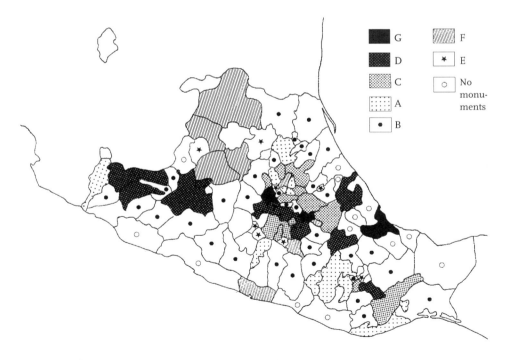

Map 6 *Different types of districts, based on building chronology and population trend*

Just to the south of the G-clusters of Mexico and Puebla-Cholula, an arc of D-districts bridges the gap between them. In these districts, there were important population concentrations and a highly developed agriculture dating from the pre-Columbian period. To the south-east there are D-districts at Oaxaca and Mitla. Other districts of the same configuration are found in the west, in the region of Guadalajara-Sayula and in Michoacán. The D-districts contain a number of colonial urban centers: Oaxaca, Atlixco, Morelia, Pátzcuaro and perhaps Guadalajara among them.

If one now imagines the G and D-districts joining the metropoli of Mexico and Puebla as one geographical entity, one sees to the north and the south a layer of C-districts clustered around this entity. The C-districts exhibit a pattern of building activity which is indistinguishable from that of the D-districts. The difference between the two is in their demographic development. Whereas the D-districts experienced average net growth in total population between 1570 and 1800, the C-districts never recovered the demographic importance they had had before the demographic catastrophe of the sixteenth century. It is as if the C-districts ceded part of their population to the D and/or G-districts during the colonial period. The C-districts are all in close proximity to the more central G and D-districts. Two C-districts are also found outside Oaxaca. There are few urban centers in the C-districts: Tlaxcala, Cuernavaca, Tepeaca.

Taken together, the G, D and C-districts closely approximate the areas which have been identified as islands of high concentration of Indian population and intensive architectural activity during the colonial period.

About the G, D and C-districts are grouped the A-districts. The A-districts, like the C-districts, lost population between 1570 and 1800. Whereas the C-districts still produced monumental architecture after 1600, however, all building activity recorded for the A-districts took place before that date. There are no urban centers of importance in the A-districts.

Still further from the central districts are the relatively isolated B-districts. Here, all recorded building activity also took place during the sixteenth century; in contrast to the A-districts, however, the B-districts had higher populations in 1800 than in 1570.

Outside the B-districts, mostly along the coasts, one finds the districts with no colonial monuments at all in the inventory. The different types of districts define a system of concentric layers or circles. At the center(s) are the islands of population and architectural production. As one moves outwards from the center, towards the periphery, the chronology of building activity shortens. Population recovery after 1620 was also more rapid at the center than towards the periphery.

The E and F-districts fall outside the system of concentric circles. They are scattered about the colony at varying distances from the central districts. In the north, however, there is a cluster of E and F-districts which practically monopolizes this part of the country, which was heavily identified with the mining of metals. Architecturally, they were late bloomers, with most or all of their building activity in the eighteenth century.

For almost all of the 129 districts we have data on total population about 1570, 1620 and 1800.[17] We can correlate the numbers of monuments with population for each type of district for these three years.

Table 6 *Population and numbers of colonial monuments, different types of districts (in descending order, from central to peripheral)*

Type	Average population per district			Monuments per district	Average population per monument		
	1570	1620	1800		1570	1620	1800
G (6 districts)	38,299	33,470	53,407	46.0	833	728	1,161
D (18 districts)	31,268	14,036	34,039	7.6	4,108	1,844	4,472
C (12 districts)	67,735	21,381	32,776	7.4	9,133	2,883	4,419
A (12 districts)	37,915	17,918	12,663	3.8	9,890	4,674	3,303
B (39 districts)	21,014	8,526	23,715	1.9	11,075	4,493	12,499
No monuments (21 districts)	8,992	3,796	13,865	0.0	-	-	-
Outside system of concentric circles							
F (8 districts)	19,168[a]	6,570[a]	38,699	12.0	2,282[a]	782[a]	3,224
E (8 districts)	13,393[b]	3,966[b]	15,246	3.0	11,480[b]	3,399[b]	5,082

[a] Data for 5 districts only
[b] Data for 6 districts only

As one moves from the centers towards the peripheral regions, the districts become geographically larger, but demographically less important; in other words, the population becomes sparser. The same can be said of the number of monuments, whose density declines even more rapidly than that of the population. The number of persons required to raise one monument increases.

According to the above criteria, the F-districts would occupy a central position with respect to the E-districts. Where E and F-districts are found together, as in the north of New Spain, the E-districts might be regarded as the periphery of the F-districts. Based on the above, we can add 5 points to the general conclusions:

10 There is a demographic shift during the colonial period in favor of the cities and the non-tributary (non-Indian) population, at the relative expense of the countryside and the tributary population.

11 The demographic shift is reflected in the architectural production: during the sixteenth century most monumental construction took place in the countryside; during the eighteenth century building activity in the cities reached its climax.

12 Parallel to these two developments, a shift in the church took place which favored the secular branch, the women's regular orders and the secondary men's regular orders at the expense of the major regular orders: Franciscan, Dominican and Augustinian.

13 The changing relations within the church influenced the development of artistic styles in colonial Mexico.

14 On the basis of building chronology and population trend we can distinguish a number of different groups of districts, each with its own characteristic pattern. The different types of districts are arranged in concentric layers of irregular form. As one moves away from the centers towards the periphery of the system of concentric layers, the density of population decreases, as does the number of monuments per district and the number of monuments *per capita*. The period of architectural productivity becomes progressively shorter as one leaves the central districts for the periphery. The demographic recovery after about 1620 was more vibrant in the centers than towards the periphery.

Economic activities in the different types of districts

The fact that there is a pattern to the local and regional variations from the general agreement found between building activity and demographic fluctuations for Mexico as a whole proves that the deviations are not to be blamed on faulty data, but answer to some other, non-demographic explanation. What accounts for these differences? Since the monuments that serve as our base material were costly to build, it is not far-fetched to search for some relation between their construction and the regional sources of economic wealth. Little is known about the conjunctural history of Mexico during the colonial period; perhaps the history of Mexico's architectural monuments can fill in a part of the void.

In their geographic descriptions, López de Velasco and Vázquez de Espinosa compiled profuse and detailed data on many aspects of life in the Indies, and thus also in Mexico.[18] They may be supplemented by similar information on economic activities registered by Vetancurt at the end of the seventeenth century for Franciscan settlements within the boundaries of that order's *Provincia del Santo Evangelio*.[19] The writers only tell us that one or another economic activity is practiced. We have no way of knowing how it fared. Further, it is impossible to say whether a given economic activity was prevalent during a long or short period of time. There are reasons to believe that the range of colonial economic activities had a rather static character, determined in large measure by factors that were not susceptible of great fluctuations.

When the data on economic activities are collected and arranged according to the same district system we have been using, it is possible to sketch an economic profile of each of the groups of districts as distinguished above. The groups of districts, distinguished on the basis of population and building activity, turn out to be distinguishable on the basis of their economic activities as well (Table 7).

Table 7 *Economic activities mentioned for districts belonging to the system of concentric circles, by type*

	No monuments	B	A	C	D	G	Total
	Number of districts, by type						
Total number of districts	21 19%	39 36%	12 11%	12 11%	18 17%	6 6%	108 100%
Number of districts with:							
Mining, quarries	8 29%	9 32%	5 18%	2 7%	2 7%	2 7%	28 100%
Livestock	14 25%	16 29%	7 13%	7 13%	9 16%	3 5%	56 101%
Cacao	4 80%	1 20%	-	-	-	-	5 100%
Pulque	- -	- -	2 50%	1 25%	-	1 25%	4 100%
Sugar	8 31%	9 35%	2 8%	2 8%	5 19%	-	26 101%
Maize	4 13%	7 22%	2 6%	7 22%	6 19%	6 19%	32 101%
Wheat	1 5%	3 14%	1 5%	6 29%	6 29%	4 19%	21 101%
Frijol, lenteja or unspecified *cosechas*	1 20%	1 20%	-	1 20%	1 20%	1 20%	5 100%
Harbors	1 13%	4 50%	2 25%	-	-	1 13%	8 101%
Cochineal or indigo	1 13%	2 25%	1 13%	2 25%	-	1 25%	8 101%
Silk culture, cotton growing or wool	2 18%	4 36%	-	2 18%	2 18%	1 9%	11 99%
Fishing	2 15%	4 31%	-	-	4 31%	3 23%	13 100%
Salt	2 33%	-	-	-	2 33%	2 33%	6 99%
Fruit	-	4 27%	-	2 13%	3 20%	6 40%	15 100%
Market or trade	-	2 15%	-	1 8%	5 38%	5 38%	13 99%
Obrejas, *textiles*	-	3 27%	-	2 18%	3 27%	3 27%	11 99%
Lime ovens	-	-	-	1 100%	-	-	1 100%
Vegetables, garden produce	-	-	-	1 14%	3 43%	3 43%	1 100%

Table 7 *Continued*

	Number of districts, by type						
	No mon-uments	B	A	C	D	G	Total
Number of districts with:							
Leather goods, finished	-	-	-	-	1	-	1
	-	-	-	-	100%	-	100%
Ducks	-	-	-	-	1	1	2
	-	-	-	-	50%	50%	100%
Chocolate	-	-	-	-	1	-	1
	-	-	-	-	100%	-	100%
Purga and *zarzaparrilla*	-	-	-	-	1	-	1
	-	-	-	-	100%	-	100%
Soap	-	-	-	-	1	1	2
	-	-	-	-	50%	50%	100%
Oficios (carpenters, smiths, ceramists)	-	-	-	-	2	4	6
	-	-	-	-	33%	67%	100%
Rosaries	-	-	-	-	1	-	1
	-	-	-	-	100%	-	100%
Flower export (to México)	-	-	-	-	1	-	1
	-	-	-	-	100%	-	100%
Tobacco cultivation	-	-	-	-	-	1	1
	-	-	-	-	-	100%	100%
Sulphur	-	-	-	-	-	1	1
	-	-	-	-	-	100%	100%
Watermills	-	-	-	-	-	1	1
	-	-	-	-	-	100%	100%
Biscuits (biscocho)	-	-	-	-	-	1	1
	-	-	-	-	-	100%	100%
Knives	-	-	-	-	-	1	1
	-	-	-	-	-	100%	100%
Wood, charcoal	-	-	-	-	-	1	1
	-	-	-	-	-	100%	100%
Ceramics and ceramic tiles	-	-	-	-	-	4	4
	-	-	-	-	-	100%	100%
Glass	-	-	-	-	-	2	2
	-	-	-	-	-	100%	100%
Processed fruit (*conservas*)	-	-	-	-	-	1	1
	-	-	-	-	-	100%	100%
Printing presses	-	-	-	-	-	2	2
	-	-	-	-	-	100%	100%
Total number of activities mentioned	12	14	8	14	21	28	97
	12%	14%	8%	14%	22%	29%	99%

What is important in distinguishing the economic character of each type of district is less the specific economic activities present, than the range and variety of economic functions represented. The peripheral districts have the shortest lists of products; the central districts have the greatest variety. The most outstanding characteristic of the central districts is the degree of economic differentiation. The peripheral zones, by contrast, tend towards monoculture. The least differentiated districts are those of the outer rings of the system of concentric circles, the A and B-districts, and the districts with no recorded monuments The B-districts and the districts without monuments, with 55 percent of the districts, only account for 26 percent of the variety of economic activities At the other extreme, the G-districts, only 6 percent of the total number, account for 29 percent of the activities mentioned In between, the C and D-districts show a relatively high degree of economic differentiation, while the A-districts are somewhat under-represented.

All the different types of districts have a few basic agricultural or mineral activities, but only the most highly diversified among them have such specialized commercial activities as the fabrication of glass or ceramics, or the printing of books. At an intermediate level one finds a lesser degree of sophistication: *obrajes* for the manufacture of textiles, and ovens for the preparation of lime.

We have tried to gain an impression of the specific economic characteristics of each type of district by comparing the share in each activity with the share in the total number of districts. If the share in the economic activity is higher, then that product or trade would seem to be especially characteristic for the type of district.

A large number of B-districts and those without monuments have a coastline and a tropical climate, factors which led in all the Caribbean to the establishment of sugar and cacao plantations. In Mexico the B-districts and the districts without monuments practically monopolized the coasts, and account for all the districts where cacao is mentioned as a product, and two-thirds of the sugar. Other characteristic activities have to do with the sea; there are harbors and fishing, and salt is won. We have seen that population was sparse in these districts. Correspondingly there is little mention of markets, the intensive forms of agriculture – horticulture, fruit growing –, and the main food crops, maize and wheat, are under-represented. Livestock and mining are about proportionately represented.

Moving inwards towards the more central districts we arrive first in the A-districts, which are characterized by a seemingly undifferentiated and labor-extensive agriculture, in which the cultivation of the maguey-cactus (pulque) and cattle are important. Mining and the production of dye-stuffs are supplementary activities, although there is no evidence that either ever flourished in the A-districts. There are at least two harbors, although here again it is doubtful if they were used much. Arable farming suffered instead of benefitting from the presence of cattle. The two activities were not coordinated, as at Zempoala, for instance, where cattle ran loose to the detriment of the crops: ' ... *hay más de quince ranchos ... y haciendas de cría de*

ganado, vacas y yeguas, a cuya causa es poco lo sembrado'.[20] The raising of livestock was
a European innovation in America. The pre-Columbian civilizations had no cows,
horses, mules, swine, goats, etc. In the A-districts, where the raising of livestock was
not coordinated with arable farming, its introduction must have had a detrimental
effect on the population, since arabe farming is the more labor-intensive activity,
and can support a larger population. In effect, we have seen that the A-districts suffered an irreversible population loss during the colonial period. We may hypothesize
that the A-districts, with their deteriorated agricultural prospects, supplied migrants
for the more centrally located zones. It is possible that cattle came to replace people
in the A-districts during the colonial period.

Continuing our journey inwards from the periphery we arrive next in the C-
districts. They are characterized by a greater diversity of economic activities than the
A-districts. Wheat, a European crop, is the most characteristic agricultural product,
followed by pulque, maize and beans. The C-districts are fertile growing areas;
Vetancurt speaks twice of '*tierra muy fértil*' (Cuernavaca and Tepeaca). There is some
irrigation, as at Tepeji del Río, which also has '*tierra fértil*'.[21] Livestock has lost much
of its relative importance, in favor of the main food crops. Moreover, in contrast to
the A-districts, there seems to be some coordination between livestock and arable
farming. There is more emphasis on small animals (pigs) and less on cattle. Here
we also find reference to the more intensive forms of agriculture: horticulture and
fruit growing. There is some primitive industry: lime ovens and textile workshops,
which process locally grown fibers and use locally produced dyes. The C-districts,
which were very populous during the sixteenth century, nevertheless lost their original demographic importance. About 1800 population levels averaged only half of
what they had been in 1570.

In close proximity to, or containing, the urban centers are the D-districts. They
are still more diversified economically. In agriculture the most intensive forms pre-
vail. The most characteristic agricultural products are vegetables, both native and
European, wheat, fruit and beans, although maize and sugar are also grown, along
with silk and cotton. The lands are fertile – Atlixco has '*las mejoras tierras de Nueva
Espana*'[22] – and intensively worked, as at Xochimilco, where land was scarce. In the
latter place farming was done on artificial floating islands, the *chinampas*. Several of
these districts have fresh-water fishing; the practice survives in the traditional form
today on the lakes of Pátzcuaro, Chapala and Cuitzeo. Trade is important; there are
markets in at least five districts. Xochimilco exported flowers and vegetables 'by
boatloads' to Mexico City, and its residents '*pudieran ser de los más ricos, si como todos
no lo gastaran en beber*'.[23] Ducks were kept, and the residents of Chalco hunted frogs.
Specialized professions are noted, especially for Xochimilco, where beds, windows,
boxes and doors were made for export to Mexico City. Oaxaca was known for its fra-
grant rosaries of *coyol*. Textiles, soap and leather goods are among the other products
mentioned for one or more of the D-districts.

At the top of the colonial economic pyramid, and at the center of the system of concentric circles, are the largest urban centers themselves, the G-districts. Whereas the districts dealt with until now produced mainly for local or regional markets, the centers of Mexico City, Puebla and Veracruz were directly involved in intercontinental trade as well. They were also the centers of European migration to New Spain. Here economic diversification reached its climax. With the exception of the plantation products, sugar and cacao, the economic activities found in other districts are found for the G-districts as well. In addition, there is a whole row of activities not found elsewhere: watermills, the manufacture of knives, ceramic tiles in Andalusian style, printing presses. The accent is more than ever on labor-intensive agriculture and on non-agricultural production and trade. Everything having to do with a complicated production process or technology is characteristic of the G-districts; there is consequently a high degree of specialization of labor. There are many professions. The most characteristic agricultural products are vegetables and fruit. Less prevalent are the main food crops: beans, maize and wheat, which were characteristic of the C-districts in particular. Although there is livestock, it is the least characteristic economic activity, along with mining, of the G-districts. These activities were seen to be typical of the periphery.

There remain the E and F-districts to be considered. We have seen that they fall outside the system of concentric circles, and that they are concentrated in the north, in the vicinity of the mines. On the basis of population and building activity we hypothesized that the E-districts might be considered the periphery of the F-districts. This hypothesis is confirmed by the distribution of economic activities (Table 8).

Table 8 *Economic activities mentioned for the E and F-districts*

| | *Number of districts, by type* | | | |
	E	*F*	*Others**	*Total*
Total number of districts	8	8	108	124
	6%	6%	87%	99%
Number of districts with:				
Mining, quarries	7	4	28	39
	18%	10%	72%	100%
Livestock	1	6	56	63
	2%	10%	89%	101%
Sugar	1	-	26	27
	4%	-	96%	100%
Cacao	-	1	5	6
	-	17%	83%	100%
Maize	-	2	32	34
	-	6%	94%	100%
Wheat	-	2	21	23
	-	9%	91%	100%

Table 8 *Continued*

	Number of districts, by type			
	E	F	Others*	Total
Total number of districts	8	8	108	124
	6%	6%	87%	99%
Number of districts with:				
Unspecified cocechas	-	1	5	6
	-	17%	83%	100%
Cotton	-	1	11	12
	-	8%	92%	100%
Harbors	-	1	8	9
	-	11%	89%	100%
Fishing	-	1	13	14
	-	7%	93%	100%
Fruit	-	3	15	18
	-	17%	83%	100%
Market	-	2	13	15
	-	13%	87%	100%
Obrajes, textiles	-	2	11	13
	-	15%	85%	100%
Garden produce	-	1	7	8
	-	13%	87%	100%
Leather goods	-	1	1	2
	-	50%	50%	100%
salt	-	1	6	7
	-	14%	86%	100%
Vineyards	-	2	-	2
	-	100%	-	100%
Total number of	3	16	97	116
activities mentioned	3%	14%	84%	101%

* District types G, D, C, A, B and districts without monuments (from Table 6).

In terms of economic differentiation, the E-districts resemble the most peripheral zones of the system of concentric circles: the B-districts and those without monuments. Whereas these latter tended towards monoculture (the plantation economy), the E-districts tend towards mono-industry: mining. The undifferentiated mining districts had a boom-bust economy depending on the discovery and exploitation of new lodes. Their architectural monuments, while few in number, were sometimes spectacular, witness the parish church of San Sebastián y Santa Prisca at Taxco or San Cayetano at Valenciana, outside Guanajuato. Only one of these districts is mentioned as raising its own livestock (Guanajuato), and it is far and away the richest of the E-districts in architectural production.

We have seen that mining is an activity associated with peripheral zones, and so it is in the north of New Spain as well, although the mines were a great source of wealth. The F-districts are much more diversified than the E-districts, and profited perhaps less from the mines they possessed themselves, than from the proximity to the E-district mines. In the F-districts mining is an important activity, but less so than in the E-districts. More characteristic are activities associated with the supply of agricultural and other products to the mines: wine and leather goods in the first place, but also food crops, livestock, textiles, vegetables, salt and fruit. The important urban centers in the F-districts grew up as commercial centers in these products: Querétaro, San Miguel de Allende, Acámbaro. With regard to their degree of economic differentiation, the F-districts fall somewhere between the G and D-districts in the system of concentric circles. This is also the case with regard to their numbers of colonial monuments. Thus in the mining economy of New Spain we can distinguish a group of central districts (F) and a periphery (E), just as in the more agrarian regions. We can summarize the above reasoning and add it to our list of conclusions:

15 On the basis of building chronology, population trend and economic differentiation we can distinguish a central group of districts, a middle group and a peripheral group. A rough economic profile of the three groups shows the following: CENTER (district types G, D, F). High degree of economic differentiation (26 percent of the districts with 56 percent of the economic activities). Characteristic economic activities: labor-intensive agriculture (horticulture, fruit growing), industry, technology, wheat, commerce. MIDDLE GROUP (district types C, A). Moderate level of economic differentiation (19 percent of the districts with 19 percent of the economic activities). Characteristic economic activities: food crops (maize, wheat), livestock pulque. PERIPHERY (district types B, E and districts without monuments). Tendency towards monoculture or mono-industry (55 percent of the districts with 25 percent of the activities). Characteristic activities: plantation economy (sugar, cacao), mining.

Conjuncture

Following the distinction made between Center, Middle Group and Periphery , it is possible to arrive at some hypotheses concerning the economic consequences of the colonization of Mexico for the different zones. Was the arrival of Europeans in Mexico a stimulus in the long run or a retarding factor? Among the great changes brought by the colonists we can mention the following: (a) demographic changes consisting on the negative side in the epidemics and mortality among the Indians during the early colonial period, and on the positive side by the immigration of Europeans and African slaves; (b) the systematic exploitation of the mines; (c) the introduction of intercontinental maritime commerce; (d) the introduction of livestock breeding; (e) the introduction of wheat as a food crop; (f) the introduction of the plantation economy (sugar and cacao). Mortality among the Indians before 1620 was devastating everywhere. Our data cover the period 1570-1620, and show that the total population in all the different types of districts declined by one-half to two-thirds in this 50-year period. Although we can expect mortality from the epidemics to have been higher in the largest urban centers (G-districts), the net population decline was less severe than elsewhere, only about one-fifth. We have no data on immigration to the G-districts, so we can only surmise that death from disease between 1570 and 1620 in the largest cities was to a large degree compensated by immigration from Europe and the surrounding regions. We do know that the largest numbers of Spanish immigrants settled in the G-districts.

Mexico's total population grew in the period 1620 to 1800, but the rise in population levels only took place in the centers and in the periphery. No demographic recovery took place in the districts belonging to the middle group. The question is why, and we believe that the answer has to do with two other changes resulting from the colonization.

We have seen that the most characteristic economic activities of the colonial middle group were the food crops and livestock raising. Among the food crops wheat had a certain predominance, especially in the C-districts. Wheat and livestock were Spanish innovations in these once heavily populated districts. We may suppose that maize had been the original staple upon which the high original populations were dependent. Wheat and livestock are land-hungry forms of agriculture, with lower yields than maize. It is logical then that to the extent that these activities were introduced, the human population had to decline to a lower level, which is what happened. Whereas in the C-districts the introduction of wheat and cattle must have led to some kind of wealth – in these districts we have notice of building activity later in the colonial period without any accompanying growth in population – in the A-districts the introduction of cattle in particular seems to have been purely destructive. The colonial period saw a heightened regional division of labor which allowed the centers to reach new highs in population and wealth, but which caused population decline in the regions specialized in wheat and cattle. It is probable that the A and C-districts supplied migrants to the centers in view of the contracting economic possibilities at home, and that this is one of the explanations why the net population decline in the cities was not as serious as elsewhere.

The most intensive exploitation of the mines took place in the E and F-districts, and especially in the sparsely populated north. There were also mines elsewhere, especially in the A-districts and those without monuments, but there mining was on a much smaller scale. The prosperity of the important mining centers came in the second half of the eighteenth century. This can be seen in the graphs of building activity, where peaks of architectural productivity are seen to be reached between 1750 and 1790. Levels of building activity responded rapidly to new *bonanzas* in the mines. A recent study of *Real de Catorce* shows that a flurry of construction of roads, bridges and churches followed on the heels of new discoveries.[24] Why should mining activity increase at different places at the same time? The answer is to be found in the large capital investments which were necessary to get a mine into operation. Sustained and intensive mining depended upon the construction of deep shafts and adits for drainage. The construction of a deep shaft 'cost as much as to build a factory or a church'. To penetrate to deep levels, gunpowder was needed. In Guanajuato this technique was not introduced until the 1720s. In Zacatecas its application was still limited in the early 1730s: in 1732 only 1,300 pounds of gunpowder were consumed. Yet all the great mines of the late eighteenth century depended on gunpowder blasting. The mining centers were thus dependent upon large initial capital investments, which would have to come from or through Mexico City or Puebla, the metropoli.[25] A relative capital surplus, upon which architectural investments depended as well, would thus have to appear in the metropoli first, and only somewhat later in the mining centers. This seems to have been what happened in the eighteenth century, as Table 9 shows. Eighteenth-century building activity was at a high level between 1730 and 1780 in Mexico City and Puebla. The high point was reached during the 1740s and 1750s. In the mining centers there is a ten-year lag. The period of heavy construction seems to fall between 1750 and 1790. We can also speculate on the consequences for the supply centers for the mines. The two largest supply centers without mines of their own were San Miguel de Allende and Acámbaro. There construction reached its peak in the decade of the 1770s.

Table 9 *Building activity at (a) Mexico City an Puebla (b) the mining centers of Zacatecas, Guanajuato, San Luis Potosí, Taxco, Valenciana and Rayas, and (c) the largest supply centers to the mines, San Miguel de Allende and Acámbaro*

Number of monuments under construction per decade								
1710-19	1720-29	1730-39	1740-49	1750-59	1760-69	1770-79	1780-89	1790-99
Mexico City and Puebla								
11	15	19	22	22	19	19	14	12
Mining centers								
3	0	0	3	4	4	4	4	2
Supply centers								
2	-	4	1	2	2	5	3	4

Especially in the sparsely populated north, the introduction of mining was thus a very great stimulus, but one which only reached its fullest development in the second half of the eighteenth century. The stimulating effect of mining can be seen in the population figures, not only or even mainly in the pure mining districts themselves (the E-districts, where population quadrupled between 1620 and 1800), but especially in the districts which sold supplies to the mines (the F-districts, where the supply function was more important, the population increase between 1620 and 1800 was sixfold). Mining was without a doubt the most dynamic economic activity during the colonial period, but it was also a risky one; the mining centers could experience a short period of great wealth, but they were rarely able to sustain one for long.

The introduction of intercontinental maritime trade probably had very little influence on the fortunes of most regions of New Spain. Puebla, Mexico and Veracruz (the G.1 districts) were the only districts directly involved. All three centers grew between 1570 and 1800. The population growth of Veracruz was the most dramatic: it was six times as large in 1800 as in 1570. Among the districts indirectly affected were the E, F and B-districts and the districts without monuments; the former two provided precious metals, and the latter two plantation products for export by sea. In all of these districts population rose between 1570 and 1800. The existence of intercontinental trade was thus of importance for the centers and the periphery. Its significance for the middle group and the D-districts is doubtful. In the middle group population levels fell during the colonial period.

Finally, the introduction of the plantation economy at the periphery was a stimulating factor. Population levels rose during the colonial period. Although they rose, the periphery remained, relatively speaking, a cultural and demographic backwater. Population levels could not compete with those near the centers, and there was little or no town life. There were very few religious institutions, and monumental architecture was largely lacking. Summarizing, we have the following points for the list of conclusions:

16 Following the demographic catastrophe, which lasted into the seventeenth century, the centers and the periphery benefited in terms of population from the colonial system, while the middle group suffered a permanent setback.

17 The economic benefits of the systematic exploitation of the mines were not confined to the mines, but were especially stimulating for the economies of the supply districts to the mines.

18 The changes introduced into the economy by the colonists were neither wholly beneficial nor wholly detrimental. Benefits in one region must be weighed off against damage to another. The good in the introduction of animals as sources of leather, meat and energy for transportation must be weighed off against the bad in their occupation of the maize fields of the original population.

Four regional economies

Combining the network of overland communications with what we know of the districts – centers, middle group and periphery – we can refine and articulate our model of Mexico's colonial economy. Whereas in the sixteenth century monumental architectural activity is recorded for a very large area (district types G, D, C, A, B, and some F), by the seventeenth and eighteenth centuries the colony had contracted, in terms of architectural production, to include only the G, D, C and F zones. Districts where new activity took place were the mining centers (E), mainly in the north. The contraction in most areas, and the expansion towards the north were the results of the decline in Indian population, a progressive concentration of population in the central districts, and the intensive mining of the eighteenth century.

Table 10 *Four regional economies of New Spain*

	1 Mexico	2 S. Miquel	3 Oaxaca	4 Guadaljara	Periphery
District types:					
G	6	-	-	-	-
F	3	4	-	-	I
D	10	3	2	3	-
C	10	-	2	-	-
A	6	-	5	I	-
B	-	-	-	-	39
E	-	-	-	-	8
No mons.	-	-	-	-	21
Total	35	7	9	4	69
Urban Centers	Mexico	S. Miguel	Oaxaca	Guadalajara	Guanajuato
	Puebla	Acámbaro			
	Cholula	S. Luis Potosí			
	Veracruz	Morelia			
	Atlixco	Pátzquaro			
	Pachuca	Querétaro			
	Tlaxcala				
	Cuernavaca				
	Otumba				
	Tepeaca				
Total Population:					
1570	1,637,231	-	296,112	-	1,095,865
1620	704,915	-	156,614	-	437,969
1800	1,167,781	383,131	146,850	-	1,346,271
Total number of monuments	415	132	41	28	100

If the centers contracted during the colonial period, the periphery grew; in the seventeenth and eighteenth centuries there was – at least in terms of our inventory – no building activity in the B and A-districts. There are four centers; three of them have middle-group appendages. They correspond to a large degree with the original tributary population islands of ca. 1570. The old population island of Michoacán has grown towards the north under the influence of the mines, and Mexico-Puebla now has its route to the sea, Veracruz. We can distinguish the four regional economies and gain an impression of their relative importance and degree of differentiation.

We see that the magnitude and degree of differentiation in the types of districts represented decreases with distance from the central region, Mexico-Puebla.

Each region has its own network of roads. The most elaborate road systems are in the most extensive and differentiated regions. Mexico's is the densest, followed by that of San Miguel. The road systems of Oaxaca and Guadalajara are more simple. Within the regional entities, the road systems are densest in the central districts, and thin out in the middle group. In the peripheries there are few overland communication routes. Between the four regional economic entities there are only one or two connecting routes; thus if one wishes to travel from Mexico to Oaxaca there is no choice of itinerary. Within each region, the network of roads has consequences for the economic differentiation of the region. We have spoken of concentric circles, in which the inner circles are characterized by high levels of population concentration, intensive agriculture, intensive religious and architectural activity, large variety of professions, etc. As one moves out towards the periphery, population levels decline as do the other criteria. In reality, however, the concentric circles are not circles at all, but resemble a pattern of contour lines, broken and distorted at points by the system of roads. In some respects the roads act as a centripetal influence; in others the influence is centrifugal. The best example is to be found in the A and C-districts to the north and south of Mexico-Puebla, where they are stretched out along the routes leading to (away from) the centers. The roads carried cattle and wheat further away from the centers, and must have acted as corridors of human migration towards the centers.

Notes to Chapter 6

* Published in *Jahrbuch für Geschichte von Staat, Wirtschaft und Gesellschaft Lateinamerikas*, 16 (1979) pp. 97-145.

1 A.C. van Oss, *Inventory of 861 Monuments of Mexican Colonial Architecture*, (Amsterdam 1978). All data used in the present article on the distribution and construction of Mexican colonial monuments are drawn from this source.

2 Peter Gerhard, *A guide to the Historical Geography of New Spain*, (Cambridge 1972).

3 The same procedure has been followed elsewhere: A.C. van Oss, 'Mendicant Expansion in New Spain and the Extent of the Colony' (sixteenth century), in *Boletín de Estudios Latinoamericanos y del Caribe*, no. 21 (1976), p. 42. Maps consulted here are those by Hector F. Esparza Torres, *Mapas de los Estados* (México: Patria) and the Atlas Euzkadi: *Caminos de México*, 2a impresión, (México 1966).

4   B.H. Slicher van Bath, 'De demografische ontwikkeling van Spaans Amerika in de koloniale tijd' in: B.H. Slicher van Bath en A.C. van Oss, *Geschiedenis van maatschappij en cultuur* (Baarn: Ambo, 1978) pp. 155-158.

5   Juan López de Velasco says that there were some 60,000 tributaries in Yucatán about 1574. *Geografía y descripción general de las Indias*, Biblioteca de Autores Españoles 248 (Madrid 1969) p. 126. See also S.F. Cook and W. Borah, *Essays in Population History*, (Berkeley, 1971, 1974) Vol. II, pp. 47-48.

6   Van Oss, 'Mendicant Expansion' p. 42.

7   Data on tributary population per district based on Gerhard, op. cit, as tabulated by B.H. Slicher van Bath, *Bevolking en economie in Nieuw Spanje, ca.1570-ca.1800*, (Amsterdam 1981) p. 215-219, totals on p. 67.

8   B.H. Slicher van Bath, op. cit., pp. 48-50, 225-231.

9   Robert Ricard, *The spiritual Conquest of Mexico*, trans. L.B. Simpson, (Berkeley and Los Angeles 1966), p. 239-263.

10 B.H. Slicher van Bath, *Spaans Amerika omstreeks 1600* (Utrecht 1979) Appendix 1, and 'De kolonisatie van het milieu: Europese flora en fauna in Latijns Amerika' in: B.H. Slicher van Bath en A.C. van Oss, *Geschiedenis van maatschappij en cultuur* pp. 196-197.

11 George Kubler, *Mexican Architecture of the Sixteenth Century*, (New Haven 1948; reprinted Westport, Conn., 1972) pp. 60-63.

12 Slicher van Bath, *De demografische ontwikkeling*, p. 144-155.

13 Van Oss, 'Mendicant Expansion', and Richard, loc. cit.

14 See the short text on p. 353 of the book by D.F. Rubín de la Borbolla, *México: monumentos históricos y arqueológicos*, Vol. 2, *México colonial y moderno* (México 1953).

15 J.A. Baird, Jr., *The Churches of Mexico 1530-1810* (Berkeley and Los Angeles 1962) p. 57.

16 Van Oss, 'Mendicant expansion'.

17 Slicher van Bath, *Bevolking en economie*, pp. 215-219 and 225-231.

18 López de Velasco, *Geografía*; Antonio Vázquez de Espinosa, *Compendio y descripción de las Indias Occidentales*, Biblioteca de Autores Españoles, 231 (Madrid 1969).

19 Fr. Agustín de Vetancurt, *Teatro Mexicano*, (México 1971; primera edición fascimilar).

20 Ibid., cuarta parte, ff. 70-74.

21 Ibid., cuarta parte, ff. 59, 60., 69.

22 Ibid., cuarta parte, f. 72.

23 Ibid., cuarta parte, f. 56.

24 Salvador Díaz-Berrio Fernández, *Real de Catorce*, SLP (México 1976) p.7-13.

25 D.A. Brading and H.E. Cross, 'Colonial Silver Mining: Mexico and Peru', in: *Hispanic American Historical Review (HAHR)* 52, no. 4 (1972), p. 545-579; M.F. Lang, 'New Spain's Mining Depression and the Supply of Quicksilver from Peru 1600-1700' in: *HAHR* 48, no. 4 (1968) p. 632-641.

7

The colonial city in Spanish America

Town life was not a Spanish innovation everywhere in America, but it certainly received a great impulse during the period following the Conquest. In contrast to other European colonizing powers, the Spanish seemed determined not only to establish a number of coastal enclaves based on the intercontinental trade of tropical plantation products, but to incorporate vast inland territories, and their inhabitants, within the ambit of their beloved Catholic Church, Castilian language, and newly united and universal Crown. The transplantation of European town life to the new territories was one of the modes of this determination.[1]

Pre-Columbian cities

Genuine cities, with concentrated permanent populations, are only known to have existed in Mexico and Peru during the pre-Columbian period. Most of the largest ones, however, had either been destroyed or abandoned long before the arrival of Europeans. The site of Teotihuacán, 46 kilometers to the northeast of present-day Mexico City, covers an area of about 22.5 square kilometers, of which 10 or 12 may be considered as having constituted a true urban core. By the time of the Conquest, however, it had been forgotten for centuries: Teotihuacán was abandoned toward AD 700 or 750. Although it had a well-defined ceremonial center consisting of a perfectly straight, fully paved esplanade 50 to 60 meters wide and 2.2 kilometers long lined by temples and pyramids (the largest having a basis of more than 200 meters to a side), the residential areas, which housed a peak population probably in the neighborhood of 85,000 persons, had no clearly defined street pattern. Houses adjoined one another or were only separated by narrow paths, sometimes no wider than 60 centimeters. The paths were more like unroofed corridors than streets. The overall impression is that of a blind labyrinth (Map 1, appendix[2]).[3] Pre-Columbian America knew neither the wheel nor – except for the Peruvian llama – the beast of burden. Wide and regular streets were thus uncommon.

The Aztec capital of Tenochtitlán, whose main temple lies buried just to one side of the massive colonial cathedral of the city of Mexico, was the largest inhabited city encountered by the Spaniards in America. The most widely accepted population for

1519, the year of its fall, used to be 300,000 (60,000 houses). Hardoy, who has tried to reconstruct the population level by multiplying the inhabited areas of the city by the probable population densities in different zones, comes to a much lower figure: between 62,000 and 166,000, probably nearer to the latter. Sanders prefers a population of around 90,000. Tenochtitlán was an island city, connected to the shores of Lake Texcoco by long causeways. It was the most important of a large number of indigenous urban centers on or near the shores of the lake (Map 2). Other central Mexican cities for which population estimates have been made are Texcoco (30,000 to 150,000 inhabitants), Coyoacán (6,000 houses), Huitzilopochco (5,000 houses), and Mexcaltzingo (4,000 houses).

Further to the east, important cities were Cholula (population between 38,000 and 100,000) and Tlaxcala. Very little is known about the original plans of these other centers, although in the case of Cholula at least, it seems to have been irregular. The Spanish, in any case, substituted a gridiron solution. According to Kubler, the 'regularization' of Cholula's original 'organic' plan was a gradual process which cost the Spanish many years to complete. Instead of suddenly leveling the existing buildings in order to start from scratch, the imposition of the gridiron plan was a kind of slow reform, lasting past the 1580s.

The densely populated lacustrine civilization of the Mexican Central Valley depended upon a highly intensive form of agriculture, the *chinampas* or floating gardens. As in other land-reclamation schemes, such as those of the fens in eastern England or the Dutch polders, land under cultivation invades the originally flooded areas. The plots which take form are of regular size and shape (in the case of the *chinampas*, rectangular, often about 100 meters long by 5 or 10 wide), and are separated by narrow canals, which serve as thorough-fares for the flat-bottomed canoes or boats of the farmers. Population pressure caused Tenochtitlán to expand rapidly in this way. Hardoy estimates that of the total surface area of the city around 1519 (about 1,200 to 1,500 hectares), only about 40 percent (480 to 600 hectares) was on the solid ground of the original islands. More than half of the city was thus composed of *chinampas*. Their regular form, and the need for a number of direct and navigable canals to handle the great volume of canoe traffic within the city (one estimate has it that the market of Tenochtitlán was serviced by a fleet of 50,000 canoes), led to a regular, almost orthogonal, city plan in which streets and canals ran parallel to, and alternated with one another (Maps 3 and 4).

The center of Tenochtitlán was defined by a large rectangular plaza punctuated by ceremonial buildings in the form of pyramids, cylindrical prisms, stairways and broad rectangular platforms. This part of the city was razed during and after the Spanish siege which led to the city's defeat. The stones of its temples seem to have been used partly as fill for some of the canals (wheeled transport and horses partly replace canoe traffic), and partly for the construction of the new colonial city. According to Kubler, there is a certain degree of continuity between the pre-Columbian and the colonial plans of Mexico City. This is no doubt due to the regularity of the Aztec system of *chinampas*, causeways, and canals. Indeed, some of the canals continued to be used into the nineteenth century, when Lake Texcoco was finally drained by means of a great tunnel.[4]

To the south, most of the so-called Mayan 'cities' were, in all probability, not true cities at all, but ceremonial centers with tiny permanent populations, surrounded and supported by large numbers of dispersed farms (*milpas*) and hamlets, whose main products were beans and maize. The centers were only inhabited by large numbers of people on specific occasions. The only permanent residents would have been priest and officials. The Mayan 'palaces' and temples of stone were of strictly limited use as residences; their interiors were small and dark. Mayan ceremonial architecture was one of open spaces, a plaza architecture articulated by carved monoliths, pyramids, and platforms. Mayan worship was an outdoor activity, and emphasized sequences of spacious, graded terraces, always orderly, but rarely symmetrical. Temples, monoliths, and stairways defined series of courtyards or plazas which often took the form of a system of interlocking trapezoids (Maps 5-7), not unlike the ordering of the Athenian acropolis or the ceremonial complex at Olympia (Maps 8-9).[5]

The Mayan ceremonial centers reached their apogee centuries before the Spanish Conquest. Beginning as early as the ninth century AD, and for reasons that remain mysterious, Maya civilization entered a period of decay, accompanied by a serious decline in population. The centers fell into disuse and disrepair; the once-great civilization declined into an aggregation of warring tribal units.[6]

A late attempt at urban life was Mayapán, in Yucatán. First constructed between AD 1200 and 1250, Mayapán was a true city, walled, with a peak population of perhaps 10,000 or 17,500 residents, and measuring about four square kilometers. Architecturally undistinguished, Mayapán became the principal economic focus of the peninsula. It was sacked, either by oppressed peasants (according to Andrews) or by dissident nobles (according to Rathje) around AD 1400. Mayapán lacked any orderly city plan. Groups of houses were separated by open spaces and paths, seemingly at random. Towards one side of the city there was a short roadway (*sacbe*), which seems to have led nowhere in particular; perhaps the *sacbe* was a processional route (Map 10).[7]

Although the Franciscan order built a number of churches and monasteries during the sixteenth and seventeenth centuries at the sites of the old ceremonial centers of Yucatán, the main Spanish settlements, Campeche and Mérida, were not influenced in their layouts by any previously existing structures. Antigua (Santiago de los Caballeros), the most important colonial city in Central America, had not been a Maya center either.[8] The normal pattern of community life in Central America at the time of the Conquest was, as elsewhere, that of the rural hamlet with a handful of modest houses.[9]

Although the hamlet pattern dominated in the Andean regions of South America as well, pre-Conquest Peru had possessed a number of urban centers. Just as in

Mexico and Central America, nevertheless, many of the most memorable complexes had flourished and died centuries before the coming of Europeans. The most impressive South American centers were built during the Pre-Incaic period. Between about 100 and 600 AD, the largest South American 'city' – there is some doubt as to whether it ever had a large permanent population or was merely a 'sacred city' on the Maya model – was Tiahuanaco, near present-day La Paz. Archaeologists have determined a built-up area of between 240 and 420 hectares, or between one-tenth and one-fifth of the size of Teotihuacán, or between one-sixth and one-third of the surface extension of Tenochtitlán.[10]

A complete plan, and population data on Tiahuanaco are lacking, as also for the pre-Inca city of Huari, which may have reached its apogee around AD 900, and was abandoned some 200 years later. The urban characteristics of Tiahuanaco are uncertain; Huari corresponded to the type of the walled labyrinth. Although archaeological investigation at Huari is not well advanced, various groups of buildings can be seen. While the buildings are rectangular, the overall impression of the plan is reminiscent of a thumbprint, and not of the rectilinear patterns of Teotihuacán, Tenochtitlán or the coastal Peruvian cities (Map 11). This has surely to do with the terrain; in Huari walls follow the contour lines of an uneven landscape. The walls of Huari betray a defensive society. There are very few windows or doors in the fieldstone walls, which are as high as 6 to 12 meters. Huari was an early imperial power. Rowe places the period of Huari's military expansion after AD 800; according to this author, both Huari and Tiahuanaco had been abandoned by 1100. Lanning's chronology of the Huari empire is earlier. According to him, the Huari empire, and Huari itself, broke up around AD 800.[11]

Huari outposts were Pikillacta and Viracochabamba, near present-day Cuzco and Humachuco, respectively. Both have orthogonal plans, and consist of plazas, corridors and rectangular rooms with very high walls and few doors or windows (Map 12). Since refuse is practically absent from the sites, it is probable that the buildings housed government stores rather than people. These were walled complexes, each with only two entrances. Pikillacta had a surface area of only about 50 hectares, and Viracochabamba covered about 32.5 hectares. The entire permanent population of Pikillacta could hardly have exceeded a few hundred. The collapse of Tiahuanaco and Huari was accompanied by a general abandonment of cities in southern Peru and Bolivia. Whatever cities there were sank into oblivion. Urban patterns of life only really reappeared with the European colonization.[12]

In the central coastal regions, large pre-Inca cities grew up at Pachacamac, Cajamarquilla, and Vista Alegre. Pachacamac was a very large city in the early part of the Late Intermediate Period (1000-1476), but declined in size, and was at least partly in ruins when the Incas took it. By the time the first Spanish exploring party arrived in 1533, many buildings were in ruins, and most of the city wall had collapsed. The Spanish chose not to settle there. Cajamarquilla may have been even larger than Pachacamac at one time, with up to 10,000 houses. Cajamarquilla and Vista Alegre were abandoned, however, sometime towards AD 800 or 1000.[13]

The great pre-Inca cities of the northern coast (Chan Chan, Pacatnamú, Apurlé, Purgatorio, Farfán) reached their apogees during the Late Intermediate Period as well. Of these, only Chan Chan has been extensively excavated (Map 13). Chan Chan was the largest city ever built in ancient Peru; its site covers an area of at least 14 square kilometers, of which some 750 hectares may be said to constitute the urban core(s). At its peak, Chan Chan may have had between 65,000 and 100,000 inhabitants. In terms of population area and surface areas it would thus be roughly comparable to Teotihuacán in Mexico. The city was laid out in 10 or more rectangular enclosed compounds (citadels) reminiscent of those at Pikillacta and Viracochabamba, averaging some 20 hectares in areas. The compound walls were multiple, and very high, reaching 15 and 20 meters. Each compound had but a single entrance; inside there were no real streets, but narrow corridors flanked by blind walls. Chan Chan's architecture, which is the same as that of the other north-coastal cities, must have a sociological explanation. But what explanation? Was Chan Chan a fortress or prison, a palace or a factory?[14]

The Incas, despite their imperial organization, were not great city-builders. The best effort was Cuzco, which consisted of a relatively small ceremonial core, inhabited by royalty, priests, and assistants, surrounded by small suburban settlements separated from one another and from the center by open fields. Lanning speaks of a 'semi-agglutinated' city. The ceremonial canter had an irregular plan of plazas and narrow streets, and lacked monumental structures. At the time of the Spanish conquest, Cuzco was estimated to have some 3,000 to 4,000 houses in and about the center, and some 19,000 to 20,000 houses scattered among the outlying villages (barrios). The Spanish conserved parts of Cuzco's center, probably in deference to its famous cut-stone walls, which still stand.[15]

Aside from Cuzco, settlements were small. Macchu Picchu, the largest Inca colony between Ollantaytambo and Vilcabamba, contained only about 200 rooms for all purposes. Ollantaytambo was a small town with a trapezoidal grid plan of 19 blocks and a central plaza (Map 14). The streets were about two meters wide. As at Cuzco, some of the original blocks still survive.

Huánuco Viejo had a highly irregular plan, except for its most outstanding feature: a huge – about 350 by 550 meters – central plaza (Map 15). What possible function could such a large plaza have had? Into it would have fit the entire main temple precinct of Tenochtitlán.[16]

Notwithstanding the plaza of Huánuco Viejo, it is doubtful if the Incas ever built any settlement larger than a small town outside of Cuzco; populations rarely exceeded 1,000 persons. By the time of the Conquest, the coastal cities had either been abandoned, or retained only a fraction of their peak population levels.[17]

Outside Greater Peru (including parts of present-day Ecuador, Bolivia, and northern Argentina and Chile), there is no evidence of urban life before the Spanish Conquest. The Chibcha peoples of what is now Colombia were excellent goldsmiths, but unprolific builders. Aside from a few monoliths they left no fixed monuments, let alone cities.[18]

Outside the Andean region, even villages were scarce. Around Barquisimeto, according to an account made up in 1579, the Indians lived in *barrios* of three to four houses each, separated from one another by interspaces ranging from shooting distance ('tiro de arcabuz') to several kilometers. In the vicinity of Trujillo (Venezuela) the Indians did not live in groups, but alone. Each family had its hut on the land which it worked. The Spanish interpretation of this pattern was that it was to protect the land from incursions by others: 'because they are great thieves, and they steal one another's crops'.[19]

In summary, we may say that at the time of the Conquest, there were but a handful of cities or towns on the American continent. They were concentrated in Mexico's Central Valley, and to a very much lesser degree in the Peruvian highlands. The Spanish did not level these previous settlements, but gradually adapted them to their needs. Modifications were necessary. Aside from the change in the religious system, which made destruction of the old temples inevitable, the introduction of new means of transport made the old street systems impractical, much as any change in ballistic technology makes existing military architecture obsolete.

Chronology of foundation of colonial towns

Since there were so few towns at the time of the Conquest, most of the colonial towns and cities were entirely new creations. No one has ever attempted a listing of all the colonial settlements, and none is possible or necessary. Especially during the early years, not every new settlement was a success. Many of the first Spanish settlements proved to be unstable, and did not survive the first years. Others were moved from one site to another. Towards the end of the sixteenth century, only a rough estimate could to be made of the number of settlements in the province of Guatemala: two cities (*ciudades*) and 300 villages (*pueblos*). In all of Central America (excluding Panamá), there were some 15 cities, 26 towns (*villas*), and 723 villages around 1800. The terms city, town, and village are sometimes misleading. There were villages with much larger populations than some cities. The 'village' of Quezaltenango had a population of around 11,000 in 1800, while the 'city' of San Pedro Sula had fewer than 400.[20]

In any case, all of the colonial centers which had or would acquire any importance as cities were in place by the early seventeenth century, Montevideo being the only exception that comes to mind. For all practical purposes, the urban network of Spanish America around 1600 or 1620 was the same as that of 1800 or 1820.[21]

We can be more exact. The period of greatest activity in the foundation of new settlements was the half-century lasting from 1520 to 1570. Lopéz de Velasco and Vázquez de Espinosa provide the foundation dates of 191 Spanish settlements up to about 1628. On the basis of these data Slicher van Bath has constructed the following graphic representation of the number of new settlements per decade.[22]

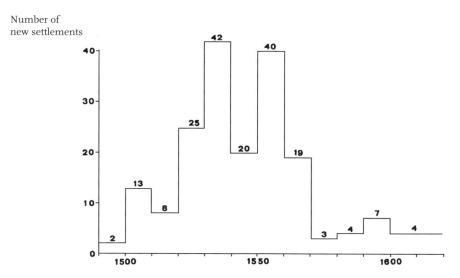

Graph 1 *Chronology of the foundation of new settlements, 1492-1620*

The graph shows three waves of new settlements. The first, small one crests in the second decade, and corresponds to the Caribbean phase of the Conquest. During the ten years 1520-1530, New Spain is opened to colonization, through the definitive subjugation of the Aztecs. In this decade and the next a second wave peaks. Only during the decade 1530-1540 does the Peruvian Conquest take place; a new wave of foundations – the final one – immediately follows. The rate of foundation of new settlements is highest during the fifty years following the fall of Tenochtitlán to the Spanish. By 1570, the initial momentum seems spent. After this date few additional settlements are founded any more.

Geographical distribution

During the first four decades of colonial expansion, the new settlements were confined to the Caribbean area, New Spain and Guatemala; this early phase of expansion was orderly and gradual, mainly limited to Hispaniola during the first two decades, spreading to Puerto Rico, Panamá and Cuba in the third decade, and to

Mexico, Guatemala and coast of Venezuela in the fourth. The pattern was that of a slowly advancing frontier. By contrast, the fifth-decade expansion covered vast distances, from New Galicia and Yucatán in the north, through the whole length of the continent to Asunción (Paraguay) in the south (Buenos Aires, also originally founded during this decade, was soon abandoned; it was founded anew some forty years later). Chile and western Argentina were opened during the 1540s. By 1550 the limits of the Spanish American expansion had already been more or less reached. Settlements founded after 1550 tended to fill in the gaps between already existing outposts; a phase of consolidation had set in.

The regional distribution of the Spanish settlements in America around 1600 reflected by and large the distribution of the subjugated Indian population: there were many Spanish towns and cities in regions with large numbers of Indian tributaries.[23] Only exceptionally were Spanish settlements founded outside the regions with the old Indian concentrations. Wherever this did happen, it was in connection with new economic activities introduced in America for the first time by the Europeans. The most obvious is the case of the mining centers. In contrast to the indigenous peoples, the Spanish were willing to go to great lengths to mine precious metals. Since the richest lodes were found in rough, inhospitable zones, often unsuitable for agriculture, population levels in their vicinity had always been very low. Potosí, Durango, Guanajuato and Zacatecas are all examples of new centers, where prior to the exploitation of the mines there had never been large indigenous populations. Similarly, the Spanish founded settlements at Cubagua and on the island of Margarita (Venezuela) based on pearl-diving. Sea transport was another Spanish innovation, and ports were founded during the early colonial years in areas with sparse Indian populations: examples are Lima (Callao), Veracruz, Cartagena, Havana, Panamá, Buenaventura, Acapulco, Trujillo and Omoa, among others.

Just as in Spain, the settlements were divided into cities (*ciudades*), towns (*villas*) and villages (*pueblos*). Slicher has found that, contrary to what one might suppose, the 'cities' were in many cases precisely very small settlements, and that they abounded in the sparsely inhabited and marginal colonial regions, especially in parts of Colombia, Ecuador, Venezuela, Central America, and south America's southern cone. The *ciudades* often had a frontier character; the title of 'city' was often granted in order to attract settlers. The pattern is reminiscent of the new cities (*villenueves*) founded in the eleventh to thirteenth centuries in Europe. In the more densely populated regions of Mexico and Peru, there were relatively few *ciudades,* but the settlements were generally larger than in the regions with higher proportions of *ciudades.* In Chile, Argentina and Paraguay, by contrast every Spanish settlement, no matter how small, was a 'city'.[24]

The size of the colonial towns

Only gradually did large numbers of Spanish come to inhabit the American cities and towns. According to Vázquez de Espinosa, there were only 14 cities in America with more than a thousand *vecinos* (non-Indian, no-slave heads of household) around 1628. In descending order of size, these cities were:

	Number of vecinos
Mexico	More than 15,000
Lima	9,000 to 10,000
Potosí	4,000
Cuzco	3,500
Quito	3,000
Puebla	3,000
Bogotá	2,000
Cartagena	1,500
Havana	1,200
La Plata	1,100
Antigua	1,000
Oruro	1,000
Atlixco	1,000
Zacatecas	1,000

The largest numbers of settlements consisted of between 50 and 250 *vecinos* around 1628. If the average family size was between four and five persons, we could say that a typical Spanish settlement might have had a total white and mixed-blood population of 200 to 1,000 persons.[25]

In the frontier areas, the cities were especially modest. In Tucamán (northern Argentina) around 1583, there were five Spanish 'cities', whose population were as follows:

City	Vecinos	Indian tributaries
Santiago del Estero	48	12,000
Córdoba	40	12,000
Talavera	40	6,000
San Miguel Tucumán	25	3,000
Lerma	?	1,500[26]

The *vecino* population was thus generally a tiny minority living in the midst of a vastly greater Indian population. The European minority did not, however, maintain itself by force of arms against the Indians. In the case of the five settlements just mentioned, not one was fortified against attack, and there was no occupying army.

In Cuyo (western Argentina) there were three cities with Spanish populations in 1610. Mendoza, the most important of them, had 32 houses, of which only one or two had tiled roofs; the rest was roofed with thatch, as were all of San Juan's 23 and San Luis's 10 houses. The small number of Spaniards living in these cities did not preclude what may seem to our eyes a large number of religious institutions. San Juan and San Luis both had parish churches. Mendoza, aside from its parish, had no fewer than three convents – Jesuit, Mercedarian and Dominican, respectively – each with only two friars, however.[27]

In general, the number of religious institutions within a town or city gives a clue to the size of its *vecino* population. The establishment of a convent or other religious institution was associated with a certain minimum *vecino* population, a threshold. On the basis of data from López de Velasco and Vázquez de Espinosa, Slicher has calculated these thresholds for 1574 and 1628.[28]

Minimum number of vecinos for the establishment of convents or other religious institutions, 1574 and 1628 (Spanish America, excluding Mexico)

Convents of the mendicant orders (Dominicans, Franciscans, Augustinians)	1574	1628
1 convent in one place	17	40
2 convents	60	80
3 convents	100	100
4 convents	300	2,000
1 Mercadarian convent	17	40
1 Jesuit house	800	40
1 nuns' convent	130	200
1 colegio	100	360
1 hospital	30	80

Within the towns: center and periphery

As we saw repeatedly during the discussion of the pre-Columbian urban forms, the Indian pattern of community was a highly decentralized one in almost all cases. There were few real cities. Where there was a dense population, this expressed itself more often in a large number of hamlets or *barrios*, separated by open fields, than in a genuine urban core. This was clearly the case in Cuzco. We also saw that the Indians of Barquisimeto and Trujillo lived scattered over large areas. In the case of Cholula, even today, outside the old colonial center are dozens of satellite villages that only thin out gradually as one leaves the center.

The Spanish pattern, by contrast, was a nucleated one, emphasizing a compact center, with administrative, religious and residential buildings all close to one an-

other, and organized around and orderly pattern of streets. As the Spanish often constructed their cities in the midst of the scattered Indian *barrios* (again, Cuzco and
Cholula may serve as examples), historians have sometimes assumed that Spaniards
and Indians lived separately, that there was a kind of *apartheid*, in which the Indians
were excluded from the Spanish center, and the Spanish avoided the outlying Indian
barrios. This model can be clearly seen in reconstructed plans of sixteenth-century La
Paz and Oruro (Bolivia) (Maps 17 and 18).

This model is too simple, as the example of Tunja (Colombia) shows (Maps
19-21).[29] Of 370 houses in the urban core, at least 38 were owned by Indians in 1623.
There was no Indian ghetto; the houses of the Indians were located among those of
the *vecinos* and *encomenderos*. It is true that the houses belonging to Indians are all
found towards the edge of the city, at some distance from the central plaza: the inner
limit of Indian penetration of the city, on the basis of the distribution of their
houses, describes a rhomboid figure around the central plaza on our plan. The diagonal axes of the rhombus are formed by the main streets diverging from the center
of the rigidly orthogonal city plan.

The same rhomboid pattern recurs if we take the distribution of the *encomendero*
houses as our criterion. The greatest concentration of *encomendero* residences sur-
rounds the central plaza. The outer boundary of the zone of the houses belonging
to *encomenderos* is ill-defined; their frequency gradually declines as one leaves the
center for the outskirts. Some *encomenderos* live scattered at the periphery. Still, the
area of the greatest concentration describes a rhombus, elongated towards the
northeast and southwest (Figure 1, corresponding to Maps 19-21, listed in the appendix).

Looking at the distribution of churches, we see that they are also concentrated in
the vicinity of the central plaza. If we trace the outer limits of the area within which
all the churches are located, we find yet a third roughly rhomboid form, elongated
along the main streets towards the north and south.

The pattern recalls a system of concentric circles or contour lines – deformed by
the rigid gridiron street plan into diamond shape – with the plaza as its center. The
encomendero houses and most of the churches are near the center: the Indian houses
are at the periphery. Scattered throughout the city are the houses of the *vecinos sin
encomienda*, which form the majority of the population. If we follow each street as it
leaves the center, we can distinguish three zones on the basis of the house owners:
(a) a central zone, which extends from the plaza until the *encomendero* houses thin
out, (b) a transitional zone in which the houses of the *vecinos sin encomienda* predominate, and (c) a peripheral zone which begins by the first Indian house. It could be
objected that there are no strict boundaries between the zones, and that therefore
even recognizing the zones is an arbitrary procedure. On the other hand, our purpose is not to establish wards or strictly separated neighborhoods, but only to identify centripetal and centrifugal tendencies within the city.

Houses
* ✳ Encomenderos
* ● Vecinos
* ○ Indians
* ||||||| Inner limit Indian house
* – – – Outer limit heaviest concentration encomendero houses
* \\\\\\\\ Outer limit churches

Other buildings
* ✳ Churches
* ① Cabildo
* ② Hospital
* ③ Jail
* ④ Caja de agua

* ⓐ Windmill
* ⓑ ⓓ Textile workshops
* ⓒ Tannery

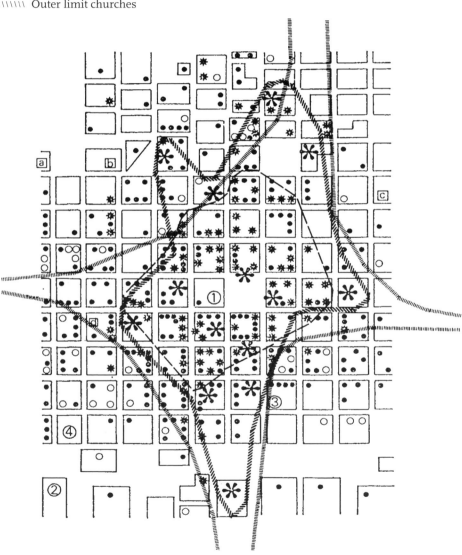

Figure 1 *Tunja 1623*

Houses
* ***** Encomenderos
* **●** Vecinos
* **○** Indians

Other buildings
* ***** Churches
* **①** Cabildo
* **②** Hospital
* **③** Jail
* **④** Caja de agua

* a Windmill
* b d Textile workshops
* c Tannery

■■■ Central zone　▨▨▨ Transitional zone　▭ Peripheral zone

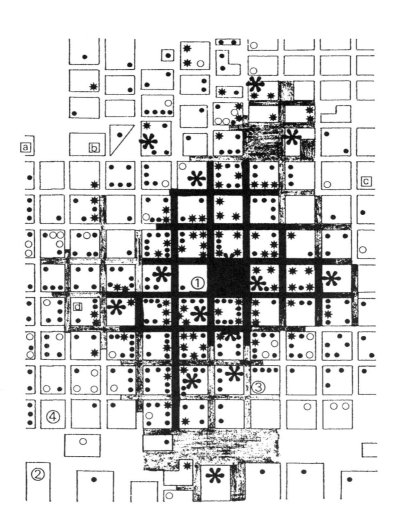

Figure 2 *Tunja 1623*

With this in mind, we have divided the city on the basis of the above criteria into a central, a transitional, and a peripheral zone, as mapped in Figure 2. The distribution of the 398 known buildings by type among the three zones is given in the table below.

The houses of the *encomenderos* were the most markedly 'central' of Tunja's buildings around 1623, followed closely by the churches. *Vecinos* without *encomienda* were characteristic of what we call the transitional zone. The public buildings were located according to function: the administrative center, the *cabildo*, was located at the center of the city; a hospital and a jail, on the other hand, were at the outskirts: in both of the latter cases, the principle of contagion explains why these buildings were placed at a distance from the center. In the case of the hospital, contagion of disease was a danger; the jail was a center of corruption of another kind. Industry (two textile workshops, a tannery and a windmill) also tended towards the periphery, as did the houses of the Indians.

Zone	Houses			Other buildings			
	Encom.	*Vecino*	*Indian*	*Church*	*Public*	*Industry*	*Total*
Central	64	65	-	9	1	-	139
	74%	26%	0%	64%	25%	0%	35%
Transitional	15	94	-	3	1	1	114
	17%	37%	0%	21%	25%	25%	29%
Peripheral	8	92	38	2	2	3	145
	9%	37%	100%	14%	50%	75%	36%
Total	87	251	38	14	4	4	398
	100%	100%	100%	99%	100%	100%	100%

The tendency of the Spanish, and especially the *encomenderos*, to group themselves around the central plaza has been noted for other Spanish American colonial cities. Lockhart, in an article on Toluca (Mexico) at the end of the sixteenth century, interprets this as a Spanish displacement of the Indians from the center: 'empujaban a los indios ... hacia los extremos'.[30] But if it is true that in almost all cases the Indian population pattern was one of widely dispersed farms, usually without an urban core, then the opposite hypothesis is at least as acceptable. It seems likely, at least in the cases of Tunja and Toluca, that the colonial centers did not displace already existing Indian concentrations, but were the first urban centers at their respective sites. It is possible to interpret the Indian presence at the periphery as an Indian penetration of an originally entirely Spanish settlement. The laws of the Indies, in fact, expressly stipulated that new towns should be laid out on hitherto unoccupied grounds: '... elijan el sitio de los que estuvieren vacantes ... sin perjuicio de los Indios ...'.[31] This rule would seem to have been followed in Tunja, as it also was in La Paz some years later.[32] In fact, there is no reason to assume that it was not generally followed throughout the Indies, with the few exceptions already noted (e.g. in Central Mexico and Cuzco), where genuine pre-Columbian cities existed. The model I am suggesting, therefore, is one of the colonial urban center acting as a population magnet, not only for Spanish immigrants, but for Indian ones as well.

Physical appearance

What did the colonial cities look like? Sources for answering this question are maps conserved in the various archives, but equally important are the many travel accounts, *visitas* and geographical descriptions made during the colonial period. There are, in all a good number of verbal descriptions of the colonial towns, which while not always of sufficient quality and detail to reconstruct every block of every city, evoke the – generally rustic – flavour of colonial urban life.

Around 1580, for example, Caracas was the largest town in what is now Venezuela, with only 60 *vecinos*. Four streets running north-south crossed another four streets at right angles, forming 25 square blocks of identical size. Precisely at the center of this matrix, one block was left unbuilt: the plaza. The streets were 32 feet wide. Caracas's houses were mostly of wattle daubed with clay (*bahareque*) or stamped earth (*tapia, tapería*), and had only a ground floor. Almost all the houses were roofed with cane mats (*cogollos de cañas*) and thatch (*paja*). Only three houses had walls of stone or brick and a second story. They and the church had the town's only tiled roofs.[33] Nearby Barquisimeto was smaller, with only eight blocks, but was also laid out symmetrically around the central plaza. Its houses were built of cane and straw. Around 1580, the first walls of *tapia* were being introduced.[34]

Tunja, while still modest, presented a more attractive physical appearance. As can be seen in the plan of 1623, there were more than 100 blocks arranged between 10 streets running north-south, and some 15 side streets. The houses were of earth and stone, and some boasted fine portals. Most were of a single story, but some had a second floor (*alto*) and an interior patio. Of the 270 houses roofed with tiles, 182 had but a single story, while 88 had *altos*; 129 houses had roofs of thatch.[35]

Around 1610, La Plata (Bolivia) had 704 houses, as many as 50 of them with their own water supply. Most of the roofs were thatched, but tiled roofs were not unknown. There were two suburbs where poor Spanish, mestizos and Indians lived. There was a central plaza, and smaller plazas in front of the Dominican, Franciscan, Mercedarian and Augustinian convents.[36] Santiago de Chile consisted of some 84 blocks in 1614, with 346 houses, of which 285 were 'well built' and had gardens, while 61 were 'poorly built' and roofed with thatch.[37] Castrovirreina (Peru) had one main street and a few side streets, and thus did not conform to the central plaza type. Towards 1628, its 100 houses were of adobe and thatch. The town had no fewer than three hospitals. Castrovirreina was a mining town, and many injuries probably occurred. Mining centers and ports in Spanish America had more than their share of hospitals.[38]

The finest colonial cities, and the largest, were of course Lima and Mexico (Maps 21 and 22). By the beginning of the seventeenth century, Lima consisted of some 350 blocks, distributed in the familiar checkerboard pattern. There were four plazas. The main plaza, which held the Vice-regal palace, the cathedral and the archepiscopal palace, was 440 feet square; Lima's streets were 40 feet wide. The houses were for the most part low, and had flat roofs, since in Lima it does not rain. Some contemporary accounts were unflattering about Lima's appearance on this account. The Inca Garcilaso commented that 'when seen from a distance, the city is ugly, for it has no tiled roofs. As there is no rain in that region or for many leagues around on the coast, the houses are covered with thatch of excellent local straw. This is covered with two or three fingers' thickness of mud mixed with the straw, which suffices for shade against the sun.'[39]

Antonio de Ulloa, writing in the eighteenth century, commented on a particularly *limeño* form of ostentation in the houses:

> The houses, though they are for the most part low, are commodious, and make good appearance. They are all of *baxareque* and Quincha [wattle and daub and plaster]. They appear indeed to be composed of more solid materials, both with regard to the thickness of the principal walls, and the imitation of cornices on them; and that they may better support themselves under the shocks of the earthquakes, of which this city has had so many dreadful instances, the principal parts are of wood ... and those which serve for the walls are lined both within and without with wild canes, and chaglias or osiers ... they afterwards add cornices and porticos which are also painted as a stone color. Thus the whole front imposes on the sight, and strangers suppose them to be built of those materials that they only imitate ...

Ulloa was equally impressed by the elegant stone bridge over the Rimac, with its gate at one end which formed the entrance to the city, whence one entered the 'very large and finely ornamented' main square with its great fountain: 'In the center is a bronze statue of Fame, and on the angles are four small basins. The water is ejected through the trumpet of the statue, and also through the mouths of eight lions that surround it, and greatly heighten the beauty of the work.[40]

Mexico City's great plaza formed the center of its rectangular grid of streets, whose surfaces were paved as early as 1558. There were seven streets north-south at that time, which crossed seven other streets at right angles. The houses were 'good and costly ... builded all of lime and stone', according to one contemporary account. Vázquez de Espinosa, writing toward 1628, speaks of Mexico as 'one of the best and greatest cities in the world', with its red stone (*tezontle*) houses, straight and wide streets and canals, four markets (*ferias*), and its great number of religious institutions, among which the metropolitan cathedral, at least 19 men's convents (several with more than 100 friars), 16 convents for women, nine hospitals and a university.[41]

Fortifications

In contrast to the great numbers of medieval and sixteenth-century fortifications to be found all over Europe of the time, Spanish America possessed very few works of military architecture. The number of walled cities was insignificant. They were, with the exception of a number of *presidios* or stockades, all located on the coasts, where there was danger from English, Dutch and French pirates. Principal works of defense were the fortifications of Havana, Cartagena, Veracruz, Callao, Panamá (second foundation), Portovelo, San Juan de Puerto Rico, Santo Domingo, and Campeche (Maps 23 and 24). Of the viceregal cities, only Lima was walled, and that was because of its close proximity to the sea. Such fortifications as there were in America were irregular and not up to contemporary European standards of military architecture. In general, although many works were proposed, only a small number were actually begun, and even fewer were completed, and then usually in cheaper versions than those called for by the plans. There were often no funds for maintaining a wall once it was built, as at Lima, where the walls soon disintegrated through earthquake damage and neglect.[42]

The 'classic model'

The majority of the Spanish American colonial towns and cities had, and have, a gridiron or checkerboard street pattern; they thus correspond to an abstract mode. Kubler speaks of the 'open grid town plan', and Hardoy of the 'Classic model of the Spanish American city'. There are two formal aspects to be considered: the shape of the perimeter of the town, and the design of the network of streets. Since very few of the American cities were walled, the shape of the perimeter was of lesser concern. As to the internal elements, Hardoy signals five characteristics:

1   The network of streets describes a checkerboard pattern made up of identical elements, most often square, sometimes rectangular;
2   the plaza is one of those elements left empty of construction;
3   about the plaza are located the main church and the buildings of civil administration (*gobernación, ayuntamiento, cabildo*);
4   the sides of the plaza and the streets leaving from its corners have arcades;
5   smaller plazas are to be found in front of the other churches.[43]

In the case of the town's growth, the gridiron was simply to be extended, as far as need be.[44]

A practical consequence of the gridiron plan – and this has to do with the shape of the perimeter – is the diamond – like, or rhomboid, form in which the city tends to grows, as we have already seen in the case of Tunja. The city grows along the main axes as defined by the streets leaving the plaza. The absence of diagonal streets makes the corners of the city less accessible from the plaza, and thus less attractive. This can be seen clearly in the 1556 map of Lima (Map 21), and in colonial maps of Buenos Aires and Caracas (Maps 25 and 26). The rhomboid pattern turns up again and again in the gridiron towns, even today, as can be seen in two maps of Sucre (La Plata, Bolivia), made in 1972 and 1974, and which show the distribution of neo-classical façades, buildings with more than one story and land values (Maps 27 and 28).

The first colonial town whose cartography is known is Santo Domingo (second foundation, 1502). Its plan already incorporates aspects of the classic model, although the fact that its streets are not exactly parallel, and are not equally spaced, makes the blocks of unequal size and shape (Map 29). It has, in any case, and orthogonal or quasi-orthogonal plan. Hardoy points to Puebla (1531) and Lima (1535) as the first perfect examples of the classic model. By the 1530s, thus, the orthogonal town plan in its fullest development had been established in America, and would continue to be repeated, with small local variations, throughout Spanish America during the entire colonial period. According to an analysis by Hardoy of 292 town plans corresponding to 134 different settlements (twenty-two of the plans dating from the sixteenth century, sixty-two from the seventeenth, and fifty from the eighteenth and early nineteenth centuries), 74 percent of the towns had orthogonal plans, while only 26 percent were irregular.[45]

Hardoy is wary, however, of generalizing from these percentages, as his sample, which emphasizes the larger cities, may not be representative for the smaller settlements as well. In this respect a study by Robertson of plans made between 1579 and 1585 of seventeen Mexican provincial towns is interesting, since most of the towns studied are small. In spite of their 'provinciality', all seventeen towns show orthogonal or quasi-orthogonal plans.[46] Other evidence supporting the view that gridiron plans had been introduced even in the smaller provincial towns by the late sixteenth century is provided by two Guatemalan plans from that period. One, a map of the province of Suchitepéquez in 1579, shows some fifty provincial settlements, with the roads and rivers connecting them.[47] The settlements are all indicated schematically by tiny gridirons, indicating that in the mind of the map's maker, at least, the idea of 'town' was inextricably associated with the checkerboard pattern of streets. The second plan is watercolor map of the lake of Atitlán dated 1585.[48] The *cabecera*, Santiago Atitlán is portrayed much as it can be seen today, with the Franciscan church on one side of its square central plaza, and houses and the civil-administrative buildings lining the other sides (Maps 30 and 31).

In Venezuela, where the towns were also on the small side, there was a chronological factor: the towns founded before 1555 were irregular; those founded later had regular plans.[49] This tends to substantiate the view, proposed by Kubler for Cholula, that gridiron plans were not instituted all at once, but were being gradually introduced during the sixteenth century.

The exceptions to the grid plan were less frequent in the small villages than in the mining centers and in some port cities. Examples of irregular plans are Acapulco, Valparaíso (ports), Guanajuato, Real de Catorce, Taxco, Zacatecas and Huancavélica (mining centers) (Maps 32 and 33). Several studies associate these irregular plans with (a) topographical difficulties (broken terrain), (b) the boom-bust economic cycles characteristic of ports and mines, and (c) large transitory populations. Probably the topographical explanation is sufficient; ports and mines depended on special topographic features – a natural harbor or an exposed vein – and were thus often located on steep slopes or in ravines. Indeed, those ports and mining towns located on relatively flat sites also had gridiron plans, as the examples of Potosí and San Luis Potosí (mines), and Veracruz, Havana, Panamá and Cartagena (ports) show.

The question of the source of the classic model has been the subject of long debate among scholars. As early as 1945 a connection was sought between the orthogonal plan of Santo Domingo and those of the military camp at Santa Fe, occupied by the Catholic Kings during the siege of Granada (1491-92), and Puerto Real on the Bay of Cádiz. It was noted that Santo Domingo's governor, Ovando, had himself taken part in the Granada campaign, and thus knew Santa Fe. Santa Fe in turn harked back to principles employed in the building of Roman military encampments, the *castra*. On the other hand, Kubler, in 1942 and 1948, Palm (1955), and Foster (1960) pointed to numerous examples from medieval Europe, the *bastides* or *villes neuves* of thirteenth-century southwestern France, and to Renaissance Italian theory (Alberty, Di Giorgio Martini, Filarete).[50]

Still others argued for an indigenous American source. According to this line of thought, such great pre-Columbian plazas as those of Tenochtitlán and Huánuco Viejo would be the precursors of the central plaza of the colonial town. The regular perimeters of certain Peruvian cities and the regularity of the plan of Tenochtitlán were supposed to be the forerunners of the Spanish American orthogonal plan.

Since Santo Domingo already had been given a plaza and a roughly orthogonal plan before any of the mainland pre-Columbian examples had even been discovered, this theory fell into discredit.[51] Also, as we have seen, the orthogonal plan was very scarce in pre-Columbian America, if it existed at all. Moreover, the pre-Columbian settlements did not have streets in the European sense.

In a 1972 article, Kubler adduced new European precedents for the Spanish American open grid plan, drawn from the history of the repopulation of the countryside between Grasse and Nice, where new unwalled towns were built on the initiative of the Benedictine abbey of St. Honorat at Lérins. These towns – Valbonne (1519), Mouans-Sartoux (1504) and Vallauris (1501) had been depopulated by plagues and abandoned until the beginning of the sixteenth century. Gattinare (Piemonte) was another unwalled grid town, built in 1526 (Maps 34 and 35).[52] The advantage of these precedents is their close proximity in time to the American urbanizing campaign.

Not to be forgotten in the inventory of Old World precedents for the American orthogonal plan are the earliest known examples, dating from Greek antiquity. The rigorous grid pattern is thought to be a Greek innovation of the fifth or sixth century BC Later it also appeared in Etruria and other Mediterranean areas colonized by the Greeks. It was observed that in Greece itself – as in Spain many centuries later – orthogonal plans were uncommon. The orthogonal plan was then associated with the Greek colonization of the Mediterranean, and by extension, with the need for new towns where none previously existed, or where previously existing ones had been destroyed.[53]

In the Old World, the orthogonal plan appeared at different times (sixth and fifth centuries BC, Roman period, thirteenth century, sixteenth century) and in different places, but always associated with to factors: (a) the need for new towns, and (b) a centralized colonial authority. These factors were of course both present during the colonization of America by the Spanish.

While the search went on for the concrete precedents for the Spanish colonial city plan, literary sources were being examined as well. Early candidates for the literary inspiration of the classic model were such Italian Renaissance theorists as Filarete, Alberti and Di Giorgio Martini, all of whom had in turn been influenced by the principle Roman source, Vitruvius. There were, however, two major problems with the hypothesis of an Italian Renaissance influence in America. In the first place, the Renaissance writers did not advocate a gridiron pattern as such, but radial or winding street patterns, which in America were very rare. Secondly, as Hardoy pointed out, their influence on patterns of American colonial urbanism was dubious if the innovations proposed by them did not become well known, even in Italy, until after the campaign of American town-building was already well underway. In fact, it was not necessary to go outside Spain for literary sources; the grid plan, and Vitruvian influence, were present in Medieval Iberian treatises: Eximenic and Sánchez Arévalo (*Suma de la política, que fabla como deven ser fundadas e edificadas las ciudades e villas*) were proposed as more probable sources.[54]

The 'classic model' was not a preconceived idea put into practice all at once. The existence of an extensive Spanish urbanistic legislation prescribing standard forms for the location, layout and distribution of lands in the new colonial towns, notably the *Ordenanzas de Descubrimiento y Población* of 1573, and titles 5, 6, 7, 8 and 12 of Book IV of the *Recopilación de Leyes de las Indias* (1681), have led some historians to assume this. The objection is, of course, that the codes are later than the period of most of the foundations. In reality the codes came into being gradually; the compilations of 1573 and 1681 are collections of earlier decrees. Of the 79 laws that make up the five titles of the 1681 *Recopilación,* one has its origin during the reign of Ferdinand II, 17 during that of Charles v, 38 during that of Philip II up to 1573, and 23 are posterior to 1573. The legislation of the colonial authorities with regard to the form of the colonial cities was a confirmation of practices that evolved during the first four decades of the colony, and not a preliminary master plan.[55]

Appendix to Chapter 7

List of Maps

1 Teotihuacán: residential district of Tlamimilolpa. Drawing by S. Linné 'Mexican Highland Cultures' (Stockholm, 1942), reproduced in J.E. Hardoy, *Pre-Columbian Cities* (London, Allen and Unwin, 1973), p. 65.
2 The Valley of Mexico ca. 1521. From M.D. Coe, 'The Chinampas of Mexico', *Scientific American* 211, no. 1 (1964), p. 91.
3 Plan of a portion of Tenochtitlán, with *chinampas*, canals and footpaths. From M.D. Coe, 'The Chinampas of Mexico', p. 93.
4 Mexico City (Tenochtitlán) prior to 1519, reproduced in Hardoy, *Pre-Columbian Cities*, p. 169.
5 Plan of Uxmal, archaeological site, reproduced in Hardoy, *Pre-Columbian Cities*, p. 230.
6 Plan of Chichen Itzá, archaeological site, reproduced in Hardoy, *Pre-Columbian Cities*, p. 231.
7 Plan of Palenque, archaeological site. After Maudsley, reproduced in I Marquina, *Arquitecture pre-hispánica* (México: Instituto Nacional de Antropología e Historia, 1964), lám. 184.
8 Acropolis, Athens, plan. From C.A. Doxiadis, *Architectural Space in Ancient Greece* (Cambridge, Mass.: MIT Press, 1972), p. 38.
9 Altis, Olympia, plan. From Doxiadis, *Architectural Space in Ancient Greece*, p. 90.
10 Map of Mayapán. After Pollock, et al., reproduced in W.J. Rathje, 'The Last Tango in Mayapán: A Tentative Trajectory of Production-Distribution Systems', *Ancient Civilization and Trade*, ed. J.A. Sabloff and C.C. Lamberg-Karlovsky (Alburquerque: University of New Mexico Press, 1975), Figure 36.
11 Plan of Huari, ruins. After Bennet, reproduced in Hardoy, *Pre-Columbian Cities*, p. 338.
12 Plan of Pikillacta. After Harth Terré, reproduced in Hardoy, *Pre-Columbian Cities*, p. 342.
13 Plan of Chan Chan. After Miró Quesada, reproduced in Hardoy, *Pre-Columbian Cities*, p. 367.
14 Plan of Ollantaytambo. After *Guía del Cuzco*, reproduced in Hardoy, *Pre-Columbian Cities*, p. 475.
15 Plan of Huánuco Viejo. From Hardoy, *Pre-Columbian Cities*, p. 478-479.

16 Plan of sixteenth-century Oruro. From J. de Mesa and T. Gisbert, 'Oruro: Origen de una villa minera', VI Congreso Internacional de Minería, *La minería hispana e iberoamericana: contribución a su investigación histórica* (León: Cátedra de San Isidro, 1970), Vol. I p. 586.

17 Plan of sixteenth-century La Paz. From J. de Mesa and T. Gisbert, 'Oruro', p. 587.

18-20 Plan of Tunja, 1623. From V. Cortés Alonso, 'Tunja y sus vecinos', *Revista de Indias*, 25, nos. 99-100 (1965), pp. 160-161.

21 Plan of Lima, 1556. From J. Bernales Ballesteros, *Lima la ciudad y sus monumentos* (Sevilla: Escuela de Estudios Hispano-Americanos, 1972), p. 40.

22 Plan of Mexico City, 1750. A.G.I. Ref. México, 178, reproduced in J. Agular Rojas, et al., eds., *Urbanismo español en América* (Madrid: Editora Nacional, 1973), p. 77.

23 Plan of Havana, 1730. A.G.I. Ref. Sto. Domingo, 160, reproduced in *Urbanismo español en América*, p. 31.

24 Plan of Panamá, 1673. A.G.I. Ref. Panamá, 84, reproduced in *Urbanismo español en América*, p. 141.

25 Plan of Buenos Aires, 1776. A.S.H.M., Ref. no. 6.268, hoja 4/Pb. 10-28, reproduced in *Urbanismo español en América*, p. 211.

26 Plan of Caracas, 1678 (?). A.G.I. Ref. Venezuela, 146, reproduced in *Urbanismo español en América*, p. 169.

27 Plan of Sucre, ca. 1974 (buildings). From W. Schoop y L.A. Márquez, *Desarrollo urbano y organismo actual de la ciudad de la Plata, Sucre, Bolivia* (La Paz: Universidad Mayor de San Andrés, 1974), Maps 5 and 4.

28 Plan of Sucre, 1972 (land values). From Schoop and Márquez, *Desarrollo urbano*, Map 9.

29 The old center of Santo Domingo. From P. Lluberes, 'El damero y su evolución en el mundo occidental', *Boletín del Centro de Investigaciones Históricas y Estéticas*, 21 (1975), p. 46.

30 Juan de Estada, Mapa de la costa de Zapotitlán y Suchitepéquez, 1579. Nettie Lee Benson Library, University of Texas at Austin, MS. JGI.XX.

31 Mapa a colores del Lago de Atitlán, 1585. Nettie Lee Benson Library, University of Texas at Austin, MS. JGI.XX fol. 306.

32 Guanajuato towards the end of the eighteenth century. A.G.I. Ref. México, 601, reproduced in *Urbanismo español en América*, p. 93.

33 Central zone of Real de Catorce, 1975. From S. Díaz-Berrio Fernández, coordinador, *Real de Catorce SLP* (México 1976), p. 40.

34 Plan of Gattinara. After Blaeu, 1682. Reproduced in G. Kubler, 'Open Grid Town Plans in Europe and America, 1500-1520'. *Verhandlungen des XXXVIII Internationalen Amerikanistenkongresses*, Band IV (München 1972), p. 118.

35 Plan of Valbonne, 1962. After Huysser, reproduced in Kubler, 'Open Grid Town Plans', p. 111.

Notes to Chapter 7

1 Frédéric Mauro, 'Prééminence urbaine et réseau urbain dans l'Amerique coloniale', *Des produits et des hommes: Essais historiques latinoamericaines XVIe-XXe siécles* (Paris: Mouton, 1972), pp. 154-172.

2 This chapter makes reference to a collection of 36 maps not reproduced here. For a list of the maps, see the appendix preceeding the notes of this chapter.

3 Ignacio Marquina, *Arquitectura prehispánica* (México: Instituto Nacional de Antropología e Historia, 1964), pp. 56-112; Jorge E. Hardoy, *Pre-Columbian Cities* (London: Allen and Unwin, 1973), pp. 35-74; Jorge E. Hardoy, *Urban planning in Pre-Columbian America* (London: Studio Vista, n.d.), pp. 22-25; W.T. Sanders, 'Settlement Patterns in Central Mexico', *Handbook of Middle American Indians* (hereafter *HMAI*), Robert Wauchope, General Editor, Vol. 10 (Austin: University of Texas Press, 1971), pp. 34-38.

4 Hardoy, *Pre-Columbian Cities*, pp. 145-202; Sanders, 'Settlement Patterns', pp. 8-9, 24-29, 31; M.D. Coe, 'The Chinampas of Mexico', *Scientific American* 211, no. 1 (1964) pp. 90-99; George Kubler, 'La traza colonial de Cholula', *Estudios de Historia Novohispana*, 2 (1967), pp. 111-127; George Kubler, 'Ciudades y cultura en el período colonial de América Latina', *Boletín del Centro de Investigaciones Históricas y Estéticas*, 1 (1964), pp. 81-90; George Kubler, *The Art and Architecture of Ancient America* (Harmondsworth: Penguin, 1962; sec. ed. 1975) pp. 55-56.

5 Hardoy, *Pre-Columbian Cities*, pp. 203-288; S.F. de Borhegyi, 'Settlement Patterns of the Guatemalan Highlands', *HMAI*, Vol. 2 (Austin, 1965), pp. 59-75; G.R. Willey, 'Urban Trends of the Lowland Maya and the Mexican Highland Model', *Verhandlungen des XXXVIII Internationalen Amerikanistenkongresses* (hereafter *Verhandlungen*), Band iv (München, 1972), pp. 11-16; G.R. Willey, G.F. Ekholm and R.F. Millon, 'The Patterns of Farming Life and Civilization', *HMAI*, Vol. 1 (Austin, 1964), pp. 446-498; J. Eric S. Thompson, 'Archaeological Synthesis of the Southern Maya Lowlands', *HMAI*, Vol. 2 (Austin 1965), pp. 331-359; W.T. Sanders, 'The Cultural Ecology of the Lowland Maya: A Reevaluation', *The Classic Maya Collapse*, ed. T.P. Culbert (Albuquerque: University of New Mexico Press, 1973), pp. 325-365; C.A. Doxiadis, *Architectural Space in Ancient Greece* (Cambridge, Mass.: MIT Press, 1972), pp. 29-38, pp. 71-91.

6 Culbert, ed., *The Classic Maya Collapse*; Thompson, 'Archaeological Synthesis', pp. 344-347; Borhegyi, 'Settlement Patterns', p. 65; E. Wyllys Andrews, 'Archaeology and Prehistory in the Northern Maya Lowlands: an Introduction', *HMAI*, Vol. 2 (Austin, 1965), p. 320.

7 Hardoy *Pre-Columbian Cities*, pp. 260-265; William J. Rathje, 'The Last Tango in Mayapán: A Tentative Trajectory of Production-Distribution systems', *Ancient Civilization and Trade*, ed. J.A. Sabloff and C.C. Lamberg-Karlovky (Albuquerque: University of New Mexico Press, 1975), pp. 409-448: Andrews, 'Archaeology and Prehistory', p. 322.

8 S.D. Markman, *Colonial Architecture of Antigua Guatemala* (Philadelphia: the American Philosophical Society, 1966), pp. 11-12.

9   S.D. Markman, 'Pueblos de Españoles and Pueblos de Indios in Colonial Central America', *Verhandlungen*, Band IV (München, 1972), pp. 189-199.

10   Hardoy, *Pre-Columbian Cities*, pp. 325-337.

11   Ibid., pp. 337-341; E.P. Lanning, *Peru Before the Incas* (Englewood Cliffs: Prentice-Hall, 1967), pp. 115, 140; J.H. Rowe, 'Urban Settlements in Ancient Peru' *Peoples and Cultures of Native South America*, ed. D.R. Gross (Garden City: Doubleday, 1973), pp. 67, 69; Luis G. Lumbreras, *The Peoples and Cultures of Ancient Peru*, trans. Betty J. Meggers (Washington, D.C.: Smithsonian Institution Press, 1974), pp. 158-165.

12   Hardoy, *Pre-Columbian Cities*, pp. 341-344, 347-350; Lanning, *Peru*, pp. 140, 162-163; Rowe, '*Urban Settlements*', pp. 67-69.

13   Rowe, 'Urban Settlements', p. 71; Lanning, *Peru*, pp. 135, 137; Hardoy, *Pre-Columbian Cities*, pp. 350-353.

14   V.A. Rodríguez Suy Suy, 'Características urbanas de Chan Chan, manifestadas en otros centros de la costa norte del Perú',. *Verhandlungen*, Band IV (München, 1972), pp. 35-59; Lanning, *Peru*, pp. 151, 153-155; Kubler, *Ancient America*, pp. 279-284. Hardoy compares Chan Chan's maze-like cityscape to Chinese cities of the same epoch, Pre-Columbian Cities, pp. 357-394.

15   Rowe, 'Urban Settlements', p. 72; Lanning, *Peru*, pp. 162-163; Hardoy, *Pre-Columbian Cities*, pp. 425-458.

16   Rowe, 'Urban Settlements', p. 72; Hardoy, *Pre-Columbian Cities*, pp. 473-495.

17   Lanning, *Peru*, p. 163; Duccio Bonavia, 'Factores ecológicos que han intervenido en la transformación urbana a través de los últimos siglos de la época precolombina', *Actas y Memorias del XXXIX Congreso Internacional de Americanistas* (hereafter *Actas*), Vol. 2 (Lima 1972), pp. 79-97.

18   Hardoy, *Pre-Columbian Cities*, p. 516.

19   'Relación geográfica de la Nueva Segovia de Barquisimeto, año de 1579', and 'Relación geográfica y descripción de la ciudad de Trujillo', in *Relaciones geográficas de Venezuela*, ed. A. Arellano Moreno (Caracas: Academia Nacional de la Historia, 1964), pp. 165, 186.

20   W. Borah, 'European Cultural Influence in the Formation of the First Plan for Urban Centers that has Lasted to our Time', *Actas*, Vol. 2 (Lima 1972), pp. 35-54; B.H. Slicher van Bath, *Spaans Amerika omstreeks 1600* (Utrecht: Het Spectrum, 1979), pp. 36-50; Markman, 'Pueblos de Españoles', pp. 193-194; Domingo Juarros, *Compendio de la historia de la ciudad,* 3rd ed., ed. Victor Miguel Díaz, 2 vols. (Guatemala: Tipografía Nacional, 1937), 1, pp. 75-94.

21   Borah, 'European Cultural Influence', p. 39; Jorge E. Hardoy, 'Las formas urbanas durante los siglos xv al xvii y su utilización en América Latina', *Actas*, Vol. 2 (Lima 1972), pp. 157-190; Graziano Gasparini, 'Formación de ciudades coloniales en Venezuela – siglo xvi', *Verhandlungen*, Band iv, p. 225.

22   Slicher van Bath, *Spaans Amerika*, pp. 36-38.

23   Slicher van Bath, *Spaans Amerika*, p. 38.

24   Ibid., p. 38.

25   Vázquez de Espinosa, *Compendio y descripción*.

26 Antonio de Egaña, S.I., *Historia de la Iglesia en la América española desde el descubrimiento hasta comienzos del Siglo XIX: hemisferio sur*, (Madrid: Editorial Católica, 1966) p. 16.

27 Ibid., pp. 146-147.

28 Slicher van Bath, *Spaans Amerika*, p. 65.

29 Data on Tunja from Vicenta Cortés Alonso, 'Tunja y sus vecinos', *Revista de Indias*, 25, Nos. 99-100 (1965), pp. 155-207.

30 James Lockhart, 'Españoles entre indios: Toluca a fines del siglo XVI', *Revista de Indias*, 33-34 (1973-1974), p. 498.

31 *Recopilación de Leyes de los Reinos de las Indias* (Madrid, 1681, rpt. Madrid: Ediciones Cultura Hispánica, 1973), Libro IV, Título VII, ley I, The origins of this law are in an ordinance of Charles V from 1523.

32 José de Mesa y Teresa Gisbert, 'La Paz en el siglo XVIII', *Boletín del Centro de Investigaciones Históricas y Estéticas*, 20 (1965), pp. 29-30.

33 'Descripción de Nuestra Señora de Caraballeda y Santiago de León. Hecha en Caraballeda', *Relaciones geográficas de Venezuela*, pp. 111-140.

34 'Relación geográfica de la Nueva Segovia de Barquisimeto', pp. 173, 196-197.

35 Cortés Alonso, 'Tunja y sus vecinos', pp. 158-159.

36 Vázquez de Espinosa, *Compendio y descripción*, parr. 1698-1704.

37 Ibid., parr. 1926.

38 Ibid., parr. 1440-1453.

39 Ibid., parr. 1224-1281; Garcilaso de la Vega, el Inca, *General History of Peru*, trans. H.V. Livermore (Austin: University of Texas Press, 1966), p. 776.

40 Jorge Juan y Antonio de Ulloa, *Relación Histórica del Viaje a la América Meridional* (Madrid: Antonio Marin, 1748; rpt. Ed. J.P. Merino Navarro y M.M. Rdríguez San Vicente, Madrid: Fundación Universitaria Española, 1978), Vol. II, Liv. I, Cap. III, parr. 70, p. 42.

41 U Vázquez de Espinosa, *Compendio y descripción*, parr. 433-463; George Kubler, *Mexican Architecture of the Sixteenth Century*, 2 vols. (New Haven, 1948; rpt. Westport: Greenwood Press, 1972) I, pp. 75-76.

42 Slicher van Bath, *Spaans Amerika*, pp. 43-47; J.E. Hardoy, 'La forma de las ciudades coloniales en la América española', *Revista de Indias*, pp. 33-34 (1973-1974), p. 342; José Antonio Calderón Quijano, *Historia de las fortificaciones en Nueva España* (Sevilla: Escuela de Estudios Hispano-Americanos, 1953).

43 George Kubler, 'Open Grid Town Plans in Europe and America, 1500-1520', *Verhandlungen*, Band IV, pp. 105-122; J.E. Hardoy, 'El modelo clásico de la ciudad hispanoamericana', *Verhandlungen*, Band IV, pp. 143-181.

44 Zelia Nuttal, transl., 'Royal Ordinances Concerning the Laying Out of New Towns', *Hispanic American Historical Review*, 5 (1922), ordinance 117, p. 251.

45 E.W. Palm, 'La ville espagnole au Nouveau Monde dans la première moitié du XVIe siècle', Dixième Stage International d'Estudes Humanistes Tours, 1966 *La découverte de l'Amerique* (Paris: Librairie Philosophique J. Vrin, 1968) pp. 241-244; Hardoy, 'El modelo clásico', pp. 143, 155-156, 173-174; Hardoy, 'La forma de las ciudades coloniales', p. 323-329.

46 Donald Robertson, 'Provincial Town Plans from Late Sixteenth Century Mexico', *Verhandlungen,* Band. IV, pp. 123-129.

47 Juan de Estada, Mapa de la costa de Zapotitlán y Suchitepéquez, 1579, MS. JGI.XX, Nettie Lee Benson Library, University of Texas at Austin.

48 Mapa a colores del Lago de Atitlán, 1585, MS. JGI.XX. fol. 306, Nettie Lee Benson Library, University of Texas at Austin.

49 G. Gasparini, 'Formación de ciudades coloniales', p. 233.

50 Kubler, 'Open Grid Plans', pp. 105-107; Kubler, *Mexican Architecture,* pp. 95-100; Borah, 'European Cultural Influence', pp. 50-52; Pedro Lluberes, 'El damero y su evolución en el mundo occidental', *Boletín del Centro de Investigaciones Históricas y Estéticas,* 21 (1975), pp. 9-66; Palm, 'La ville espagnolle', pp. 241-244.

51 Lluberes, 'El damero y su evolución', p. 53; Borah, 'European Cultural Influence', pp. 47-49; Kubler, 'Open Grid Town Plans', pp. 105-106; Hardoy, 'Las formas urbanas', p. 165.

52 Kubler, 'Open Grid Town Plans'.

53 Fernando Castagnole, *Orthogonal Town Planning in Antiquity* (Cambridge, Mass.: MIT Press, 1971); Lluberes, 'El damero y su evolución'.

54 Borah, 'European Cultural Influence', p. 53; Palm, 'La ville espagnole', p. 244; Lluberes, 'El damero y su evolución', pp. 28-32, 43, 56-57; Hardoy, 'Las formas urbanas', pp. 171-172.

55 Borah, 'European Cultural Influence', pp. 42-43; Hardoy, 'El modelo clásico', pp. 144-148; Hardoy, 'Las formas urbanas', p. 170.

8

The 'colony' at Acámbaro

In the writing of history, as in the reading of it, the natural tendency is to gloss over the dull parts, searching out the heart of the matter in dramatic confrontations that seem to bring out the contrasts inherent in an age. The stuff of history is change, and change tends to concentrate itself in a few large centers and in times of crisis. One looks at the 'islands of intensity' – centers of conflict and innovation – and may forget the great seas of conservatism and isolation which surround them and make them possible. For the Platonists, change was a repetitive and insignificant part of the universe, a sign of unimportance, a mode of non-existence.

In the historiography of colonial Spanish America, the preference of historians for the dramatic confrontation is as clear as anywhere else. In the historical demography, the main attention goes to the catastrophic decline in America's Indian population as a result of the Conquest. In economic history interest is concentrated on the forms of European exploitation of the native and Negro labor forces – generally portrayed as a passive mass, malleable in the hands of the new white masters – in the mines, the plantations, along the roads. In political history, one tends to forget that another history exists than that one which prefigures the wars of independence, which pitted one continent against another. In cultural history one spends innumerable hours trying (unsuccessfully) to identify the contribution of each separate race to the greatest of the American colonial monuments.

In all these aspects, one looks at the great centers of population, where the contrasts are greatest, and where innovations and experiments followed on one another's heels, and project this picture onto the whole of the land. In Mexico, where the historiography, as almost everything else, follows the demography and is almost as ill-spread as the incidence of colonial Mexican painters, one asks, how was it in one place? A place removed from the centers of political importance. Was all change and drama there? Or did it have its share of that, but also some measure of quiet, of continuity?

The plan of sixteenth-century Acámbaro – which is the plan of twentieth-century Acámbaro (State of Guanajuato) – shows no sign of having been influenced by any previous, pre-Columbian, settlement. No permanent structures seem to have existed before a Spanish priest, Juan Bautista of Tula, placed a high wooden cross at the center of the site which henceforth would be known as *el pueblo de San Francisco de*

Acámbaro on the 19th of September 1526. If we are to believe the document which describes the foundation, the very same day the plan of the streets of the new town was laid out: five streets running from north to south, intersecting five other streets at right angles to form sixteen nearly square blocks within the resulting *traza*. A small hermitage was set up, and from two long poles, with a third short one fastened between them, two bells were hung; and on the next day, Sunday the 20th of September, the first Holy Mass was said, and the village was declared to exist.[1]

How much of it actually existed may be doubted. But in 1527, Fray Antonio Bermul was occupied for a full year in fashioning a primitive system for transporting water from springs in the mountains near Ucareo, a primitive aqueduct so long that when water was first allowed to flow in at the upper end, it took 24 hours to reach its destination.[2] This undertaking certainly presupposes some kind of settlement at the other end. In 1529, authorization was given to begin construction of a convent, and work actually began two years later in 1531. As soon as an early convent and church were completed, a provisional hospital was added on grounds adjoining those of the convent.

By mid-century, more and larger projects of construction were being carried out. The town had a shape, defined by a checkerboard pattern formed by the ten streets crossing one another at right angles. In the plan of the town, the central parts were the large open *plaza*, the Franciscan convent and church, and the adjoining 'Hospital Real de los Naturales para enfermos; e asimismo para los caminantes'. The plaza took up the space of three blocks of the traza; the hospital and conventual's complex took up another two, leaving eleven blocks for houses and gardens. The extension of this primitive nucleus was 500 *brazadas* (ca. 1000 m) in one direction, and 400 *brazadas* (ca. 800 m) in the other.[3] The population of the *pueblo* towards 1535 was given as twelve *indios caciques* and 400 *naturales*.[4] These figures surely refer to heads of families. Multiplying the total by 4.5 gives a rough estimate of the total Indian population: about 1,850.[5]

In the sixteenth century there is no mention of any civil authority aside from the Franciscan mission: there was no *ayuntamiento*, no jail. Although small bands of unsettled *chichimecas* must have worried the settlement from time to time, there were no public works of fortification, and no walls around the town. Such public services as there were – in the form of a cemetery, baptismal and marriage facilities, and a primitive kind of justice – were administered apparently by the friars in conjunction with the *caciques*. Already during the first decades the Franciscan establishment was rather large for a rural town. There were four resident friars; in 1586 there were seven.[6]

From the beginning, the *solares* within the traza were distributed among the native Indians – Otomíes and Tarascos – 'in sufficient size for houses and gardens'.[7] Spanish settlers were also admitted. From the sixteenth century onwards Spanish *vecinos* – including *encomenderos* and landgrant holders – constructed houses in the

town, and administered *haciendas de campo* in the surroundings. The only appreci-
able colonial houses that still survive, however, date from the eighteenth century.
Until 1964, all houses but two were of but a single story.

In 1586 Acámbaro was visited by Ponce. His secretary (who wrote the work for
which Ponce is famous) described the houses of Acámbaro as being built of adobe,
mostly covered with thatch (*paja*), but some of them having roofs of stamped earth.
The river Lerma, on whose left bank Acámbaro lies, was rich in fish (*bagre*), and the
land supplied nuts, figs peaches, oranges and other fruits, as well as vegetables
(*hortalizas de Castilla*) and wheat, and especially 'much abundance of maize'. Cattle
and smaller livestock were raised in the area.[8]

The building activity

The building activity provides a guide to the economic life of the town. A study of 21
individual colonial monuments provides an index to the fluctuations in building
activity that have left their mark on four and a half centuries of life in Acámbaro.
There are three phases of intense building activity during the colonial period in
Acámbaro (for data on the individual buildings, see the appendix at the end of this
chapter). They can be summarized as follows:
− *Phase 1*: (1526 – early 1530s): the town is founded, a traza is laid out (ten streets), a
provisional hospital church and convent are built, the original distribution of lands
takes place, adobe houses are built for/by the inhabitants, a primitive aqueduct is
built.
− *Phase 2*: (ca. mid-sixteenth century, ending before 1586, perhaps with the epidemics of 1576-1581 which raged throughout New Spain): from this period date large
permanent masonry structures, new convent, church and hospital.
− *Phase 3*: (ca. 1734 – ca. 1800/1810): this is the phase of greatest apparent activity;
from it date the third and largest version of the conventual's complex, alterations to
the hospital, the chapels of the *Via'crucis*, the churches of San Antonio, La Soledad,
and Guadalupe. Civil buildings include the bridge over the Lerma, repairs or rebuilding of the water supply system, the monumental public fountain, and all of the
houses which remain of architectural interest today.

Periods of active building cover limited stretches of time. Taken generously, they last
50 years during the early colonial period and about 65 years during the later part of
the eighteenth century. Between these two dynamic periods, an enormous rupture
occurs, a period during which only a single repair to the aqueduct breaks the silence
of a century and a half, a silence which embraces half of the colonial period. Rojas
points out two post-colonial periods in which growth recurred,[9] without giving par-
ticulars; indeed they are periods of scant architectural interest. The first of these

periods is during the tenure of Porfirio Diaz, who presumably was no personal
source of inspiration, but who happened to govern at the time that the railroad came
to Acámbaro.[10] The other period of active building began ca. 1935, as it did in other
areas as well, and we still have not seen the end of it.

Demographic fluctuations

Towards 1535 the population of the *pueblo* was about 1,850 Indians (see above). During the first decades of its existence it was the only settlement of mixed population in
the immediate area.[11] The large number of resident friars at Acámbaro (four, increasing to seven by 1586) may indicate that the original settlement grew rapidly as a result of immigration. In 1600 the population is given as 1,500 tributaries (x 4.5 =
6,750 Indians).[12] Such a net increase from 1535 to 1600 is unlikely, since it is known
to have been a period of high mortality among Indians everywhere in New Spain,
who were afflicted with repeated epidemics. The cited figure for 1600 must therefore also include all the dependent villages which fell to Acámbaro for administrative
purposes (the *sujetos*; in 1580 there were 44 of them).[13] Nevertheless, it is hard to find
any evidence of a net population drop either in Acámbaro during the period 1535-
1600. Immigration would seem to have neutralized mortality in the total population
trend.

In 1698, there are supposed to have been 5,612 tributaries in Acámbaro, and in
1743, there would have been 7,530 (respectively 25,254 and 33,885 Indians).[14] These
figures are far too high for the town itself; present-day Acámbaro has only about
23,000 inhabitants.[15] Moreover, they would have the period 1600-1743 as one of
rapid population growth, clearly impossible in view of the complete stagnation in the
building activity. The figures therefore again include large numbers of tributaries
living outside Acámbaro, but technically within its jurisdiction.

It is known that in large parts of Hispanic America, as in Spain itself, the seventeenth and early eighteenth centuries were characterized by deep economic crisis.
Murdo J. MacLeod has described in detail the demographic results of the disastrous
economic developments for Central America.[16] Two generally observed trends are of
interest here. First, increased economic pressure on the Spanish community led
them to attempt to exact higher levels of tribute from the Indian population, a population which had declined in size drastically. One consequence was a tendency on
the part of the Indians to withdraw from the towns where Europeans were settled to
subsistence farming outside these places.

Secondly, as commercial and other non-agricultural possibilities dried up, the
Spaniards themselves were increasingly forced to seek a living in direct agriculture,
for their own consumption. This development further de-emphasized the importance of town-living, and helped give rise to the self-contained rural hacienda. Two

tendencies, therefore, which tended to decrease the importance of the town within its rural setting. Thus the rising population figures for 1600, 1698 and 1743 probably have more bearing on the rural areas around Acámbaro than on the growth of the town itself.

Urban expansion on the ground

In dealing with the urban extension of Acámbaro, we have the advantage that the Spanish checkerboard street arrangement continued to be followed in the late and post-colonial periods. Since the blocks formed by the intersecting streets are of roughly the same size, we can speak of the area of the town in terms of blocks. The approximate situation at three different moments is:[17]

	Total blocks in use	Church	Plaza(s)	Housing & gardens
Ca. mid-C16	16	2	3.0	11.0
End C18	±36	1 ?	0.5	34.5 ?
1967	±60	1	1.0	58.0

The area of the town dedicated to housing has increased more than fivefold since the middle of the sixteenth century, and has grown by more than half since about 1800. Between the mid-sixteenth century and about 1800 the area of the town devoted to, housing about tripled. From what we know of the building activity, we suppose that the size of the town on the ground must have remained about the same between the middle of the sixteenth century and ca. 1734; the period ca. 1734–ca. 1800 is therefore when the growth must have occurred. We can now fill in a fourth tentative 'moment' in the urban extension:

	Total blocks in use	Church	Plaza(s)	Housing & gardens
Ca. 1734	16 ?	2 ?	3 ?	11

Urban expansion on the ground and demographic fluctuations

The number of blocks in use for housing is not directly proportional to population: the number of inhabitants fluctuates more rapidly. In the case of urban expansion, even for a small town practically free of buildings of more than one story, the population growth will be more pronounced than the growth in area, since the concentration of population on the ground will rise.

We know the beginning and end points. Towards 1535 the population was about 1,850; the area of the town dedicated to housing was eleven blocks. In the 1960s the population was 23,000; the area on the ground was in the neighborhood of 58 blocks. In terms of population density this is:

- 1535: 168 persons/block;
- 1960s: 396 persons/block.

The population increase is therefore only partly compensated by an increase in the built-up surface area of the town. This makes it possible to project a probable range of population for the questionable 'moments' in the demographic history of Acámbaro. The probable population range for the pueblo of Acámbaro, based on a maximum population density of 396 persons/block and a minimum of 168 persons/block is:

	No. of blocks for housing	Population at 168 p./b. (min.)	Population at 369 p./b. (max.)
1535	11.0	1848	-
ca.1600	11.0 ?	1848 ?	4059 ?
ca.1698	11.0 ?	1848 ?	4059 ?
ca.1734	11.0 ?	1848 ?	4059 ?
ca.1800	33.5 ?	5628 ?	13,266 ?
1967	58.0	-	23,000

Immigration must have been an important factor in Acámbaro's growth; during the period of the great epidemics it must have offset high Indian mortality to a great extent, and during the depression of the seventeenth century the agricultural possibilities of the lands around Acámbaro must have attracted many farmers from more urban areas. This is indicated by the total population figures from 1600, 1698 and 1743, which, as we have seen, reflect the situation in the countryside rather than in the town, which stagnated. The large farming population in the countryside near to Acámbaro must have provided the base for the urban prosperity of the second half of the eighteenth century, when presumably new commercial possibilities opened up for agricultural products.

Religion

There seems to be little to distinguish the post-Conquest religious life of Acámbaro from that of many other towns in New Spain. There is no record of religious strife or of persistence of pre-Hispanic religious observances. No pre-Columbian temples were apparently found, or caves sheltering pagan idols; there were no idols behind alters hiding in the Christian buildings. On the contrary, if anything is remarkable about the colonial religious history of Acámbaro, it is the impression of relatively intense evangelical activity (carried out here by the Franciscan order) combined with an almost stifling impression of religious harmony, a combination which – perhaps due to its lack of dramatic possibilities – is hardly emphasized in the literature dealing with American missionary activity, a literature which often dwells on conflicts within the Church, the destruction of native relics, the exaggerated idealism of the first missionaries, and the exaggerated cynicism of the later ones. In Acámbaro there is every sign of an unspectacular, but quite substantial religious conversion and colonization.

We have already noted that the Franciscan Fray Antonio Bermul was responsible for first bringing water to the new village. His sole companion during the first years was Fray Juan de Lazo y Quemada. Later they were joined by others. After a permanent convent was established around 1532, there were four resident friars; in 1586 there were seven. This number, which is relatively large by sixteenth-century Mexican standards (two was nearer to the normal size), indicates that Acámbaro was considered to be an important concentration of Indian population by the Franciscans. This is reinforced by the fact that it was one of the very first Franciscan missions in Michoacán (being roughly contemporary with that of Pátzcuaro).[18]

An exceptional feature in Acámbaro's religious history is that it was never secularized during the colonial period, as most parishes were. It always remained in hands of the Franciscans, who were therefore also responsible for the three new churches and the chapels of the *Vía crucis* in the eighteenth century. This stability cannot be explained by geographical isolation, as Acámbaro was located on the way towards more remote settlements which were secularized. The explanation might lie in the economic importance of the community, which might have made it indispensable to the community, or in the hospital which they administered, or in some other knot which bound it strongly to the community; in any case, its position was not challenged either by another order or by the secular church during 300 years.

The Franciscan presence was not confined to the spiritual side of life; their convent was no 'ivory tower'. Their worldly activities were probably quite pronounced in the small town, and their economic fortunes – as reflected in their building activity – were intimately bound to those of the community on the whole. They must have played an important role in the economic (agricultural) life of the town, and in its administration. After having undertaken the first public works (the traza, the first division of lands, the water supply), the construction of the convent, hospital and presumably other works were carried out by religious and natives in conjunction. It is hard to see how there can be any question, in Acámbaro's case, of forced Indian labor. The friars were always a tiny minority within the community and did not dispose of coercive means to enforce their will upon an unwilling population. One must suppose that a kind of community came into being in which collective interests overshadowed whatever class, racial or cultural differences existed – a situation which exists in farm communities the world over.

Art

Acámbaro is not known for its works of painting or sculpture. Toussaint does not mention it once in his massive *Pintura colonial en México*.[19] There is, however, one large painting of interest; it is in the sacristy of the church of Guadalupe. Painted in oils on cloth, it portrays the genealogy of the Virgin (of Guadalupe). The tree springs from the reclining body of David, and the 39 patriarchs and kings of the Old Testament are arranged on five pairs of branches.[20] In view of its style and its situation in the church of the same devotion as the painting itself, it is reasonable to date it from the same period as the church: the second half of the eighteenth century. Since it is by no means the work of an amateur, one must suppose that it was commissioned to an artist from outside the town. The absence of other works means that there was not sufficient demand to justify the presence of a resident painter.

Aside from this, the monuments of artistic interest are architectural, and are limited to the hospital; the Franciscan convent; the three eighteenth-century churches of San Antonio, La Soledad and Guadalupe; the public fountain; and a number of eighteenth-century houses. The hospital, as it existed in the sixteenth century, had 25 beds and ample infirmaries.[21] Its basic plan did not differ from that of the typical Mexican convent, with a chapel alongside a square building enclosing a square patio with arcaded walks around the four sides. The entire complex was of masonry. The chapel was a simple, single-naved structure, without transept, with a choir raised above the main entrance, much in keeping with the normal practice of Mexican sixteenth-century conventual churches.[22] It is a substantial building which remains intact – with alterations – today. In the appendix, data are given as to the periods of building activity, which are roughly the same as for the Franciscan conventual buildings.

The parts of the hospital which give it its individual character are the façade and, perhaps to a lesser extent, two small pairs of windows in the tower. They both date from the middle of the sixteenth century. The two small paired windows in the tower are, according to Toussaint: 'de indudable ascendencia mora', so primitive as to merit their inclusion in a catalogue of Moorish survivals in Mexico.[23] Inscribed in stone rectangles according to Moorish practice, a roughly worked Christian motif, that of the tree of life, frames in each case tiny pair of arched windows in an improbable setting: a hospital built by Spaniards and Indians in a small town to the West of Mexico. The façade of the hospital is no less extraordinary in its allegiance to imported models, and is also of complicated extraction. The portal and the rectangular choir window are framed by a large, flat *alfiz* frame of Moorish derivation. The wide, rectangular field of the *alfiz*, divided in half by a horizontal cornice, is composed of smooth stone masonry covered by projecting six-pointed stars at regular intervals in perfect concordance with sixteenth-century Spanish metropolitan usage (see for example the Casa de las Conchas at Salamanca). Six stylized roses surround the arch of the doorway, recalling the hospital's devotion to Mary, the rose without thorns.

The decoration of the archivolt of the doorway, also carved in stone, includes a Franciscan cord, a 'tree of life' topped by pineapples, and two birds who hover above the fruits. In the jambs, two Renaissance medallions enclose busts of St. Peter and St. Paul (the two poles of the church), and angels in the form of birds with human heads are carved in the rough manner which some associate with the Indian crafts-man's hand.[24] The style of the portal may thus be said to fit easily into the European/Christian tradition iconographically, the Spanish/*mudéjar* tradition compositionally, and the native tradition technically: a cosmopolitan work for a small Mexican village. This said, the façade cannot be said to be a copy of any other known work, and it re-tains its own special place – somewhat larger than that of the town itself – in the his-tory of European as well as of American art.

The structure of the present Franciscan convent church dates from the eighteenth century – it is some 200 years younger than the essential fabric of the hospital. Yet it differs from the hospital only superficially, and is, for its time, every bit as conven-tional. While the plan of the church has changed – the single nave has been retained, but now with a projecting transept and a dome above the crossing – the relationship between church and square conventual edifice with patio has been conserved.

The church adjoins one side of the rectangular conventual building following the normal pattern established in New Spain since the sixteenth century, and which dates back in Europe to the early Middle Ages. The two-story masonry square clois-ter, with arcaded walks (four arches per story per side), has at its center a wide foun-tain of mixtilinear plan, which identifies it as an eighteenth-century product. Details betray the stylistic changes of two centuries: the form of the vaults (domical) of the upper cloister walks, refectory and chapter room, the capitals, archivolts and decora-tion of the face of the second-story arcade, the *fleur-de-lis* finials which adorn the cor-nice, and the characteristic moldings of the second-story archivolts. These moldings – which in themselves are simple and sober enough – are borrowed from the Fran-ciscan convent of Celaya (finished in 1728),[25] and reappear in almost all the other eighteenth-century buildings of Acámbaro, thus forming a sort of local trademark based on the example of the convent. The moldings are repeated in the jambs of the side portal of the hospital, the side portal of the convent church, the stone lantern atop the cloister building, the door jambs of the refectory, the tower and main portal of the church of San Antonio, the portal of La Soledad, the sacristy door of the church of Guadalupe, and several of the colonial private houses; all are works of the second period of prosperity in Acámbaro, which dates from the mid- to late eight-eenth century.

The ornamentation of the convent, and of all the eighteenth-century buildings of Acámbaro remains limited to small flourishes here and there, and does not disturb the generally classicizing and sober, and slightly archaic, order of the façades and buildings of the town. There is no sign of the wildly experimental 'baroque' surface decoration which is known as the most striking feature of eighteenth-century architecture in New Spain. The dominant tone at Acámbaro is not so much one of novelty and innovation, as one of continuity with long-standing architectural tradition. This is not to be interpreted as total lack of sophistication, or of unredeemed provinciality: the works are elegantly fashioned and labored. The geometrical rigor of the convent, for example – its basic proportions are determined throughout by the golden 'rectangle' principle[26] – is attenuated by the delicate application of restrained ornament, as has been remarked.

The portals of the eighteenth-century churches of Acámbaro – the convent church, San Antonio, La Soledad and Guadalupe – are likewise almost archaic in their compositional simplicity: while contemporary Mexican churches elsewhere were experimenting with Salomonic columns and *estípite* non-architectonic pilasters, the portals of the Acámbaro churches recall more than anything the austere façades of the sixteenth-century mendicant missions. As in the case of the cloister, only small details give away their eighteenth-century dates of construction: the moldings (which have been spoken of), their somewhat elevated and narrow proportions, a narrow mixtilinear molding which frames the niche above the choir window of the convent church, *fleur-de-lis* finials which continue the verticals of jambs or window frames above (non-broken) pediments, etc.

In all these churches, certain features are shared; others are quite distinct from church to church. In structure and style, conservatism wins from experimentation; is this a reason to deny them a place in the literature?[27] By emphasizing the innovative side of Mexican architecture – which is not always its strongest side – at the expense of conservative provincial buildings, the literature risks the romantic and false impression of a backward and copy-cat architecture, 'decorative' in its pejorative sense. This while most Spanish towns of the size of Acámbaro, an ocean away from the metropolis, might well pride themselves to possess a complex of such quality and refinement as that of the Acámbaro convent, hospital and plaza. In most cases they lack one.

One monument of ingenuous local fantasy and frank amateurism adds a touch of lightness perhaps lacking in the ecclesiastical architecture. The 'pila historiada', the public fountain, is thus called because the sixteen faces of the basin are covered with scenes of local life carved with little plan and less skill. Nevertheless, it is possible to make out the most picaresque of the scenes, which include a man being scolded by two female neighbors, scenes from a bullfight, a public whipping (?), a pair of dolphins (?), and various other animal and vegetal motifs, placed with no apparent regard to any kind of order.

Life in Acámbaro: means and ends

Community life has a material as well as a spiritual or cultural side. The two are intertwined in a subtle way, where neither has absolute mastery over the other. In the history of colonial Acámbaro, a number of interworkings of these two sides of human life are visible. On the economic side are demography and the economic fluctuations; on the spiritual side art and religion. There are six possibilities for mutual interaction. The most important ones seem to be:

a) *Demography-religion.* In an earlier study, it has already been established that there was an intimate connection between the sixteenth-century distribution of population in New Spain and missionary activity: the European friars tended to distribute themselves in such a way as to reach the largest concentrations of Indian population.[28] It is the demographic significance of Acámbaro which is responsible for the size of the Franciscan convent. The relation demography-religion is not one-sided: in the building of a hospital, and in the bringing of mountain water for the first time to the site, the Franciscans made contributions which must have had a salutary effect on the demographic possibilities of the town. The work of the religious was not limited to preaching; they were just as concerned with improving the material conditions of life. Another contribution must have been of great importance: as we have seen, a large variety of agricultural products were recorded by Ponce's secretary in 1586. It is noteworthy that among the products listed, many were unknown in pre-Conquest America, and were therefore introduced by the religious: figs, peaches, oranges, wheat, cattle and other livestock, and vegetables ('hortalizas de Castilla'). More intense agriculture and a varied diet are thus to be counted among the works of the Franciscans, with obvious demographic implications.

b) *Economic fluctuations-art.* We have seen that the most important artistic monuments of Acámbaro are architectural. While demographic growth must have been the impulse for most of the building, the economic fluctuations determined the possibilities to do so, and in an 'artistic' way. The periods of building activity coincide with periods of economic prosperity, and are dependent upon economic conditions. This said, it cannot be claimed that there is any economic significance in the artistic content of the works: they follow patterns which have parallels which are not bound by strict geographical limits, and which are to be found in areas of greater as well as lesser economic prosperity. Of great importance for the content, is of course the relation art-religion.

c) *Art-religion.* This relation is always very close in all places and at all times. Eliot has gone so far as to practically identify the one with the other.[29] Although the relation is sensitive, in a mysterious way, to economic conditions and crises, the prime motives of both religion and art are non-economic, and to a very great degree the content of art and religion are answerable only to each other. In Acámbaro, as we have seen, the colonial period is marked by an almost extreme degree of continuity in its artistic styles. The ruptures in activity, due to economic fluctuations, are not accompanied by stylistic ruptures or dramatic changes in content. On the religious side, the Franciscan order enjoyed a monopoly position for the entire colonial period, which must also have ensured a large measure of religious continuity.

Appendix to Chapter 8

Building activity in Acámbaro (Gto.), individual buildings according to Rojas.

Religious:

- Hospital Real de los naturales (de la Concepción): 1532, mid-C16, C18, 1792.
- Convento de Santa María de Gracia (OFM): 1531-1532, mid-C16 (before 1586), 1734-1743, 1744-1749.
- Capillas de la Vía Crucis: mid-C18.
- Iglesia de San Antonio: ca. 1750-ca. 1780?
- Iglesia de la Soledad: second half C18.
- Iglesia de Nuestra Señora de Guadalupe: between 1749 and 1772, after 1802 (probably shortly afterwards).

Civil:

- Puente sobre el río Lerma: mid-C18 (existed already in 1767), between 1810 and 1874 (probably during 1860s).
- Acueducto: 1527, 1679, ca. 1781(?), 1791.
- Fuente 'del Aguila' o de 'los toritos': second half C18.
- Casa de 'Sámano', Avenida Hidalgo no. 476: 1772.
- Casa, Calle de Allende no. 2, second half C18.
- Casa, Calle de Madero no. 504: second half C18.
- Casa, Calle de Guerrero no. 7: second half C18.
- Casa, Calle de Matamoros no. 3: second half C18.
- Casa, Calle de Leona Vicario no. 122: second half C18.
- Casa, Calle de Guillermo Prieto no. 2: second half C18.
- Casa, Calle de Guillermo Prieto 4: second half C18.
- Casa, Avenida Hidalgo no. 315: second half C18.
- Casa, Calle Madero no. 452: second half C18.
- Casa, Avenida Hidalgo no. 353: second half C18.
- Casa, Calle Benito Juárez no. 445: ca.1800?

Notes to Chapter 8

1   P. Beaumont cited a document purporting to describe the foundation of Acámbaro; it is reproduced in Pedro Rojas, *Acámbaro colonial: estudio histórico, artístico e icono-gráfico* (México: Universidad Nacional Autónoma de México, 1967) pp. 143-150. It includes a detailed description of the formalities involved. Some (Kubler, among others) have called its veracity into question. Indeed the 19th of September 1526 was

a Wednesday, and the 20th a Thursday. It is possible that the 29th and 30th are meant (Saturday and Sunday); the document is dated the 25th of November, 1535, nine years after the foundation itself; this may explain the confusion of the dates. It is probable that the document contains inaccuracies and exaggerations, but its detailed nature, and the fact that much extraneous information is included make it unlikely that the document is an essential falsification of the facts.

2   Ibid., pp. 146-147.

3   The conversion is based on the measurement to scale of the plan published by Rojas, ibid., plan 1.; it is however possible that with *brazada*, the measurement *braza* is meant. A braza is about 1.65 m; this would make the size of the traza somewhat smaller: ca. 825 m by ca. 660 m.

4   Ibid., pp. 15 and 21.

5   W. Borah and S.F. Cook, *The aboriginal population of Central Mexico on the eve of the Spanish Conquest* (Berkeley and Los Angeles: University of California Press, 1961), p. 67, use this coefficient for the pre-Conquest population; this will serve in this region too.

6   Rojas, op. cit., pp. 49 and 53.

7   Ibid., p. 14.

8   Antonio Ciudad Real y Alonso de San Juan, *Relación breve y verdadera de algunas cosas de las muchas que sucedieron al padre fray Alonso Ponce en las provincias de la Nueva España* (Madrid, 1873), cited by Rojas, ibid., p. 53.

9   Ibid., p. 117.

10   Traffic opened on the line Acámbaro-Maravatio (-Toluca-México) on the 6th of April, 1883. Daniel Cosío Villegas, et al., *Historia moderna de México*, 9 vols. (México: Editorial Hermes, 1955-1972), Vol. 7, p. 552.

11   Peter Gerhard, *A guide to the historical geography of New Spain* (Cambridge, 1972), p. 66.

12   Ibid., p. 66.

13   Ibid., p. 66.

14   Ibid., p. 66.

15   Rojas, op. cit., p. 117.

16   M.J. McLeod, *Spanish Central America: A socio-economic history 1520-1720* (Berkeley, Los Angeles and London: University of California Press, 1973).

17   Based on Rojas, op. cit., plans 1 and 11, and the aerial photograph reproduced in the same work of Acámbaro as it was during the 1960s (illustration 1).

18   See A.C. van Oss, 'Mendicant expansion in New Spain and the extent of the colony (sixteenth century)', in: *Boletín de estudios latinoamericanos y del Caribe*, 21 (1976). See also this volume.

19   Manuel Toussaint, *Pintura colonial en México* (México: Universidad Nacional Autónoma de Mexico, 1965).

20   Rojas, op. cit., lámina a color; pp. 114-115.

21   Carmen Venegas Ramírez, *Regimen hospitalano para indios en la Nueva España* (México, 1973).

22   George Kubler, *Mexican Architecture of the sixteenth century* (New Haven: Yale University Press, 1948; reprinted Westport, Conn.: Greenwood Press, 1972), pp. 21-282.

23 Manuel Toussaint, *Arte mudéjar en América* (México: Porrúa, 1946), p. 31.
24 There is a large literature on the Indian contribution to Hispano-American architecture. An excellent survey article is, 'El problema del arte mestizo: contribución a su eslarecimiento', by Mario J. Buschiazzo, *Actas y memorias del XXXVI Congreso Internacional de Americanistas*, Vol. 4 (Sevilla, 1966): pp. 229-244. The latest work in the field, which deals with the Andean area but whose argument is more or less applicable as well to colonial Mexico, seems to be Ilmar Luks, 'Tipología de la escultura decorativa hispánica en la arquitectura andina del siglo xviii', published as a special issue (no. 17) of the *Boletín del Centro de Investigaciones Históricas y Estéticas* (Caracas, 1973). One of the criteria which art historians have used to establish the ethnic origin of colonial works of architecture is that of carving technique; flattened, crudely cut reliefs would be considered as being of Indian or *mestizo* craftsmanship. The idea of identifying the ethnic origin of an artist on the basis of his carving technique has been greeted by other authors with well-deserved scepticism, however. See also Kubler, op cit., p. 396.
25 Rojas, op. cit., pp. 66-87.
26 Ibid., pp. 65-66.
27 Aside from the work by Rojas (ibid.), which deals extensively with the works mentioned here, there is little mention of Acámbaro in the architectural studies. Kubler (op. cit.) reproduces a photograph of the hospital chapel façade (fig. 414), as does Pablo C. de Gante in *La arquitectura de México en el siglo XVI* (México: Porrúa, 1954) (fig. 190). Kubler's text dealing with the hospital façade is limited to three lines (on pp. 385 and 399-400). His text on the convent is five lines long, and is only concerned with the dating (p. 488). De Gante gives a brief description of the façade of the hospital chapel (p. 234), and a short mention of the fountain (p. 285), with a photo (fig. 247). Luis MacGregor, *El plateresco en México* (Porrúa, 1954), produces a photo of one jamb (the north one; fig. 52) of the main doorway of the hospital chapel, and the following text: 'Iglesia y convento franciscanos, fundados en 1526. Construidos por Fray Antonio Bernal [sic] y por Fray Juan Lazo [sic]. Mejorados por orden de Nuño de Guzmán. La portada del Hospital es gótico-mudéjar con decoraciones platerescas' (p. 34).
28 See Van Oss, op. cit., pp. 39-41. See also this volume.
29 T.S. Eliot, *Notes towards the definition of culture* (London: Faber and Faber, 1972; originally printed 1948).

9

The church in Hidalgo towards 1930[*]

The Church strike of 1926-29 and the Cristero rebellion against the government of Plutarco Elías Calles formed the most dramatic episode in Mexico's long history of confrontation between civil and ecclesiastical authority. From the sixteenth century onwards, laws and decrees were passed which aimed at limiting the wealth and influence of Church institutions. During the nineteenth and twentieth centuries the frequency of such measures increased: the anti-religious laws enacted during the presidency of Gómez Faría in 1833 ended the civil obligation to pay tithes; the Lerdo Law of 1856 was meant to divest religious corporations of their real estate holdings. The constitution of 1857 reaffirmed the Lerdo Law; the Reform Laws of Juárez began to take effect in 1859. And the constitution of 1917 collected, reaffirmed, and elaborated on the earlier anti-clerical statutes. The immediate cause of the Church-State crisis of the 1920s was the attempt by the Calles government to implement the religious clauses of the 1917 Constitution.[1]

But the real effects of government pressure on the Church were minimal. The results of the legal measures always disappointed their designers, usually because the laws remained a dead letter. It was all very well for the central government of the moment to promulgate new legislation, but the officials charged with its execution were unwilling or unable to carry it out. In the lower reaches of a chronically weak bureaucracy, orders from above were viewed with skepticism: 'obedezco pero no cumplo' was the old formula.

The Church found ways of circumventing laws that were to its disadvantage, and continued to grow in spite of them. This can be illustrated by a simple comparison between Mexico's total population and the increase in the number of Mexican dioceses since 1525. During the past four centuries the growth of the Mexican Church has kept pace with that of the population it serves. The anti-clerical statutes have never been consistently enforced, and have never succeeded in weakening Mexican Catholicism.

If the Church-State conflict in Mexico over the long term shows signs of having been much noise and little substance, what about the period of greatest crisis, the Church strike of the late 1920s? What were the real effects of the government's new offensive against the Church, and what were the results of the strike itself? I believe that the effects were limited, and that in great parts of Mexico the Church strike was not observed. This belief is based on the study of the physical evidence provided by the church buildings in one Mexican state, Hidalgo, at the end of the Church strike.

This implies an archaeological approach to the religious history of the period. Such an approach is possible in the case of Hidalgo, because of the existence of a remarkable catalogue of religious buildings: the *Catálogo de construcciones religiosas del estado de Hidalgo.*[2] This catalogue was originally conceived around 1925, but only began to be published fifteen years later. Ironically, it owes its existence to the nationalization fever of the Calles government, which was one of the prime irritants inflaming relations between Church and State in the first place. The initiative for the project went out from the Secretaría de Hacienda y Crédito Público, and foresaw the publication of a series of catalogues that would eventually cover the religious buildings of the Republic. Having decided to apply all such buildings to the national patrimony, the government wished to know what it was acquiring. No such inventory as the one contemplated by the government existed. It was thought that the entire national inventory would take a few years to complete.[3] Nevertheless, this estimate proved to be excessively optimistic. In the end, only two inventories, covering the states of Hidalgo and Yucatán respectively, were ever published. The Hidalgo catalogue appeared first, volume I in 1940, and volume II in 1942. By the time it finally became available, the government's passion for physical acquisition of Church property had cooled. The catalogue became a scholarly tool, especially prized by architectural historians. The staff of the commission charged with the compilation of the work consisted of more than 35 historians, architects, draftsmen, and government officials. The team was led by one of Mexico's foremost art historians, Justino Fernández, and counted with the support and collaboration of the dean of Mexican art historians, Manuel Toussaint. The took Quadrado's *España Monumental* as its model, and upon publication of the first volume, Kubler compared it favorably as an art historical source with the catalogue drawn up by the British Royal Monuments Commission.[4]

The catalogue presents data on 805 religious buildings, listed by municipio. Because of editing errors, volume II ends with building number 800. Buildings 801-804, in the municipio of Francisco I. Madero, are to be found in volume I, between numbers 299 and 300. The 805th monument appears in the catalogue as number 171 bis. For each monument, the exact name and geographical location are given, as well as a specification of the type of building and ecclesiastical rank (catedral, parroquia, iglesia, capilla, etc.). Each entry includes a section on what is known of the history of construction, use and maintenance of each building, and a bibliographical note where applicable. Local archives have been consulted in many cases. For every building there is a plan, and there are elevations, diagrams and sketches of the more noteworthy among them. Finally, there is a note about the present use and material condition of each monument at the time of writing. The data presented in the catalogue were collected in the years 1929-32, that is to say, immediately after the settlement of the Church strike of 1926-29.

Ecclesiastically, Hidalgo was divided among three different dioceses. The south-western part of the state belonged to the archdiocese of Mexico, the middle zone to Tulancingo, and the Northeast to Huejutla. The largest towns were and are in the south of the state, in the dioceses of Mexico and Tulancingo. The diocese of Huejutla was more rural in character, with many small villages, but few towns of consequence.

The catalogue lists 731 Catholic religious structures for Hidalgo in 1929-32. According to the compiler it is a complete listing.[5] There was a hierarchy among the structures, ranging from the cathedrals at Tulancingo and Huejutla, through the parish churches (parroquias) and churches of lower-than-parish rank (iglesias, santuarios), down to the chapels (capillas, humilladeros, oratorios, ermitas). The distribution of the different types per diocese is given in Table 1.

Table 1 *Different types of catholic buildings in Hidalgo 1929-32, by dioceses*

Diocese	Parishes	Churches	Chapels	Total
México	18 (11%)	18 (11%)	125 (78%)	161 (100%)
Tulancingo	36* (9%)	43 (10%)	333 (81%)	412 (100%)
Huejutla	12* (8%)	2 (1%)	144 (91%)	158 (100%)
Total	66* (9%)	63 (9%)	602 (82%)	731 (100%)

* Including the cathedrals of Huejutla and Tulancingo

Most Hidalguenses went to pray in humble structures. Hidalgo was a land of chapels, many of them short, whitewashed, shoebox-like constructions with thatched roofs, hardly more elaborate than the houses of the faithful themselves. Fully four-fifths of Hidalgo's religious structures in 1930 were chapels. The concentration of chapels was greatest in the north, where, as we have seen, there were many small villages. In the diocese of Huejutla more than ninety percent of the religious buildings were chapels.

Towards the south, in the dioceses of Tulancingo and Mexico, we find clusters of chapels around the major sixteenth-century monastic centers: Tula, Tepeji del Río, Ixmiquilpan, Actopan, Huichapan and Tecozautla. The monastic establishments had been founded as centers of conversion of the rural Indian population to Christianity; in the sixteenth century as in the twentieth, the areas surrounding the convents had a concentrated Indian population. The chapels are the religious expression of age-old patterns of rural life.

The distribution of the parish churches, on the other hand, is less an indication of settlement patterns than a product of administrative convenience. Geographically they are spread relatively evenly in order to avoid excessive distances between the different points in each parish. In all three dioceses of Hidalgo around 1930, the parish churches accounted for about ten percent of the Catholic structures. In most cases the sites of the parish churches had long been established, and the buildings themselves show this. Of 53 parish churches whose original construction dates are known, 40 were built during the sixteenth century, 11 during the seventeenth or eighteenth, and only two during the twentieth century. Indeed, when we look at who built them, we find that most (39 out of 49) were originally monastic foundations of the Franciscan and Augustinian orders. Only about one-fifth of the parish churches were originally built by the secular clergy. The great majority of the parish churches thus belong architecturally to the early colonial phase of the religious conversion of the Indians. The cathedrals of both Tulancingo and Huejutla also occupy buildings originally constructed by the mendicants during the sixteenth century.

Some of Hidalgo's most opulent religious structures were its 'churches' (iglesias, santuarios). The reason they never attained parish status is that as a group they were built later than the parishes. Of Hidalgo's 63 churches, we only know the original construction dates of 23, but of these 23, only five correspond to the sixteenth century. Thirteen date from the seventeenth and eighteenth centuries, and five from the nineteenth. They thus belong to a later phase of construction than the parishes. Most of the iglesias are found in the areas where there are few or no chapels, and especially in the thinly populated center of the state. There were many mines in this region during the colonial period. It is possible that some of the iglesias were financed by rich miners, who found the patronage of a church an appropriate way of advertising their prosperity. In other areas of Mexico this was a common practice, and resulted in some of the colony's most luxurious churches. In any case, the northeast of Hidalgo had very few iglesias in 1930; the rural diocese of Huejutla had only two of them.

If it were so that the years 1926-29 had been a period of great hardship for the Church, this would be reflected in the physical condition of the temples. The religious buildings described in the catalogue were visited by staff architects between 1929 and 1932. The material condition of each building was noted at the time of the visit. Sometimes the descriptions are very detailed, expressing consternation at every crack in every wall, a sagging staircase, a leaking roof. In other cases, only a one-word evaluation is given, an overall impression. Usually in the cases of the more detailed evaluations, a summary of the general impression is given at the end in a short phrase. The compilers of the catalogue tried to standardize their evaluations, giving a consistent meaning to each of a small number of short phrases describing the material conditions of the religious buildings: 'muy bueno', 'perfecto', 'bueno', 'regular', 'malo', abandonado', 'en ruinas'. This is essentially the same system followed by the Departamento de Monumentos Coloniales of the Instituto Nacional de Antropología e Historia for the purposes of conservation and restoration today.

I have tried to summarize these summaries, in order to get an idea of the general physical state of the Church in Hidalgo at that moment when the period of greatest crisis for the Church would seem to have just ended. The religious edifices were in surprisingly good shape at the end of the Church strike, as Table 2 shows. The architects of the survey found three-fourths of the Catholic buildings to be in good to excellent condition. Only one building in twelve was found to be seriously deteriorated. Only one in twenty-five was in a state of abandonment. The religious constructions of the diocese of Huejutla were in especially good condition, and the buildings in both Huejutla and Mexico were better maintained, on the whole, than in the bishopric of Tulancingo.

Table 2 *'Estado material' of Catholic buildings, 1929-32*

Diocese	Muy bueno, perfecto	Bueno	Regular	Malo	Abandonado, en ruinas	Total
México	4 (3%)	127 (81%)	20 (13%)	2 (1%)	3 (2%)	156 (100%)
Tulancingo	13 (3%)	274 (67%)	82 (20%)	19 (5%)	22 (5%)	410 (100%)
Huejutla	12 (8%)	122 (77%)	13 (8%)	6 (4%)	5 (3%)	158 (100%)
Total Hidalgo	29 (4%)	523 (72%)	115 (16%)	27 (4%)	20 (4%)	724 (100%)

It was the rural chapels, on the whole, that were the best maintained of all. In Huejutla, especially in the municipios of Tlanchinol, Yahualica, and Orizatlan, there were more buildings in very good to perfect condition than in poor condition or in state of abandonment. In the diocese of Mexico, the chapels in the vicinity of the already mentioned sixteenth-century monastic establishments were well maintained. On the other hand, in the diocese of Tulancingo, the religious buildings in the vicinity of the Augustinian monastery of Metztitlán were in notably poor condition on the whole. This is an interesting exception, because Metztitlán was the only monastery in Hidalgo that had still not been secularized by 1930. While in ecclesiastical matters it was subjected to the authority of the bishop of Tulancingo, it remained property of the Augustinian order, and a small community of friars continued to live there. It is possible that for this reason it was discriminated against as an intrusion upon the episcopal hierarchy.

Many Catholic structures were dilapidated in the sparsely settled central zone of the diocese of Tulancingo as well. It will be remembered that many of the churches in this area had been established during the period of mining prosperity; by 1930 this part of Hidalgo was in economic and demographic decay. In general, therefore, the higher percentage of deteriorated religious constructions found in the diocese of Tulancingo is due to local conditions, and not to the effects of the Church-State conflict.

A number of chapels were in poor condition because they had been abandoned in favor of newer buildings. An old chapel would simply be replaced by a new one. Thus, for example, there were two chapels in the village of El Espíritu (municipio Ixmiquilpan), both named 'El Espíritu'. One was a complete ruin, while the other – which had of course replaced it – was in 'very good' condition, and was being enlarged in 1930. Similar pairs of chapels, one in excellent material conditions, and another in ruins, were in Almoloya (Apam) and Calnali (Calnali). Sometimes there would seem to have been a rivalry between the chapels of neighboring villages. In the south-eastern corner of the municipio of Acatlán, the parish church and chapel of the cabecera were both very deteriorated in 1929, while the chapels in the neighboring villages of Totoapa el Grande and San Dionisio were both described as being in very good repair. Of course we must not forget the role of Providence in any study of the condition of religious buildings. The Capilla de la Natividad in Santa María (Juárez Hidalgo) was destroyed by a bolt of lightning on 15 July 1929, just before it was examined by the architects of the inventory.

The physical state of the Church in Hidalgo at the end of the Church strike was therefore good. There is no evidence of deterioration resulting from neglect or abandonment, much less violence, during the period of the 1926-29 conflict. Where Church buildings showed signs of abandonment or disrepair, it was for other reasons. The material condition of the rural chapels was especially good.

Far from being neglected or abandoned during the Church strike, Hidalgo's places of worship were being actively repaired and renovated. The catalogue provides many cases of such works of maintenance and restoration. The most common type of repair carried out was the renewal of a defective roof. In 1926 roofs were renovated at the chapels of San Francisco Atotonilco (Acaxochitlán), Huitznopala (Lolotla), Escobar (Mineral del Monte) and Olotla (Tlanchinol). In the following year the chapels at Boca de León (Tlahuiltepa), Cuatencalco (Xochicoatlán) and Zacatipán (Tianguistengo) were also given new roofs, as were those at San Bartolomé (Huasca), San Nicolás (Juárez Hidalgo), Chantasco (Lolotla), Zacualtipanito (Tepehuacán de Guerrero) and San Miguel (Tianguistengo) in 1928-29. All of these chapels are located in the rainy northern and eastern part of Hidalgo. Probably in the other parts of the state there was less wear and tear on the roofs. The rains were apparently too much for the chapel at Ocotlán (Lolotla); its roof caved in sometime in 1928. The loss was not grave, however, since the chapel had already been abandoned at an earlier date.

A number of other chapels, and at least one church, underwent more general renovations or rebuildings. This was the case with the chapels at San Antonio (Molango, 1926), Tlazcantitla (Tlahuiltepa, 1929) and Cuatatlán (Tlanchinol, 1928). In 1929 the sacristy of the chapel at Itztacapa (Metztitlán) was renovated, and a tower was added to the one at Portezuelo (Tasquillo). Pachuca's capilla de San

Miguel Cerezo received a needed buttress in 1927. Statues were placed in the atrio of the chapel at Cuatolol (Tepehuacán de Guerrero) in the same year. The atrio at Cuazáhual (Tlahuiltepa) received a new surrounding wall (barda) in 1926. And at the time it was visited in 1929, the chapel at Tlacolula (Tianguistengo) was in the process of being rebuilt.

Unspecified repairs were carried out on the parish church of Huazalingo (Huazalingo, 1927 and 1929), and the chapels at Bondojito (Huichapan, 1928), San Miguel (San Salvador, 1927 and 1929), San Nicolás (Tenango de Doria, 1929), Chipoco (Tlanchinol, 1928), Santa María Catzotipan (Tlanchinol, 1929), Xochitlán (Tula, 1928), the capilla de Guadalupe at Tulancingo (Tulancingo, 1928), and the iglesia of Tlahuelompa (Zacualtipán, 1928). After a fire in 1927 the walls of the chapel of Zacatipán had to be refinished; this was done early in 1928.

Surprisingly for a period in which no Church services were officially held, no fewer than thirteen completely new chapels were constructed: in 1926 at El Zapote (Alfajayucan), Jacalilla (La Misión) and San Miguel (Tlanchinol). In 1927 new chapels arose at Baxthé (Alfajayucan), Xalcuatla (Lolotla), Olvera (San Salvador), Tenexco (Tianguistengo) and Xilocuatitla (Tlahuiltepa). This last chapel was built on land especially granted by the municipio for the purpose. In 1928 work was begun on a chapel at Barrio (Chapulhuacan), and 1929 saw chapels constructed at San Andrés (Actopan) and Santa Cruz (Zempoala). A vault dated 1929 in the chapel at Bocajhá (San Salvador) probably refers to the year in which it was completed. Finally, a chapel was under construction in Ixtacuatitla (Yahualica) in 1929.

If all this building activity seems strange during a time in which the Church officially lay dormant, one place seems to have taken the strike more seriously. In Calnali (Calnali) the reconstruction of the parish was interrupted in 1926, 'al iniciarse el conflicto religioso'. But in view of the fact that the religious conflict formed no impediment at all in so many other places, we may well ask if in the case of Calnali it was not simply an excuse given for a work stoppage caused by other, more mundane reasons. Work in progress on a new chapel in La Peña (Pisaflores) was also interrupted, in 1927, for unknown reasons. In this latter case the work stoppage did not coincide with the outbreak of the religious conflict.

New chapels were not only built, but were also opened and consecrated. This took place in five cases of which we know, although the catalogue is surely incomplete on this point. The official inauguration of the chapel of El Zapote took place in 1926, those of the chapels of Xalcuatla and San Miguel in 1928, and that of the chapel of Baxthé in 1929. The chapel at Xilocuautitla was built in 1927 and opened immediately: 'El primer oficio tuvo lugar le 12 de octubre del propio año y estuvo a cargo del Presbítero Angel Huidobro'.

It is also certain that at least the day of the Virgin of Guadalupe was being celebrated in Hidalgo chapels, for the roof of the one at Zacatipán burned down during a religious observance held on the 12th of December, 1926.

In fact, the catalogue only contains two hints at an interruption of services in the churches of Hidalgo, possibly as a result of the Church strike. In Tultitlán (Orizatlán), the vecinos had constructed a new chapel between 1923 and 1924. According to the catalogue's sources, it was used as a school from 1926 through 1929, on account of the Church strike. On the other hand, this report is suspicious, because the same catalogue lists the building as unfinished in 1929: 'se está acabando actualmente su construcción'. The second case, which is also dubious, concerns an unnamed chapel in Zontecomate (Zempoala). It was closed in 1926, perhaps at the outbreak of hostilities. But there must not have been much demand for it anyway, since in 1931, two years after the end of the Church strike, it still had not been reopened. It was abandoned, and the roof was in poor condition.

On a brighter note, the early mornings of a number of Hidalgo's towns rang with the sound of new church bells. Between 1926 and 1929 new bells were cast for the chapel of Pueblo Nuevo (Ixmiquipan, 1926), Capula (Ixmiquilpan, 1927, 1928, 1929), Jacalilla (La Misión, 1929), Xicopantla (Zacualtipán, 1927), and San Pedro (Zimapan, 1928). There were also new additions to the belfries of the church of Xoxoteco (Metzquititlan, 1926) and Pachuca's parish church of Santa María (1926).

How did the level of building activity during the period of the Church strike compare to earlier levels of activity? Data from the catalogue allow us to make a statistical comparison between the number of religious structures that underwent some kind of repair, modification or construction during the period of the strike, and the number of building that underwent similar works in the preceding periods. For the sake of convenience I have worked with five-years periods going back to 1895. For the period before 1895 the data become more fragmentary and imprecise. The results of this comparison are given in Table 3.

Table 3 *Catholic buildings in construction 1895-1929, by five year periods*

Period	Catholic buildings in construction
	(numbers refer to specific monuments in the catalogue)
1895-1899	12, 15, 69, 112, 121, 137, 191, 195, 266, 497, 529?, 532, 533, 546, 548, 549, 646, 647, 654, 694, 783 (21 buildings)
1900-1904	9, 123, 165, 171 bis, 201, 236, 247, 517, 545, 565, 567, 579, 636, 702, 714, 753 (16 buildings)
1905-1909	8, 38, 93, 111, 127, 262, 286, 303, 420, 436, 437, 521, 531, 602, 622, 630, 666, 699, 717, 723 (20 buildings)
1910-1914	32, 137, 197, 287, 293, 347, 443, 537, 613, 634, 639, 653, 720, 773

In terms of constructive activity, the late 1920s were not only not a particularly bad period for the Church in Hidalgo, but one of relative prosperity. More religious buildings were being built and renovated than at any other time in the twentieth century up until then. The decade of violence which followed the outbreak of the Mexican Revolution, by contrast, was clearly a period of troubles for the Church as well: constructive activity reached its lowest levels in those years. A possible hypothesis would be that political adversity under the Calles government somehow galvanized the religious sentiments of the people and clergy of Hidalgo, inspiring a surge of new church-building. But on the other hand, the elevated level of activity during the period 1925-29 can also be considered as a continuation of the rising trend already set during the previous five-year period, before the worsening of the political situation.

Actually, a comparison of the record of religious constructive activity with the demographic trend of Hidalgo, according to the population censuses taken in 1900, 1910, 1921 and 1930, tends to make any political hypothesis superfluous. The level of ecclesiastical building faithfully reflects the general population movement. If the Church in Hidalgo remained relatively impervious to the effects of national political turmoil during the late 1920s, this was especially true for the rural areas, where the chapels followed their own rhythms, and not those the federal government would like to have imposed. Of the 61 religious constructions that took form or were renovated during the years 1925-29, all but three were chapels. Since the chapels only accounted for 82 percent of the total number of Hidalgo's Catholic structures, but 95 percent of the building activity, we can say that their share in such activity was disproportionately large. Conversely, the effects of political strife were felt more acutely near the administrative centers: parishes and iglesias, while making up 18 percent of the Church buildings, only accounted for five percent of the constructive activity between 1925 and 1929.

One of the liberal governments' goals, incorporated into Mexican law since the times of Lerdo and Juárez, had been to establish civil authority over, and later to gain actual physical possession of ecclesiastical real estate, whether in landholdings, houses rented by the Church to private individuals, or the temples, monasteries, and other purely ecclesiastical buildings themselves. By the 1920s, this liberal principle had only been very fragmentarily applied in actual practice. When Calles assumed the presidency, only a small part of the total ecclesiastical holdings had been nationalized. The Calles government aggressively reasserted the principle of civil ownership of ecclesiastical properties, and announced its intention to complete the unfinished process of expropriation. This program, which was to affect Church holdings in the entire Republic, was one of the immediate causes of the Church strike and the Cristero War, and formed a leitmotif in the ecclesiastical protest literature.[6]

The catalogue gives insight into the process of nationalization as it was carried out in Hidalgo. It shows that in Hidalgo at least, the theory and the practice of nationalization lay far apart. Between 1856 and 1932 only 48 properties once belonging to the Catholic Church had been or were in the process of being nationalized. This is less than seven percent of the properties that had ever been in Church hands, and because of the subdivision of properties after nationalization, even this figure may be considered inflated. Moreover, it was often the marginal or unused ecclesiastical holdings that were redirected by civil authorities to non-ecclesiastical ends; in short, the impact of nationalization on the Church must have been minimal.

One-third of the nationalized properties were terrains without any buildings at all at the time of expropriation. In Zacamulpa a piece of land was applied to the federal fisc in 1889. By 1930 it remained unbuilt. The field in Temuthé known as 'El Sabino' belonged to the Cofradía de la Santa Cruz until it was nationalized in 1856. In possession of the Secretaría de Hacienda y Crédito Público in 1929, it was not being used in any way. Also in possession of the same Secretaría was another plot of land in Olontenco (Zacualtipán), nationalized at an unknown date. In Pachuca an unnamed field and the ex-cemetery of San Rafael (which had belonged to the Franciscan convent of Pachuca) were subdivided and partially sold to individual developers after their nationalization around 1860. A happier fate was that of the main burial ground of the same Pachucan convent, which was converted into a public park around 1881. Now it is familiar as the Jardín Colón. The ex-atrio of the Augustinian convent of Atotonilco el Grande and an unoccupied square of land in Omitlán were likewise turned into paseos públicos. Until its nationalization in 1888, the atrio at Atotonilco el Grande had served as a cemetery. At Tenango de Doria and Jaltepec (Tulancingo), plots adjacent to the local places of worship were nationalized at unknown dates. By 1930 both were occupied by private houses. An unoccupied terrain in Tepeji del Río, nationalized and used for army barracks in the nineteenth century, had reverted to its original status by 1930: 'solar sin uso'. In Nopala (Nopala), good use was made of the atrio of the parish church by the municipal government. They constructed a new Municipal Palace there in 1874, and – probably at about the same time – two schools. The inhabitants of San Bernardo (Zacualtipán) had also hoped for a school. A chapel begun in the village around 1904, but still not completed, had been destroyed by a storm. The owner of the land – it was apparently to have been a private chapel – thereupon decided to cede the land to the federal government for the purpose of erecting a school. But by 1929 construction had still not begun, and the San Bernardinos were asking for their land back in order to undertake the project themselves.

Many Mexicans had taken advantage of the 1833 law abolishing the civil obligation to tithe, to discontinue payment of this ecclesiastical tax.[7] As a result, the many tithe administration buildings maintained by the Church fell into disuse. Consequently, the nationalization of a number of these buildings at a later date could not have represented a very great inconvenience, although it must have been felt as a classic case of adding insult to injury. Ex *colecturías de diezmos* were nationalized in Apam in 1866, Pachuga (probably around 1860), and Metztitlán and Tulancingo at dates unknown. In Pachuca the building was put to use as a normal school, and in Apam as a military barrack. In Metztitlán (1929), the Ayuntamiento rented the building out: in view of its poor material condition and reduced size, it cannot have generated much income in rent.

Aside from the old *colecturías*, only five Catholic buildings were nationalized in their entirety between 1856 and 1930. In Calnali, a chapel and cemetery were demolished in 1889. To what immediate purpose the land was put is not certain, but in 1929 it was an orchard. And the loss of the chapel in question in 1889 had been immediately compensated by the construction of a new one, begun in the same year that the old one was demolished, and finished in 1901. In Mineral del Chico, the ancient capilla de la Cruz passed into the hands of the municipio in 1857. Possibly already in disuse at that time, it was an abandoned ruin in 1930.

Other Catholic buildings nationalized by 1930 were the old quarters of the Archicofradía del Santísimo in Tulancingo, occupied by a school run by the Ayuntamiento since the promulgation of the Reform Laws, and an originally Catholic school in Tezontepec, taken over by the Ayuntamiento sometime after 1901. In Pachuca, the old hospital of San Juan de Dios was nationalized and converted in 1869 into a Scientific and Literary Institute administered by the state of Hidalgo.

In 1929, the original Augustinian monastery in Metztitlán, that was known as 'La Comunidad', was being employed to house offices of the municipality and state, but it is hard to see this as a real loss to the Augustinians, since they had already moved from this original convent to a new one in the same town ('Los Santos Reyes') in the sixteenth century. Predictably, La Comunidad was found to be in poor condition when it was visited in 1929.

The largest number of nationalizations affected dependencies and annexes of churches and parishes, in which civil offices, military barracks and other institutions came to occupy parts of ex-curacies or ex-convents. Such was the case at San Pedro Tlachichilco (Acoxochitlán), where the upper floor of the curacy housed the minuscule Federal School no. 657 in 1929. Likewise, the ex-curacy of the parish church at Jacala (Jacala) was shared by a school and municipal offices, and that of Omitlán had been taken over by the Ayuntamiento of that town. In Pachuca as well, the curacy of the parish La Asunción had been nationalized at an unknown date, but its destination in 1930 is not given in the pages of the catalogue. On the other hand, at least one curacy was nationalized in name only, with no practical effect at all: the curacy of Santuario (Cardonal) is listed as part of the national patrimony, but the sacristan of the church was still living there at the time it was visited.

By far the biggest single nationalization took place in Pachuca, upon the exclaustration of the Franciscan monastery around 1861. This monastery was a sprawling complex, almost a city in itself. After it was nationalized it was partitioned among a number of different federal, state and municipal agencies. Among other purposes to which portions of the ex-convent were applied, we find mention of a school of mining, several barracks, two jails, a stall for horses, a public park, the municipal slaughterhouse, a state hospital, a public bath establishment, and private houses. In

1932 nationalization proceedings were still underway for a number of houses which had been constructed on lands originally belonging to the monastery, but which had been subdivided and sold without authorization by the municipality during the nineteenth century.

In Tulancingo another large nationalization took place: parts of the ex-monastery, by then secularized and raised to the rank of cathedral, were broken off from the original convent block between 1870 and 1922. One part was in the legal possession of the Secretaría de Educación Pública by 1930, but was not being occupied, while another piece of the building had been pressed into military service as a barrack as early as 1914, 'aunque sin las formalidades de ley'.

To summarize, most of the Church properties nationalized in Hidalgo up until about 1930, while not without value, were largely marginal holdings, underutilized by the Church, and in most cases probably not sorely missed. On the other and, the monastic complexes of Tulancingo and Pachuca were mutilated, that of Pachuca beyond recognition. In 1977, Pachuca's authorities were trying to rehabilitate portions of the convent as a cultural center, but as a result of the depredations of the past century, Pachuca has irrevocably lost the greatest part of its principal colonial monument.

Some of the expropriated Church properties were put to good use by the civil authorities. In some cases schools and hospitals were established. On the other hand, the monastic buildings in particular seemed to lend themselves especially well for military functions, or refitting as prisons. Perhaps only a military man will be able to appreciate the conversion of the ex-monasteries of Tulancingo an Pachuca into housing and drilling grounds for soldiers.

But most surprising is the number of nationalized Church properties which were put to no use at all, and which were left fallow, in the case of the terrains, or left to deteriorate in the case of the buildings. In these cases nationalization can only be interpreted as a symbolic act against the Church, not particularly harmful, but a needless aggression serving none of the proclaimed goals of the Constitution.

Geographically, the nationalizations were concentrated in a few important towns. Pachuca alone accounted for 20 of the 48 nationalized properties. Tulancingo and Nopala followed, with five and three respectively. More than half of all the nationalizations took place in these three towns. Almost 90 percent (42) of the nationalizations took place within the municipal administrative centers, the *cabeceras*. Of the six that took place outside the cabeceras, five affected plots of land without buildings. The nationalization process only affected the civil administrative centers, and had practically no impact in the countryside. Regionally, this is also clear; only one nationalization took place in the isolated northeast, the diocese of Huejutla. And then it was in a cabecera, and it was only an abandoned chapel.

The chronology of the nationalizations shows that not much came of Calles's new offensive on the nationalization front. The majority of the expropriations were not carried out in the name of the 1917 Constitution, but much earlier, especially in the time of Juárez. A number of nationalizations were also carried out in Hidalgo during the years 1888-89; Knowlton has pointed out that these two years were a period of increased governmental activity on this score in all Mexico.[8] After 1889 few nationalizations were effected any more. During the period of the Church strike, only three properties in Hidalgo were with any certainty effected by nationalization procedures: all three were dependencies of the ex-convent of San Francisco in Pachuca, and all had long since been in use as barracks. Now they were officially transferred to the Secretaría de Guerra y Marina. A questionable case is that of the curacy of the parish church at Zimapán, which may have been nationalized in 1929, but which was still not in use in 1930. The expropriations carried out by the Calles government during the period 1926-29 were merely formal procedures, and had no practical effects.

Although not explicitly a part of anti-Catholic policy, the establishment of Protestant churches in Mexico broke the old Catholic monopoly. Freedom of religion was a Liberal invention in Mexico, and the spread of Protestantism was at least a potential threat to the older Church. Hidalgo was not immune to Protestantism, but neither did it make much headway. The catalogue lists 21 Protestant buildings, or 2.6 percent of all the religious buildings in Hidalgo. This percentage seems in agreement with the overall percentage of non-Catholics in Mexico that, according to repeated censuses, hovers in the region of 1 to 3 percent.[9] The majority of the Protestant temples were of the Methodist denomination. In 1930 the Methodist Church in Hidalgo was still young; none of its establishments antedated 1892.

The Protestant temples were clustered together in only eleven municipios, mainly in the south of Hidalgo. The municipios with Protestant churches adjoined one another, forming three separate zones of Protestant influence. The Protestants were strongest in and around Pachuca and Napola in 1930. No Protestant churches had penetrated into the northeast (Huejutla). The Methodists were not particularly adventurous; their churches were located in places with good rail communications, or near the main roads. There is some agreement between the distribution of the Protestant church and the nationalizations. The eleven municipios with Protestant buildings accounted for 57 percent of the nationalizations. If the Methodist Church had not made dramatic advances by 1930, it could take solace in the knowledge that the government also had difficulty moving against the Catholics of Hidalgo.

President Calles complained early in 1926 that the religious clauses of the 1917 Constitution still remained without effect; it was his government's threat to rectify this 'irregular' situation that prompted the Mexican bishops to invoke the Church strike, a decision only rescinded in 1929 as part of a wider settlement with the government. Hidalgo was as caught up in the conflict as most other regions of Mexico, and its own bishop of Huejutla, Manríquez y Zarate, earned a reputation as perhaps the most intransigent of the bishops opposing the government.

Yet the harsh rhetoric surrounding the Church-State conflict was largely a façade, hiding a much milder reality. In Hidalgo, the anti-clerical principles proclaimed by the government made little or no headway. A law proposed late in 1925 to limit the number of priests in the state to sixty was quietly abandoned.[10] It is doubtful whether any new nationalizations took place, and even if they did, they concerned only marginal properties, of little use either to the Church or to the government. As far as can be judged from the catalogue of Hidalgo's religious monuments, no Catholic schools were closed or taken over by the civil authorities. Hidalgo's only male convent – the Augustinian establishment at Metztitlán – continued to exit, in violation of article five of the Constitution. In short, at the end of the period of the Church strike, the ecclesiastical situation in Hidalgo was as far from 'regularity' under the Constitution as it had been in 1926.

As far as the Church strike itself is concerned, there is no evidence that it was observed, at least in the countryside. On the contrary, existing churches were maintained, repaired, and in some cases improved. New chapels were built and consecrated. Services continued to be held – perhaps clandestinely; old habits are hard to break. In the atrium of the ancient Franciscan convent of Calpan (Puebla) towards the end of 1978, an elderly woman pointed in the direction of the parish church across the way. 'There we said mass in those years, at twelve or one at night. In the morning no one was the wiser. We never talked about it. Sólo Dios sabía'.

Notes to Chapter 9

* Spanish translation: 'La Iglesia en Hidalgo hacia 1930', in *Historia Mexicana*, 22, no. 2 (1979), pp. 301-324.

1 J. Pérez Lugo (J. Ramírez Cabañas), *La cuestión religiosa en México, recopilación de leves, disposiciones legales y documentos par el estudio de este problema político*, (México; Centro cultural Cuauhtemoc, 1926); M. Cuevas, *Historia de la iglesia en México*, 5 Vols. (El Paso: Edit. 'Revista Católica', 1928); E. Gruening, *Mexico and its Heritage* (New York: Century, 1928); W.H. Callcott, *Liberalism in Mexico, 1857-1929* (Hamden: Archon books, 1965); A. Olivera Sedano, *Aspectos del conflicto religioso de 1926 a 1929: sus antecedentes y consecuencias* (México: Instituto Nacional de Antropología e Historia, 1966); J.H. Wilkie, 'The Meaning of the Cristero war against the Mexican Revolution', in: *A Journal of Church and State*, VII: 2 (1966), pp. 214-233; R.E. Quirk, *The Mexican Revolution and the Catholic Church, 1910-1929* (Bloomington: Indiana University Press, 1973); J. Meyer, *La cristiada*, 3 Vols. (México: Siglo XXI, 1974); D.C. Bailey, *¡Viva Cristo Rey! The Cristero Rebellion and the Church-State Conflict in Mexico* (Austin: University of Texas Press, 1974).

2 *Catálogo de construcciones religiosas del estado de Hidalgo*, 2 Vols. (México: Talleres Gráficos de la Nación, 1940-1942), further abbr. CCREH.

3 CCREH, 1940, I, p. xxi; *Excélsior* (México, D.F.), 17 y 29 marzo de 1926.

4 Review of the *Catálogo de construcciones religiosas del estado de Hidalgo*, in *The Hispanic American Historical Review*, XXII: 1 (1942) pp. 188-189 by G. Kubler; CCREH, I p. xiii.

5   CCREH, II p. xi: 'El presente volumen completa el material relativo al Estado de Hidalgo, pudiendo asegurar que no ha quedado una solo construcción religiosa sin catalogar, es decir, hasta la fecha de la formación del inventario'.

6   For example, A.M. Carreño, *Páginas de historia mexicana, Colección de obras diversas,* Vol. 3 (México: Victoria, 1936), and R. Planchet, *El robo de los bienes de la iglesia, ruina de los pueblos* (El Paso: Revista Press, 1936). The Church-State conflict provided material for a great number of inflammatory pamphlets and books, written from the point of view of the Church as well as from that of the State. For a brief overview of the Church protest literature see Ch. C. Cumberland, *Mexico, the Struggle for Modernity* (New York: Oxford University Press, 1968, p. 359).

7   P. Costeloe, 'The Administration, Collection and Distribution of Tithes in the Archbishopric of Mexico, 1800-1860', in: *The Americas,* XXIII: 1 (1966) p. 22.

8   R.J. Knowlton, *Church Property and the Mexican Reform, 1856-1910,* (DeKalb: Northern Illinois University Press, 1976) p. 239.

9   J.W. Wilkie, 'Statistical Indicators of the Impact of National Revolution on the Catholic Church in Mexico', in: *A Journal of Church and State,* XII: 1, (1970), p. 91.

10 *Excélsior,* 2 y 3 de enero de 1926; D.C. Bailey, op. cit., p. 61.